HAUNTED HOLLYWOOD

HAUNTED HOLLYWOOD

Tinseltown Terrors, Filmdom Phantoms,
and Movieland Mayhem

Second Edition

Retold by Tom Ogden

Globe
Pequot

Globe
Pequot

An imprint of Rowman & Littlefield

Distributed by NATIONAL BOOK NETWORK

British Library Cataloguing in Publication Information Available

Library of Congress Cataloging-in-Publication Data

Ogden, Tom.
  Haunted Hollywood : tinseltown terrors, filmdom phantoms, and movieland mayhem / retold by Tom Ogden. -- 2nd [edition].
    pages cm
  Includes bibliographical references.
  ISBN 978-1-4930-1577-1 (pbk.) -- ISBN 978-1-4930-1578-8 (e-book) 1. Ghosts--California--Los Angeles. 2. Haunted places--California--Los Angeles. 3. Hollywood (Los Angeles, Calif.)--Miscellanea. I. Title.
  BF1472.U6044 2015
  133.109794'94--dc23
                                            2015013306

For Sarah and Rebecca

CONTENTS

Contents

ACKNOWLEDGMENTS

This book would not have been possible without the help of many friends and colleagues. Since it all starts with the stories, let me first thank Cindy Freeling, Michael Gingras, Milt Larsen, Joan Lawton, Bryan Lee, Betty Jean Morris, Mark Nelson, Marty Rosenstock, Kate Ward, and Jeremy Vargus for sharing their personal tales of ghost encounters.

My gratitude goes out to Greg Lyczkowski, the staff at the William S. Hart Museum, and the rangers and visitor center at Griffith Park; also to Tom Ewing, Manon Rodriquez, and George Schindler for their help tracking down information on the Houdini Mansion. I also want to show my appreciation to Hollywood historian Marc Wanamaker, coauthor with Laurie Jacobson of the indispensable book *Hollywood Haunted,* for his insights. George Siegel and Tanja Barnes provided important new insights regarding the schoolhouse that supposedly stood on the site of the Vogue Theatre, and Richard Carradine (president and co-founder of Ghost Hunters of Urban Los Angeles, or Ghoula.org) and David Markland (CreepyLA.com and ScareLA.com) also made many helpful contributions to the book.

Also special thanks to Michael Kurland, Bill Harris, Max Maven, Joan Lawton, Mark Willoughby, and David Shine for their advice, feedback, and assistance.

Finally, thanks to my agent, Jack Scovil, and my original team at Globe Pequot—editor Mary Norris, project manager Jennifer Taber, copy editor Antoinette Smith, and group publisher Gary Krebs—as well as my editors for this second edition, Erin Turner and Lauren Brancato.

INTRODUCTION

To paraphrase the tagline from the blockbuster movie *The Sixth Sense*: I'm surrounded by ghosts. All the time.

But that's to be expected if, like me, you're lucky enough to live in a place that has as rich of a history as Hollywood.

That's right: Movieland. Where wishes come true, and stars are born. Over the past hundred years, thousands of actor wannabes have swarmed to this hamlet in the foothills of the Santa Monica Mountains in the hopes of getting their faces up there on a twenty-foot silver screen, trying to grab for themselves one small slice of immortality.

It's said that Native Americans once called this patch of Earth "the land of shadow and light." What an apt description for the ephemeral art of moviemaking! Where once nothing but citrus trees and fields for grazing flourished, today a multibillion-dollar industry has made these 9 square miles (of the 498 making up Los Angeles) the film capital of the world.

It's hard to say, though, exactly how large Hollywood is because, to many people, it extends far beyond its actual geographic boundaries. It's more of a state of mind.

Besides, most of the major studios, including Warner Brothers, Universal, Twentieth Century Fox, and Sony Pictures (on the former MGM lot), either moved out long ago or were never located in Hollywood in the first place. They're found in outlying areas such as Burbank, Universal City, Culver City, and the San Fernando Valley.

For the purpose of putting together this set of eerie tales, I've allowed "Hollywood" to mean not only the town itself but also the places where the stars lived, worked, and played. And, hoping to place the legends into context, I've done my best to surround my fictional retelling of the folk-tales with historical information about Hollywood and the people who have called it home.

There are dozens of ghost stories and haunted places in Tinseltown, many more than would fit in a single volume. For every tale I did select, there seemed to be a dozen more begging to be included. Anyone for the collection *Haunted Hollywood II*?

(In the meantime—and here's a shameless plug—if you want to check out other Hollywood ghost stories, you can read about James Dean and Telly Savalas in my book *Haunted Highways*. Accounts of several movie stars bumping into phantoms on the stage, including the Pasadena Play-house located just a few miles east of Hollywood, can be found in my *Haunted Theaters*.)

It seems that after their deaths, some of the biggest stars in film history decided that they just weren't ready for their final bows and returned to the city that made them world-famous. Many have quietly returned to their old homes, places where they were comfortable and that made them happy while they were alive, away from the prying eyes of the public. Others revisit the places where they died. Then there are the stories of celebrities who, while they were still alive, became the "haunted."

Are these Hollywood ghost stories true? Are phantoms "alive" and walking the streets of Tinseltown? Who can be sure? After all, Hollywood is a town where fantasy constantly intermingles with fact. In an industry that depends upon illusion, it's hard to tell how much of anything is real and how much is make-believe.

Perhaps a look at the early days of Hollywood is in order. The community didn't start out to become the center of movies worldwide. In fact, it didn't even start out as its own city.

In 1781 eleven families that had traveled from Mexico settled on a site along a riverbank that became the pueblo of Los Angeles. Within a hundred years, almost five hundred people had moved approximately seven miles north to found a hamlet in a former fig orchard close to a pass in the mountains that led to the San Fernando Valley.

In 1887, Horace J. Wilcox, a real estate speculator, laid out the streets of this new community, and it's on his map of the prospective town that the name Hollywood first appears. There are competing claims as to the origin of the name, but the most commonly accepted story is this: On a train trip back east, Wilcox's wife, Daeida, struck up a conversation with a woman who described her estate outside of Chicago, which she had named Hollywood because of the holly trees that grew there. Mrs. Wilcox liked the name so much that when she returned home, she gave the sobriquet to the Wilcox estate. Soon the entire town was going by the name Hollywood. Unfortunately, the Wilcox home (at what is today 1721 Cahuenga Boulevard) has long since been razed, and no marker exists to identify where it stood. In 1910, Hollywood officially became part of the City of Los Angeles in order to share in its water supply, sewage system, and other city services.

Although earlier film "shorts" were shot in the area, the first real movie to be made in Hollywood itself was *In Old California* (1910), directed by D. W. Griffith for the Biograph Company, whose studio was on East Fourteenth Street in Manhattan. At the time, movie production was based on the East Coast, centered on New York City and the Fort Lee area in New Jersey, and production continued there well into the

1930s. Moviemakers finally moved their main studios west for the good weather, the scenery, and the open spaces.

The first full-length feature film made for a Hollywood-based studio (the Jesse L. Lasky Feature Play Company) was 1914's *The Squaw Man*, directed by Cecil B. DeMille and Oscar Apfel. (Technically, the two men were billed as—get this—"picturizers.")

And the rest, as they say, is history.

I'm happy to be back with Globe Pequot for another collection of ghost stories. It's a personal pleasure to write this particular book because I've made Hollywood my home for more than thirty years. During that period, I've had the chance to visit (or, in the case of private residences, see the exterior of) every one of the haunted landmarks, theaters, parks, hotels, cemeteries, and other places mentioned in this book.

Please remember as you flip through these pages that the chapters start out with new, fictional "campfire" stories, but they're based on previously existing Hollywood folklore. The original legends, in turn, are based on multiple and often conflicting accounts that have arisen over the years. These tales aren't intended to be taken as the definitive word on the alleged hauntings or offer evidence or proof. We're talking ghost stories, not documentaries.

My goal has simply been to make you shiver as you read some really spooky ghost stories. If even one of these Tinseltown tales gives you goose bumps, I've accomplished my goal.

Happy hauntings.

Part One

FAMOUS PHANTOMS OF FILMLAND

Hollywood is the place where dreams come true—though sometimes they may turn into nightmares! After death, some of the biggest stars in film history have decided that they just weren't ready for their final bows and returned to the city that made them world-famous.

Many have quietly returned to their own homes, places where they were comfortable and that made them happy while they were alive, away from the prying eyes of the public. Others revisit the place where they died. Then there are the stories of celebrities who, while they were still alive, were not the "haunters" themselves but became the "haunted."

Where better to start than with the first megastars of Hollywood: Douglas Fairbanks and Mary Pickford. In short order we'll visit the haunted homes of Thelma Todd, William S. Hart, Harry Houdini, Jean Harlow, Clifton Webb, Jayne Mansfield, Elke Sommer, and George Reeves. We'll even take a sail on John Wayne's beloved yacht, the *Wild Goose*.

Time to start our tour of Haunted Hollywood.

Chapter 1
The Pickfair
Phantoms

The cream of Hollywood attended the lavish parties at Pickfair thrown by its owners, Douglas Fairbanks and Mary Pickford. After their deaths, at least four phantoms (perhaps including Fairbanks and Pickford themselves) haunted the mansion up until its demolition.

Frank couldn't believe it. He was actually inside the fabled walls of Pickfair. Everyone who was anyone wanted to receive an invitation to attend one of the fabulous parties thrown there by its owners, Hollywood's "golden couple" Douglas Fairbanks and Mary Pickford. The Roaring Twenties had just ended, and Fairbanks and Pickford were Hollywood royalty.

It's good to be the king. And the queen. Especially if the realm over which you reign, Pickfair, is only a few acres, and you have no real duties except to be loved and admired. And in Hollywood in the 1930s, Fairbanks and Pickford fit their roles as the Monarchs of Moviedom to a T.

Both came from humble beginnings. Fairbanks was born Douglas Elton Ullman in Denver in 1883 and began acting in amateur theater productions in the Mile High City when he was still a teenager. He moved to New York City around 1900 and made his Broadway debut in *Her Lord and Master* in 1902. He had performed in eighteen shows by the summer of 1915, when he moved to Hollywood with his wife and their son, Douglas Fairbanks Jr.

Once there, Fairbanks began working with D. W. Griffith and Anita Loos at Fine Arts Film Company before switching to Paramount. By 1918 he was one of the most popular male stars in silent films.

By that time he had also met and begun a clandestine relationship with Mary Pickford. "America's Sweetheart," as she was known, had been born Gladys Louise Smith in Toronto in 1892. She made her first stage appearance at the age of six or seven, and by the end of 1900 she was touring in minor stock productions throughout the United States.

(She was accompanied, of course, by her mother as well as her two younger siblings, both of whom also became actors. Her little brother Jack would go on to marry Ziegfeld Follies star Olive Thomas in 1916. Thomas died four years later from accidentally ingesting too large a dose of what was most probably a syphilis medication prescribed to her husband, and her ghost has haunted the New Amsterdam Theatre in New York, where the Follies were held, ever since.)

Still billed with her real name, Smith appeared briefly on Broadway in 1905, her first notable role came two years later in *The Warrens of Virginia*, written by William C. DeMille, older brother of Cecil B. The play was produced by impresario David Belasco, who gave her a new stage name: Mary Pickford. (Today, Belasco's spirit haunts his namesake playhouse, the Belasco Theatre.)

In April 1909, D. W. Griffith gave Pickford a screen test in the Biograph Company's New York studio and was impressed. By the end of the year, Pickford had made more than fifty films for Biograph at ten dollars a day—twice the salary given most of their actors.

In January 1910 they sent her to Los Angeles to shoot, and before long she had appeared in dozens of Biograph's shorts. Movie audiences soon started recognizing her talent. Actors didn't receive billing in those days, but Pickford became so much in demand that movie theaters—most of which were nickelodeons back then—started advertising out front that "The Girl with the Golden Curls" (the tresses were her trademark) or "Blondilocks" was appearing in the film. Her name first appeared in an above-the-title credit in 1914's *Hearts Adrift*.

Because of her association with Biograph, Pickford also became known as "The Biograph Girl." But she left them to work for, first, Independent Motion Pictures Company (which later became Universal Studios) and then Majestic Film Corporation, because the two offered her the astounding sum of $175 and $225 a week, respectively. In January 1911, she married fellow actor Owen Moore.

Unhappy with the movies in which she was appearing, she took a cut in salary to return to Biograph in 1912, which was producing better quality pictures. But Pickford longed to return to the stage and dreamed of starring on the Great White Way. She returned to New York to appear in Belasco's *A Good Little Devil*, which opened in January 1913.

What she discovered, much to her surprise, was that she actually preferred the more intimate medium of film. When the show closed in May, she returned to Hollywood and never looked back. She joined Adolph Zukor's new film company, Famous Players, which would one day evolve into Paramount Studios. Incredibly popular with the public, and a canny businesswoman, Pickford had control over the production of her own films and was making $10,000 a week by 1916 when she met Fairbanks.

By then both actors were unhappy in their marriages. Soon, friendship blossomed into an affair. Conveniently, in

1917, they set out on a nationwide tour by rail (along with Charlie Chaplin) to sell war bonds.

Perhaps it was during these travels that Fairbanks, Pickford, and Chaplin compared notes. All three believed that the established studios were holding them back commercially and financially. In February 1919, along with D. W. Griffith, they founded their own studio, United Artists, which gave them complete artistic control and distribution of their films.

Meanwhile, the romance between Fairbanks and Pickford continued. Although they were concerned how their fans would react if they divorced their spouses to marry each other, they couldn't deny their love. On March 5, 1919, Fairbanks and his wife divorced; Pickford's divorce became final on March 2, 1920. A mere twenty-six days later, the movie stars were wed.

They need not have worried about their followers. The couple was swarmed during their honeymoon in Europe, and riots broke out wherever they went in London and Paris. Their return to the States was celebrated by both the public and the press.

In 1919 Fairbanks purchased (possibly with Pickford) about eighteen acres on Summit Drive in Benedict Canyon above Beverly Hills. At the time, the only building on the land was a modest hunting lodge. The couple renovated and expanded the house into a twenty-two-room mansion and, by combining their names, dubbed it Pickfair.

The pair loved to entertain. And it wasn't just movie industry people who coveted an invitation to Pickfair. Over the years guests included Nöel Coward, Jack Dempsey, Sir Arthur Conan Doyle, Amelia Earhart, Albert Einstein, F. Scott Fitzgerald, Charles Lindbergh, Helen Keller, George Bernard

Shaw, H. G. Wells, the Duke and Duchess of Windsor, and the Crown Prince of Japan!

Added into the mix were a few commoners for good measure. Like me, thought Frank, as he stood in the massive entryway, trying to soak in the lavish surroundings. The mock Tudor home had been designed by Wallace Nell, one of the top architects in Los Angeles. It had two wings, one 95 feet long, the other 125 feet, overlooking the canyon below. The first floor had a living room (the size of a small ballroom, Frank noted), screening room, dining room, kitchen, breakfast nook, sun porch, and rooms for the staff. Upstairs were five guest bedrooms in addition to the master bedroom suite, and a third floor held a billiards room and bowling alley.

Frank marveled at the frescoes on the ceiling as well as the expensive but tasteful art and furniture throughout what could only be considered a palace. Although he probably wouldn't get a chance to visit the grounds, he knew they contained formal gardens, stables, and a crescent-shaped swimming pool. *Just think of that,* Frank marveled, *having your very own swimming pool.* People said it was the first pool on private property anywhere in Hollywood.

Of course, the couple could afford it. Some of Pickford's films were grossing over $1 million, and it was fair to say she was probably the most famous woman in the world. And Fairbanks was no slouch either. Beginning in 1920 the actor, who had always shown athletic grace in his films, began to star in a series of wildly successful costume dramas. Before Tyrone Power, before Errol Flynn, Douglas Fairbanks became the first great swashbuckler of the silent-film era, portraying a dashing hero in such films as *The Mark of Zorro, The Three Musketeers, Robin Hood, The Thief of Bagdad,* and *The Black Pirate.*

The two were not only rich but beloved by their peers as well. In 1921 they helped establish the Motion Picture Fund to assist actors in need. In January 1927 they were among thirty-six founding members of the Motion Picture Academy of Arts and Sciences, and Fairbanks was elected its first president. That April 30, they were the first to place their hands and feet into wet concrete outside Grauman's Chinese Theatre. Fairbanks and Pickford were partners in the syndicate that financed the Roosevelt Hotel on Hollywood Boulevard across the street from the Chinese Theatre, and when the first Academy Awards were presented in the hotel's Blossom Room in 1929, Fairbanks hosted the event.

From where he was standing in the central foyer, drink in hand, Frank let his eyes sweep in a grand circle. They came to rest on the wide staircase leading up to the second floor. And then, something strange started to happen.

Maybe it was the dim lighting; maybe it was the late hour, or perhaps it was the alcohol. But as he stared, a petite, translucent female form slowly began to appear half-way up the stairwell, less than twenty feet away from him. She wasn't dressed formally, as were the guests. She seemed to be one of the staff members, and, for some inexplicable reason, she was holding sheet music. Her eyes rested briefly on Frank, neither acknowledging nor ignoring him; then she turned, walked up one or two stairs—or did she float?—and then simply faded into nothingness. The spirit was gone.

Frank freaked out. But whom could he tell? "Excuse me, Miss Pickford, Mr. Fairbanks, but did you know your house is haunted?" There was no way he was going to approach anyone about what he had just seen.

Not being a confidant of his hosts, Frank didn't know that Fairbanks and Pickford had already seen the phantom for themselves—on four separate occasions. At first they were, well, not exactly frightened, but certainly startled. After they told a few close friends about the experience, an absurd rumor started around town that the spectre was a female servant who'd been shot to death in the house. Preposterous. They would have known if anyone, especially one of their own employees, had died there. Nevertheless, the story persists to this very day.

By the time of the party, trouble was brewing in paradise. Pickford was growing too old to play the waifs that had made her famous, and although her 1929 film *Coquette* (her first sound movie) had won her critical acclaim (and an Oscar), her admirers never warmed to her new persona. Her next film, *The Taming of the Shrew*, the only movie in which she costarred with her husband, was Fairbanks's first talkie, but the novelty was not enough. Audiences stayed away in droves.

Pickford made only three more films, retiring from the silver screen in 1933. Fairbanks made four before throwing in the towel in 1934. Meanwhile, he had begun an affair with Lady Sylvia Ashley, and when news of the relationship became common knowledge, he and Pickford separated. They divorced in January 1936.

As part of the settlement, Pickford received the mansion, which Neff, the original architect, had remodeled in 1934 and 1935, turning it into an English Regency–style manor.

In March 1936 Fairbanks and Lady Ashley married. Then in June of the following year, Pickford married actor-bandleader Charles "Buddy" Rogers, with whom she had costarred in *My Best Girl* in 1927.

Fairbanks died of a heart attack in 1939. His health had been failing for several years, caused at least in part by his heavy smoking. He was buried in Forest Lawn Memorial Park in Glendale, but two years later his widow transferred his remains to Hollywood Forever Cemetery, where he was entombed in a massive marble sarcophagus.

Pickford stayed active as a producer, but she eventually sold her shares of United Artists in 1956. In her remaining years, she became more and more of a recluse, no longer entertaining or seeing many friends, and seldom leaving the shelter of Pickfair. In 1976, when she received an honorary Academy Award, rather than attend the ceremony she taped her acceptance speech at the mansion in advance.

Pickford died of a cerebral hemorrhage in 1979 and was buried in Forest Lawn Memorial Park in Glendale. For a time, Rogers lived in the empty mansion. But he was not alone. It wasn't long before he saw a ghost for himself.

But this time it wasn't the phantom on the stairwell that Fairbanks and Pickford had observed. No. Rogers—and his friends!—was visited by a beautiful woman in a long, white ruffled gown walking in the vestibule and the living room.

"Mary?" he croaked in a soft, disbelieving whisper. "Is that you?"

Shortly thereafter Rogers moved into a smaller home, and the Pickfair property was subdivided and put on the market. The house remained vacant for several years before Dr. Jerry Buss, longtime owner of the Los Angeles Lakers, bought it in 1980.

According to legend, the hauntings didn't just continue during the Buss years at Pickfair: They increased! In addition to seeing the Woman in White (who was never definitively identified as Pickford), some guests spotted a male phantom in the entrance hall that they thought looked a lot like Fairbanks. At least one other unidentifiable spectre also appeared in the hallway from time to time. And then there was a ghostly maid, a different apparition than the one carrying sheet music Frank had seen, who would pop up in the servants' quarters.

In 1988 businessman Meshulam Riklis and his wife, Pia Zadora, purchased Pickfair. Two years later, in what many in the Hollywood community considered an act of sacrilege and historic desecration, Riklis and Zadora razed the mansion and built a new one in its place. They defended their actions by saying that the seventy-year-old building was in such bad condition that repairs and renovations were impossible.

If nothing else, they exorcised the spirits.

There have been no new reports of hauntings since the demolition of the old mansion, so whatever spectral forces were there must have lost interest once the original Pickfair was gone.

In 2005 Pickfair and its remaining 2.7 acres were purchased by UNICOM International Inc. as its headquarters. Today, all that remains of the original, magnificent estate are the tall wrought-iron gates, still topped by a large, ornate "P," and the enormous swimming pool.

But if you ever get a chance to enter the property, keep your eyes peeled. Many times ghosts don't leave forever; they just go into hiding until the time is right to return. "America's Sweetheart" could simply be waiting for you to visit!

Chapter 2

The Hot Toddy

Was it suicide? An accident? Or murder? After the suspicious death of early screen actress Thelma Todd, her ghost began appearing in the building that housed her speakeasy as well as in the garage where her body was discovered. So far, her phantom hasn't given any clues as to the circumstances of her demise.

How dare he!

After all, *she* was the movie star! *And* most of the money behind their partnership. Besides, it was *her house*! If it weren't for her, he'd still be living with his wife in the place up on the hill. He had no right to lock her out!

Thelma Todd banged on the door again. She'd wake up the whole neighborhood if she had to.

"Roland! Damn it! Open the door!"

Finally, a light appeared in one of the bedrooms. Heavy steps made their way to the front door, and Thelma heard a small click as the door was unlatched. It cracked open, and Thelma could just barely make out her lover's face, silhouetted by the light coming from down the hallway. After making sure it was Todd—and that she was alone—the man opened the door wider. But as she started to wobble inside, he suddenly blocked her path.

"Let me in, baby. Why'ja lock the door? I thought I was gonna freeze out here."

"Toddy, you're drunk. And late. I told you I was going to lock the door at two. And I did."

Roland West had had it with Todd. Tonight was just the latest of an increasing number of lovers' spats, most of them caused by her incessant drinking. In fact, that's why the actress had been driven home from the party on the Sunset Strip. She had so many car accidents while under the influence that the studio demanded she have a chauffeur. They had too big of an investment in her.

"C'mon, honey. So I'm a little late and had a coupla drinks." Her words were badly slurring by now. "It was a special night."

But her pleas fell on deaf ears. "It's always a special night with you. Go somewhere else and sleep it off!"

And with that, he slammed the door in her face.

That no good bastard, thought Todd. She turned to peer into the darkness. The road was empty. Where was her driver? Oh, right, she had told him he could go, that she could make her own way up to the house. Well, what was she to do now?

It would be hard for anyone, especially one of her fans, to believe that Todd could be stuck in such a situation. After all, she was famous, adored by millions!

But like many film actors, Thelma Todd had been born nowhere near the glitz and glitter of Tinseltown. Brought up in Lawrence, Massachusetts, she had studied to become a schoolteacher. But her life changed dramatically after she entered a beauty pageant and was named Miss Massachusetts. Paramount scouted her, and she was enrolled in its acting school on the East Coast. In 1926, at the tender age of twenty, she appeared in her first movie, *Fascinating Youth*, shot in Paramount's Long Island studio.

Soon she was sent out west, and by 1930 Todd had appeared in forty movies, mostly in supporting roles. Then in 1931 she was paired with Zasu Pitts for the first in a series of slapstick comedies for Hal Roach. Before long, she had also starred in *Monkey Business* and *Horse Feathers* with the Marx Brothers and played opposite Jimmy Durante and Buster Keaton. She caused such a sensation on the screen that she was nicknamed "The Hot Toddy," which inspired a drink by the same name. Others called her "The Ice Cream Blonde."

By the time West locked Todd out of her own house that night, she had made more than 130 shorts and features. Standing there on the doorstep, she remembered how half on a lark but also with a keen eye for business she had opened up a roadhouse on the coast highway in Pacific Palisades. (It was also a kind of insurance. Even though she hadn't been affected by the film industry's switch to sound, she had seen how people's careers could evaporate overnight.) She dubbed the three-story Spanish-style building Thelma Todd's Sidewalk Café.

The first floor housed a restaurant. Upstairs she opened a private club called Joya's, and above that were her private apartments. Hers and Roland's, that is.

For two tempestuous years, she had been married to Pasquale "Pat" De Cicco, who was involved in a number of criminal activities, most probably including prostitution and bootlegging. But as the old song goes, De Cicco "done her wrong," with frequent fights and physical abuse. In 1934 Todd finally got up the courage to divorce the louse, on the grounds of incompatibility and cruelty.

When Todd met West while cruising on a yacht off Catalina Island in 1930, he was a well-established movie writer, producer, and director, having been at the helm of at least a dozen films, perhaps most notably *The Bat* and *Alibi*. The following year, he directed her (in a minor role) in *Corsair*. It would turn out to be the last film of West's career.

When he went into business with Todd at the café, West wasn't single. In 1918 he had married Jewel Carmen, a spirited blonde actress who'd been in movies for six years. For a time, she was in Mack Sennett's stable of actors at Keystone, working under the name Evelyn Quick, before moving on to Fox Film Corporation. Carmen retired when she married West, but he convinced her to return to the screen in 1920 for two of his own films. Then in 1926 she made her final film appearance in *The Bat*.

When Carmen and West split up, the former director moved with Todd into the rooms over the café. They lived in separate bedrooms, connected by a sliding door.

Though the restaurant's address was 17575 Pacific Coast Highway, their apartment was numbered on a street that hugged the cliff above the speakeasy, at 17531 Posetano Road. The doorway didn't open out onto Posetano, however. To get there, it was necessary to leave the apartment and climb a steep staircase up a hillside—almost three hundred steps.

And it was at that staircase that Todd now stared in the darkness of the chilly Sunday morning, December 15, 1935. Her garage was at the top of all those steps. Maybe Todd could catch some sleep in her car. Carefully, methodically, she started the climb.

The events of the evening began to swirl around in her head. British hall comedian Stanley Lupino and his daughter Ida (who was still coming up through the ranks in Hollywood but was already one of Todd's best friends) had thrown a party in her honor at the fabulous Cafe Trocadero on the Sunset Strip. When Todd heard that her former husband would be there, she asked Lupino to seat De Cicco next to her. (God help her, despite everything she still had feelings for the jerk.)

But De Cicco had shown up with a Warner Bros. actress, Margaret Lindsay, on his arm. Todd was sure he had brought the woman to deliberately humiliate her in front of her friends, and she threw a fit. The exchange was short but particularly spiteful, and after staying just an hour, De Cicco left.

By that time, it was already 1:00 a.m., and Todd, embarrassed and dejected, began to drink heavily. It was almost a quarter to three when she stumbled out of the Troc and into her waiting limousine. With so little traffic at that hour, her driver, Ernest Peters, had gotten her home quickly, somewhere between 3:15 and 3:45.

Which brought her to her current predicament. So here she was, making her way up to the garage. It was only a few more steps, and she'd be there. She couldn't have seemed more out of place. She was still stunning at thirty, dressed in her mauve and silver silk evening gown, mink coat, high-heeled sandals, and thousands of dollars' worth of jewelry. Anyone who saw her would have wondered how a vision like that could be trudging her way, all alone, up the side of a hillside at almost four in the morning.

Thelma finally made it to the top of the stairs, paused, straightened her dress, then walked across to the double doors of the garage. Thank God it was unlocked! Her car, a brown 1934 Lincoln Phaeton convertible, was safely parked right where it belonged, and she quickly slid in behind the wheel.

As she started to doze, she unconsciously shivered. Even with the doors to the garage closed, the early winter winds whipping off the ocean and up the cliff were able to find her. Thelma fumbled in her purse for the car keys. Maybe if she ran the engine for just a few minutes the heater would warm her up.

As Shannon crept along narrow Posetano Road in the Castellammare section of Pacific Palisades, she could see Pacific Coast Highway at the bottom of the embankment. Directly below her stood a three-story red-tiled building.

This was the landmark her friends had told her about. When she saw it she was to start looking for a place to park. Their house would be along this stretch.

It hadn't been the easiest place to find. The streets in the area formed a mini-labyrinth, full of dead ends and cul-de-sacs. Even the two halves of Posetano were separated by an outgrowth of the cliff and didn't connect with each other.

Shannon parked, locked the door, and looked for some house numbers. Her friend's apartment had to be close.

It was late afternoon, and the sun was just beginning to set over the Pacific. Without thinking, she let her eyes follow one of the long shadows spreading across the street to the twin blue doors of a garage about a half block in front of her—17531.

Then, out of the silence, Shannon suddenly noticed the low murmur of a car engine idling, just a few feet down the road. But it wasn't coming from one of the cars parked on the street. It was coming from . . . that garage.

That's not good, she thought, *starting up your engine before you open the garage door. Doesn't the driver know how dangerous carbon monoxide fumes can be?* She waited patiently, expecting the doors to open and the car to back out at any second.

But it never did. Shannon inched closer to the garage. She could smell the unmistakable scent of car exhaust coming out from under the closed blue doors. The left-hand door had a small window cut into it, and, although she knew she was snooping, Shannon stepped up to the glass, shielded her eyes with both hands, and peeked inside.

Instantly, the rumbling of the engine stopped. A last whiff of exhaust wafted in the wind; then it, too, was gone. The room was empty.

No car? Then what had been making the sound? And what about the car fumes?

She peered through the window into the vacant space one more time. Nothing there. Well, perhaps she had imagined it after all. She turned and started down Posetano. Her friend's place had to be there someplace.

About ten-thirty on Monday morning, Todd's maid, Mae Whitehead, made the long climb up to the garage. Todd had been expected at the Hal Roach Studios, where she was shooting *The Bohemian Girl* with Laurel and Hardy. But she had never shown up. Frantic calls followed, her house was searched, and her usual haunts were checked. The garage seemed to be the one place no one had looked.

Whitehead flicked on the light as she walked into the garage and immediately spotted the actress slumped behind the wheel of her car. Was she sleeping off a bender? The maid crept forward, not sure whether—or how—to disturb her boss.

It was then that she saw the blood.

It seemed to be everywhere. On Todd's face, on the seat beside her, on the running boards, on the floor of the garage. Whitehead screamed.

The true cause of Thelma Todd's death, or at least the full story, may never be known. There was only a cursory investigation. The coroner quickly concluded—some say under pressure—that Todd passed out from her heavy drinking and injured herself as she struck the steering wheel. (The alcohol content in her blood was so high that police were surprised she'd been able to make it up the stairs.) Then, after she had fallen asleep, she was overcome by the toxic exhaust from the car. The coroner's official verdict was accidental carbon monoxide poisoning.

But rumors immediately began to circulate that Todd had been murdered, either by West or De Cicco, or perhaps by the mob, which was upset that she wouldn't allow them to control gambling inside her club. After her viewing and funeral at Forest Lawn Cemetery in Glendale, Thelma Todd was cremated—proof positive to some that there had been a cover-up because her body could never be reexamined. When Todd's mother died, she had her daughter's ashes placed in her coffin and buried with her back in Lawrence.

One of the most unsettling aspects of the police inquiry was that several people claimed to have seen Todd alive and kicking well after she was already deceased. Foremost among these was Jewel Carmen, who recognized Todd driving her car down Vine Street. She followed in her own vehicle for a few blocks but could never get Todd's attention. When Todd turned right onto Santa Monica Boulevard heading toward the beach, Carmen gave up the chase. She figured she'd see Todd soon enough. She had no way of knowing that Todd was already dead, sitting behind the wheel of that car.

Ever since Todd's death, there have been reports of a diaphanous female form, assumed to be hers, appearing at the top of a staircase inside what was her old café. The

15,000-square-foot building still stands, owned today by Paulist Productions, which makes and distributes religious films. The apparition is said to show up from time to time, hovering above the steps and then gliding down the stairs toward an open courtyard. Could that have been the route Todd used at some point on the last night of her life?

And that's not all. People have heard the engine of a phantom car running inside the garage where the body was found, and some have caught the telltale odor of exhaust fumes even when no vehicle was parked there.

In life, Thelma Todd, the Hot Toddy, was a free and effervescent spirit. Why shouldn't she remain one after death?

Chapter 3
The Cowboy Spirit

The silent screen cowboy William S. Hart loved the outdoors, so he built his ranch north of Hollywood in the Santa Clarita hills. Today, the house is a museum, but that doesn't stop the movie star, his sister, and the family dogs from continuing to make themselves at home.

The docent, tired after her long day, decided to take one last swing through the house—just for herself—before security started locking up for the night. Several classes of elementary students had come on a field trip to visit the museum that day, and she was exhausted. But something told her— some odd, indistinct feeling—she should make the rounds one more time on her own.

Busy days like today didn't happen much anymore. School budgets, like everybody's budgets, were tight, and more students now experienced the museum through its outreach program than actually got to visit the ranch.

The students today had been well-enough behaved on the thirty-minute tours, but they were still children, so Patti had had to keep her eyes on them the whole time, even while she was trying to guide them through the mansion explaining who had lived there and why he should be remembered. Just as important, she had to make sure nothing got broken and nobody strayed from the group.

Patti loved the place. She had first seen it as a little girl, when she was seven or eight. Her family had regularly gone riding out of a stables located in nearby Santa Clarita, so when she'd found out that a real live cowboy had lived in the area and his ranch was open as a museum, she'd begged her mom and dad to take her for a visit.

It never occurred to Patti at the time that the rugged, six-foot-two William S. Hart wasn't actually a cowboy. She knew that all those people she saw in cowboy-and-Indian movies and the Westerns on TV were actors—she lived just twenty-five miles north of Hollywood—but she thought (or at least hoped) that maybe Hart was the real thing.

And in a way, he was.

Hart was most likely born in 1864, far away from the Wild West and the open prairies, in Newburgh, New York, on the Hudson River, just fifty miles north of Manhattan. His father, who ground millstones for a living, dreamed of owning his own mill. He knew his best chances would be in the burgeoning west, so he moved the family to Illinois. Unfortunately, he was injured when a metal chip hit one of his eyes, and his vision problems plagued the family for years.

After successful surgery back in New York, Hart's father was on the move again, this time to Iowa and Wisconsin. Along the way, young William came in contact with Native Americans, especially the Sioux, and he came to admire and respect their culture. By the time the Harts arrived in Minnesota, William had fallen in love with the frontier.

Around the time Hart turned seventeen, the family moved back to Newburgh, then down to New York City. The boy did a variety of odd jobs to help support the family, including messenger and delivery work, for which he sometimes received theater tickets as tips. What he saw on the stage cast its spell over him, and Hart decided to become an actor.

He first traveled to London for acting lessons, then went on to visit the theaters of Paris before returning to New York to study. His first stage appearance was in his native New-burgh in 1887, and he made his Broadway debut eight years later in the drama *Mistress Betty*.

Hart appeared in thirteen plays in New York City—fourteen, if you count the original 1899 Broadway production of *Ben Hur* and its return engagement as two separate shows. In both versions, Hart played the role of the Roman charioteer, Messala. (And, yes, the show did have an actual chariot race onstage, accomplished by the use of a treadmill.)

Then, in 1905, Hart was cast in a Western drama, *The Squaw Man*, in which he got to portray a low-down ornery villain. He realized that, with his background, it was a per-fect role for him, and he made sure that the press publicized that he was an actual frontiersman.

And with good reason. America was enthralled with a romantic notion of the Old West. If anyone needed proof, Annie Oakley had just spent years touring with Buffalo Bill's Wild West and Congress of Rough Riders of the World. Teddy Roosevelt had even borrowed part of the show's name for his cavalry during the invasion of Cuba in the recent Span-ish–American War.

Hart's Western roles continued. After eighteen success-ful months in *The Squaw Man*, Hart went on the road in a stage adaptation of the popular 1902 Western novel *The Vir-ginian*. The year 1912 brought him the Broadway production of *The Trail of the Lonesome Pine*, and it was while touring in the show the next year that Hart caught his first cowboy movie.

He was appalled by what he saw. The wardrobe was all wrong. The plots were too melodramatic and the actors unconvincing. Suddenly, William S. Hart had a calling. He would become a movie cowboy and let America see what the real Old West (or at least his memory of it) was like.

When his troupe reached Hollywood, he called an old friend, Thomas Ince, by then a film producer and director, with whom he had already discussed the possibility of appearing in Westerns.

Although studios could shoot interior scenes on sound-stages, Westerns required grand, rugged vistas and miles of open space. Ince established an outdoor studio/camp (which he named Inceville) in the San Ynez Canyon for shooting cowboy pictures. It was located where Pacific Coast Highway meets Sunset Boulevard (very close to the spot that, two decades later, Thelma Todd would build her now-haunted Sidewalk Café). In addition, Ince hired a company of cow-pokes and Native Americans to populate the picture, and many of them lived in Inceville on a regular basis.

Hart toured the compound with his friend, and by the time he left he was convinced that Western movies were his future. After the run of *Lonesome Pine* was over, Hart returned to Los Angeles to make his transition—at the age of forty-nine—to motion pictures.

His first films, in 1914, were the two-reelers *The Bad Buck of Santa Ynez* and *His Hour of Manhood*. That same year he also portrayed the title character in *Two-Gun Hicks*, which led to the nickname that stayed with him for the rest of his life: Two-Gun Bill.

Hart began to work with Triangle Studios, built in 1915 by Ince, D. W. Griffith, and Mack Sennett in Culver City, just a few miles west of Hollywood. (Three years later, the company became Sam Goldwyn Studios; after a merger with two other studios in 1924, it became the storied Metro Goldwyn Mayer Studios, or MGM.)

In 1917, when Ince moved to the Famous Players–Lansky studio, Hart followed suit, where Adolph Zukor put him under contract. As Hart's fame rose, so did his salary. He earned $125 per week while making *The Disciple* in 1915; for *The Narrow Trail* in 1917 he earned $150,000 plus a percentage of the profits. His 1919 contract with Artcraft (which became part of Paramount) raised the figure to $250,000, plus percentages.

By the end of the decade, Hart had made an astonishing sixty movies, many of which he had also directed. But his era was rapidly coming to a close as audiences wanted more lighthearted pictures and colorful cowboy heroes, which they found in the Tom Mix/Hoot Gibson mold.

(Hart's career was also hurt in 1923 by a paternity suit, in which his wife, already in the middle of divorce proceedings, accused Hart of fathering a child with another woman. The case was later dismissed.)

During the 1920s, Hart made just thirteen more films. His last movie, *Tumbleweeds*, was released in 1925, right before the end of the silent-film era.

Back around the time Hart had started working for the Triangle Picture Company, he brought his younger sister Mary Ellen, an invalid, out to Los Angeles to live with him. (His other two sisters, who were both married, remained back east.) The cowboy star briefly became engaged to a twenty-four-year-old actress, Jane Novak, around 1920 before marrying a different young actress, Winifred Westover, in December 1921. Within six months, though pregnant, she moved out, some say because Mary Ellen was more important to Hart than she was. A son, William S. Hart Jr., was born in September 1922. Then, after years of litigation, the Harts were divorced in 1927.

When Hart retired from the movie business, he was around sixty years old—and very wealthy. He had always admired the scenery in the ranch lands surrounding Los Angeles, and in February 1921 he had bought the 229-acre Horseshoe Ranch in Newhall, in the rolling hills about twenty-five miles north of Hollywood where many of his later movies had been shot. He then hired architect Arthur Kelly to design a two-story, twenty-two-room ranch house high on a hilltop on the property.

Between 1925 and 1927, while the home was being completed, Hart spent his time between his Hollywood adobe and a small house that had been built in 1910 at the entrance to the ranch. He named his new estate La Loma de los Vientos, or Hill of the Winds. It was built in a Spanish Colonial Revival style, with white stucco walls, a low pitched roof covered with red tiles, and a wooden porch extending out from the second floor. The front door opened into a circular entrance-way, which featured a high ceiling decorated to resemble an eight-spoked wagon wheel.

As Patti walked through the dwelling, she realized Hart's love for the Old West could be seen everywhere in the way he'd furnished it. There were paintings and sculptures by Frederick Remington, Joe De Young, Charles Christadoro, and "America's Cowboy Artist" Charles M. Russell; cowboy movie memorabilia; Native American pieces including bows and arrows, wardrobe, textiles, wampum—a veritable kaleidoscope of artifacts. His collection also included numerous rifles and pistols, although for safety reasons only a few long arms were kept on display—very high up on the walls, out of reach of small hands.

In the living room, an enormous bearskin rug was spread out in front of the fireplace. It was flanked by Navajo rugs, and another Indian carpet hung on the wall as a tapestry. In the dining room, one of the walls was ornamented with horseshoes.

You could tell, Patti reflected, that Hart was not just acting in his movies: He was a true fan of the Wild West—so much so that both legendary lawmen Bat Masterson and Wyatt Earp were personal friends. (In fact, Hart acted as one of Earp's pallbearers in 1929.) Perhaps it was the adventure-some spirit of the frontier that attracted Hart. After all, hadn't he also befriended that pioneer of the skies, Amelia Earhart? (They had met after he found out she was the one disturbing his peace by flying her plane over his house.) Patti glanced over at the photo of the celebrated pilot, still sitting in the same spot Hart had put it on display so many years before.

Patti walked up the large circular staircase to the second level and passed the telephone booth in the hall outside Mary Ellen's bedroom suite. To think: not just a phone but an entire telephone booth! Patti smiled involuntarily. She had once checked the directory hanging inside. It was all of one page, listing just forty-five names.

Mary Ellen had passed away in 1944, and the Western superstar followed two years later. He left all of his land, buildings, and furnishings to the City of Los Angeles Department of Recreation and Parks to be maintained as a museum and public park; and, for the most part, the house remained exactly the way Hart left it.

Something drew Patti to Hart's private rooms. In the outer sitting area she couldn't help but notice the raised wooden platforms with cushions on them that Hart had constructed for his Harlequin Great Danes. And there, sitting in the corner, was the black iron safe—a prop Hart had kept from one of his movies in which he'd supposedly kept old bones for his pets to chew. (After their deaths, many of the dogs were buried right there on the grounds down by the ranch hands' old bunkhouse. So, too, was Hart's favorite horse, Fritz, which he had first ridden way back on his initial visit to Inceville.)

Patti passed quietly into the master bedroom. With the house all but deserted, she could feel the silence envelop her. She stared at the photo of Hart's son resting on the dresser, the slippers by the bed, a box of cough drops and a cowboy hat on the nightstand.

The sun was low coming through the windows, and the room was starting to fall into dark shadows. Patti's eyes widened as she turned her gaze to the writing desk at the far side of the bed. She was *sure* she'd been alone upstairs. But there by the chair was a man, or at least the faint figure of a man. He stood with his back to Patti, and at first, he seemed to take no notice of her. Then he turned around.

With a gasp, Patti raised her hand to her lips. She would recognize that face anywhere. It was Hart!

Even as the apparition evaporated into the aether, the docent fled out of the room and down the stairs. Her supervisor never knew why Patti, one of the most dedicated volunteers at the museum, resigned without explanation the next day. Pity. If she had, the director could have assured Patti that she wasn't alone.

Yes, Patti's encounter that day was not the only one that had been experienced by people in the old Hart mansion. In fact, far from it. And Hart's ghost wasn't always found by the chair at his bedroom desk. He's also been seen reading the newspaper in the downstairs living room. Others have spotted him standing by the French doors in the "dogs' room"; sometimes he doesn't bother to manifest but simply taps people on the shoulder as they walk by.

Interestingly, Hart isn't the sole ghost that appears there. A security guard has reported seeing the phantom of a white dog in the room, and others have felt a disembodied canine rubbing up against them as they passed through the anteroom.

Some have even witnessed the ghost of the wheelchair-bound Mary Ellen seated by her bed.

Thousands of guests pass through the William S. Hart Museum every year. Most spend just a few leisurely hours there, touring the old ranch house and the main residence, stopping by the corral or the buffalo pens, maybe taking a light lunch at Mary Ellen's Tea House out back or walking one of the many hiking trails. They get to go home at the end of the day, however. The spirits of Hart, his sister, and their pets have decided to stay.

Chapter 4
The Man from
Beyond

Although primarily a stage performer, the master escape artist Harry Houdini also starred in several movies. His spirit, or some sort of glowing orb from the Other Side, has reportedly haunted the site of his Hollywood home for years. But did the great illusionist ever in fact live there? It's all part of the mystery that surrounds his life, death, and beyond.

Of course Justin knew it wasn't really Houdini's mansion. And it may or may not be haunted. Still, he had to see it for himself.

According to Hollywood legend, shining balls of light dart over the grounds of an estate where Houdini lived back around 1920, and people have claimed that they've seen an astral form hovering over the still-standing staircase in front of the ruins. Because Houdini, perhaps the most famous magician in history, supposedly stayed there, surely the apparition must be the great illusionist himself, right?

Well, Justin wasn't so sure. There was no proof that Houdini ever actually resided in the house. And during ten years of séances after his death, Houdini never appeared to his widow, Bess. If he wouldn't show up for her—which he'd promised he would try to do—why would he turn up someplace where he would have spent, at most, a few months?

But Justin had the disease: He was an amateur magician, one of those thousands of people, mostly men, who had received a magic kit when he was a kid and discovered that he enjoyed fooling people. By the time he was in his teens, he was performing at birthday parties, Cub Scout banquets, and church shows, making enough money that during his high school years he never had to ask "Would you like fries with that?" for a living.

Now, just out of college, he had decided to take his first trip out west and visit a famous private club for magicians known as the Magic Castle. While he was in Hollywood, he would also take a drive across town and see what remained of the mansion where Houdini *the actor* may have lived while he was in town—*and* find out whether all the rumors were true. Was the place really haunted by Houdini?

The pass over the Santa Monica Mountains between the San Fernando Valley and the coastal plain to the south in which the estate was located was a stagecoach route in the early days of Los Angeles. The first recorded owner of Laurel Canyon, as the area became known, was the Laurel Canyon Land Company, which took control of it in 1907.

One of the group's major shareholders was Ralf M. Walker, who ran a prestigious department (or possibly furniture) store in downtown L.A. About 1915 he began construction of a mansion at the intersection of Laurel Canyon Boulevard and Willow Glen Road, just north of the western end of Hollywood Boulevard. Over the next several years he hired dozens of European craftsmen to create Mediterranean-style landscaping in the rustic surroundings.

When work was completed, the three-story mansion had eleven bedrooms, nine baths, a ballroom, a separate ballet room and rehearsal hall, and an indoor aviary and pool. The four-acre property was dotted with stone walkways, fourteen terraces, grottoes, fountains, and an artesian spring that was channeled to produce man-made streams, water-falls, and ponds. A large masonry staircase led from the lower grounds up to the front of the mansion. Anyone who visited couldn't help but be impressed by the estate's size and splendor.

And one of those visitors was probably Houdini. By 1919, when Harry Houdini came to town to appear in movies, the escape artist was already world-famous. He had been born Erich Weiss in Budapest, Hungary, in 1874 but was brought to America as an infant. He grew up in Appleton, Wisconsin, before moving with the family to New York City in 1887. He "became" Harry Houdini in 1891, naming himself after a famous nineteenth-century French prestidigitator, Jean-Eugène Robert-Houdin. After the escape artist was discovered by vaudeville impresario Martin Beck in 1899, his career took off. For five years beginning in 1900, Houdini, assisted by his wife, Bess, toured Europe; by the time he returned to America he was an international sensation.

Houdini understood the power of the new medium of motion pictures early on. While in Paris in 1901, he performed a number of his escapes on a short film produced by Pathé called *Merveilleux Exploits du Célébre Houdini à Paris* (*The Marvelous Exploits of the Celebrated Houdini in Paris*), and he was a special effects supervisor for one of the company's other films, *The Mysteries of Myra*. He was offered the (nonmagical) leading role of Captain Nemo in Pathé's version of *20,000 Leagues Under the Sea*, but unfortunately the movie never got made.

In 1918, movie producer B. A. Rolfe offered him the chance to come to Hollywood to star in a fifteen-part serial called *The Master Mystery*, which was released the following year. When Rolfe's production company went out of business, Houdini moved over to the Famous Players–Lasky Corporation, where he made two films: *The Grim Game* in 1919 and then *Terror Island* in 1920.

Back in New York, Houdini founded his own company, the Houdini Picture Corporation, for which he produced and starred in two movies. *The Man from Beyond* (1922), for which he also wrote the screenplay, was particularly interesting because it explored the possibility of life after death and reincarnation. His last film, *Haldane of the Secret Service,* was released in 1923.

Houdini was many things, but a great actor was not one of them. Or perhaps the films didn't catch on because the daring stunts and escapes he performed in most of the story lines simply had to be experienced live. Whatever the reason, his movies weren't successful, so in 1923 he reluctantly gave up the business.

(His fame and involvement in the film industry were important enough, however, that in 1975 he would receive a star on the Hollywood Walk of Fame.)

At some point during his years in Tinseltown, the illusionist met Walker. Although he became a friend and possibly a business partner—he is said to have become a silent investor in the land company—Houdini most likely never lived in the Walker mansion.

But he *may* have lived across the street.

In addition to his main residence, Walker built a four-bedroom guesthouse on the other side of the boulevard, high on a bluff overlooking the gatehouse at the end of the driveway to his estate. The visitor's house in which Houdini probably stayed had an elevator that descended into the bedrock and was connected to the gatehouse via a tunnel under the road.

If the Houdinis *did* stay with Walker during their nine months or so in Hollywood, it was almost certainly in the guest facilities. The problem is, there is no lease or deed that shows Houdini as a tenant or owner of either house on the Walker estate.

Justin drove west on Hollywood Boulevard. After a slight curve at Fairfax, the road came to a T at Laurel Canyon Boulevard. He turned right and started up the hill. The house he sought would be about two miles up on the right.

After leaving Hollywood, Houdini entered perhaps the most controversial part of his career: He became a passionate debunker of Spiritualism, and during his performances he exposed the methods used by fraudulent mediums to deceive the unwary at séances.

Some say Houdini's crusade was really an attempt to find a true medium that had the power to get in touch with his beloved mother, who had died in 1913. People would point to the secret pact he made with Bess as proof that he believed in at least the possibility of communication with the dead. Harry and Bess promised each other that whichever one of them died first would try with all his or her might to contact the other from the Next World.

Houdini was the first to go—on Halloween 1926—as a result of peritonitis caused by a ruptured appendix.

(This may have come as the result of a blow he received from a McGill University student while in his dressing room at the Princess Theatre in Montreal. The most commonly heard version of the story is that the young man asked whether it was true that Houdini could take a blow to the stomach without being injured. When the magician nonchalantly affirmed that he could, the young man took the reply as an invitation and punched the performer several times before he was prepared. Although highly unlikely, some have suggested that the assault was, in fact, a concerted attack orchestrated by the so-called Psychic Mafia as retribution for Houdini's campaign against Spiritualism.)

Sometime later, Bess Houdini, along with her personal manager, Edward Saint, definitely moved into the Walker guesthouse, so it's likely (though not proven) that the widow had either stayed there previously or, at the very least, knew the owner from the magic duo's earlier stay in Hollywood.

Some say that Walker himself referred to the guest residence as "Houdini House" while the magician was there. Others believe that the claim Houdini owned the Walker estate stems from the Pacific Coast Association of Magicians convention that was held in Los Angeles in 1935. Bess invited about five hundred magicians and their wives to a reception held in the gardens below the main house on July 24, and newspapers covering the event referred to Walker's house as the "Houdini mansion." Regardless of how the nickname started, it has stuck to the property all these years.

Walker died in 1935, and Bess Houdini moved when the property was sold, thus ending any connection the legendary magician may have had with the estate. Bess lived for eight more years, and although she ended her public attempts to communicate with her husband (including a final séance on the roof of Hollywood's Knickerbocker Hotel on Halloween 1936), she never fully gave up hope that one day she might receive a message from him.

In 1928 a medium, the Reverend Arthur Ford, claimed to have contacted Houdini's mother during a séance, and he told Bess that the spirit had said, "Forgive." Knowing that Houdini hoped this word would be part of any legitimate message from his mother (and forgetting that she had mentioned that fact to a newspaperman the previous year), Bess agreed to attend a séance with Ford.

Initially Bess reported that during the subsequent sitting Ford received the code word she and Harry had worked out in advance—"believe"—but by 1930 she had modified her stance. Perhaps she changed her mind after some accused the pair of being in collusion; at one point she claimed she was ill at the time of the séance and was therefore unsure what she may have heard. Others pointed out that she had already revealed the supposedly secret message to many people, any number of whom could have given the information to Ford.

Did Bess ever really "believe" she had heard from Harry? Justin wondered. There was no way to tell. He saw the intersection with Lookout Mountain Avenue, so he knew the Houdini property would be ahead on the right at any second.

And there it was! A magnificent, crumbling medley of concrete walkways, staircases, rock-reinforced walls, stucco niches and . . . wait, there was a small lane to the right, just at the end of the property. Willow Glen Road. Justin made a sharp turn onto the side street and found himself at the end of the gated driveway that led up to what was left of the mansion.

If he wanted to get a good look at the property, he'd have to park the car. But where? He'd didn't dare leave it on Willow Glen. It was signposted as a No Parking zone, and he didn't want to come back and find that his rental car had been towed away. The last vehicles he'd seen parked along Laurel Canyon were a mile or more back. Reluctantly he started down the boulevard.

Justin tried to remember what had happened to the mansion after Houdini's time. Following Walker's death, a real estate broker, Charles Wilson, bought the estate. He in turn leased it to an ex-con-turned-evangelist named Joe Jeffers, who renamed the house the Temple of Yahweh and opened it as a retreat for his faithful followers. Before long, the group's unusual activities, including predawn rituals and prayers in the gardens, disturbed neighbors, who brought suit against Jeffers. In 1947 Jeffers's mismanagement of church funds led to charges of fraud, and he was returned to prison on a parole violation.

The next resident was no less colorful: a wealthy heiress who had taken the sobriquet Eve, the Green Virgin. She was well known for her unique hairstyle—she wrapped it to look like a turban—and for wearing sheer, almost see-through clothing.

Wilson died in 1954, and the mansion was next bought by Fania Pearson. She was its owner when a brush fire swept through the canyon in 1959, reducing the house to charred rubble. It stood there unoccupied, a magnificent ruin until 1968, when the city of Los Angeles demanded that the site be leveled out of safety concerns. Not only were trespassers—of which there were many—at substantial risk, but traffic slowed to almost a standstill as drivers gawked at the derelict site when they passed by.

In 1969 and 1970, Pearson allowed noted ghost hunter Hans Holzer to visit the property, which by then had acquired a reputation for being haunted. People were reporting ghostly illuminated globes and apparitions floating over the grounds.

Naysayers pointed out that the unusual lights and strange noises had all-too-human causes: probably those damn hippies! Apparently, during the decadent decade of the psychedelic '60s, occultists held nighttime séances on the property. (Though she offered no proof, Pearson claimed that Houdini had also conducted séances in the parlor of the mansion.) Then, too, by the late 1960s, the tall grass and secluded caves covering the property had become home to vagrants, so it shouldn't have been surprising if now and then someone spied unidentified shapes strolling over the ghostly ruins in the nighttime hours.

But there were those who were sure the phenomena were otherworldly. And for many of those believers, it was obvious that the phantom form seen roaming the gardens, the terraces, and especially the remains of the ornate stone staircase had to be none other than Houdini himself.

In June 1997 Patrick Williams, an antiques dealer and magic aficionado from Georgia, bought the property, primarily because of its Houdini association, for just under $400,000 and began the daunting task of restoring the estate.

For over a year curiosity seekers watched as the brush was cleared and the paths and stone relics were revealed. Some paranormalists thought that maybe it was all this activity that roused spirits from the past. Justin didn't know about that. But he *did* know that, if he was ever going to see the ghost—whether it was Houdini or not—it had to be that night. It was his last evening in town.

The workers were long gone by the time Justin had parked far down the ravine and walked the long stretch up Laurel Canyon. The sun had begun to set, casting deep shadows across the narrow canyon, and traffic thinned out. Cars were already beginning to turn on their headlights; many, unaccustomed to seeing a pedestrian along the road, flashed their high beams in warning as they passed.

Justin knew better than to wander around the extensive grounds. It was private property, and he didn't want to trespass. So at the southern end of the gardens, just off the street and slightly hidden under a low palm, he spread out a small mat, took out a bottle of water and his binoculars, and waited.

As twilight and then a quiet darkness settled in, he felt completely alone. No wonder people fought to buy property in this wooded glen. If he didn't know better, it would be impossible to convince him that he was less than five miles from the rowdy din of the Sunset Strip.

It was after nine now, and he suddenly became aware of how chilly the night had become. A low breeze brushed against his face, carrying the scent of freshly mown grass to his nostrils. From where he sat he had an unobstructed view of the ruins farther up the hill.

Without warning, a cool glint of white light appeared on the large central staircase, causing Justin to involuntarily raise the binoculars to his eyes. What was that?!

There, standing halfway up the set of steps, was a shining, translucent shape, not tall, but definitely human. And it was moving, slowly, up the flight of stairs. Justin tried to focus on the form's face, but it was impossible. Whatever it was, it seemed to be emitting a soft, iridescent radiance that prevented him from zeroing in on any of its features.

Stunned, he lowered the glasses and simply stared at the glowing spectre. As it drifted higher toward the landing at the top of the staircase, the light from the figure began to intensify. Brighter. And then, as if a switch had suddenly been turned off, the apparition was gone.

Justin jumped up, his eyes still glued to the spot on the stairway where the spirit had vanished. He stood riveted to the ground, waiting to see if he could catch any other sign of movement by the ruins. He scanned the roadway and then the hillside to his right. But no, nothing.

In years to come, Justin would have to convince himself time and again that what he'd experienced that night was not just his fertile imagination, making him think he had seen Houdini's ghost. But right now, here on the grounds of the old mansion, he was convinced that the master illusionist had paid him a house call.

A word, unbidden, popped into Justin's mind. He *believed*.

A ten-room structure known simply as "the Mansion"—a fabled site in music history—is located within a quarter mile of Harry Houdini's alleged Hollywood home on Laurel Canyon Boulevard (although the homes are completely unrelated). In the 1960s and 1970s many artists such as the Beatles, David Bowie, Jimi Hendrix, and Mick Jagger stayed there.

Owned in recent times by music producer Rick Rubin, the combination residence–recording studio was built on the ashes of a building that burned to the ground in the 1950s. Hauntings at that house had started in 1918 after the son of a prominent furniture store magnate pushed his lover off the balcony.

The first major recording at the Mansion was the Red Hot Chili Peppers's 1991 LP *Blood Sugar Sex Magik*. Because of recurring paranormal activity while they were in the studio, the band's drummer Chad Smith wouldn't live in the house, but guitarist John Frusciante thought the spirits were nice enough. One of the photos that was shot for the album art had an odd light orb floating in the background. (Many spirit researchers think such balls of light are ghostly presences.)

While recording there in 2002–2003, Cedric Bixler-Zavala of The Mars Volta returned to find open doors that he was certain had been closed. The band refused to live in the bell tower because of its unsettling vibes. Joey Jordison, drummer for Slipknot, wouldn't go back down into the basement after he was groped by an invisible spirit in the cellar during a 2003 recording session. Slipknot's vocalist, Corey Taylor, captured photos of two spirit orbs near the thermostat as the temperature changed. Daron Malakian, guitarist for System of a Down, maintains that when the band was recording there in 2004, his amplifier tubes acted up every day at four o'clock.

Perhaps it's only a matter of time before a spirit voice is captured on a recording.

Chapter 5

The Harlow
Hauntings

Film siren Jean Harlow died at only twenty-six. She may be buried in Forest Lawn, but many believe she's still "living" in her old home outside Beverly Hills. And then there's the strange case of Sharon Tate. Was it the ghost of Harlow's husband, Paul Bern, that appeared to Tate in his old house off Benedict Canyon?

Sharon couldn't sleep. She wasn't used to staying alone in the big house, and, quite frankly, she was frightened. The wind in Benedict Canyon had kicked up early and especially strong that evening, and she could hear it whistling through the eaves. The house, built to resemble an old Bavarian chalet, was full of cracks and crannies that caught even the slightest breeze and amplified it into chillingly spooky howls.

She would have thought that the wooden sentinels on the roof stood guard against such frights. One of the curiosities of the old building, one of the things that drew her boyfriend, Jay, to it, were the hand-carved statuettes of silent film stars at each end of the rain gutter. An actress herself, she easily recognized a few of them—Douglas Fairbanks, Mary Pickford, Rudolph Valentino . . .

Sharon Tate had been born in Dallas in 1943, and for most of her childhood she traveled from one city to the next, wherever her father, an officer in the army, was stationed. During her childhood she entered a few beauty pageants, but then around 1960 her family was sent to Verona, Italy.

While she was there, she got work as an extra in films and appeared on a Pat Boone TV special that was taped in Venice. On the set of the movie *Adventures of a Young Man,* she met the handsome star Richard Beymer. They dated briefly, and Beymer suggested Tate try her luck in Hollywood.

When her family returned to the States, she called Beymer's agent, who agreed to represent her. Before long she was cast in an assortment of small roles and began modeling in print ads.

In October 1964, at a party in the famous Whiskey A Go Go on the Sunset Strip in what is today West Hollywood, she met Jay Sebring, a celebrity hairstylist whose clients included Warren Beatty, Kirk Douglas, Steve McQueen, and Jim Morrison. Tate and Sebring hit it off immediately, and it was perfect timing for both of them. She was ending a bad relationship with French actor Philippe Forquet; Sebring was getting a divorce. After the divorce was finalized in 1965, the couple got engaged.

Sebring bought a dream house, the one in which Tate was now trying desperately to get to sleep, from the recently retired former MGM actress-dancer Sally Forrest. Sebring was out of town on business; besides his Los Angeles studio, he had successful salons in New York and London. Sharon was holding down the fort.

As she tossed and turned she couldn't help but think about the history of the house and the notorious suicide that had taken place there. Paul Bern, the husband of superstar Jean Harlow, had killed himself there—perhaps in that very room—just two months after their wedding night.

Harlow was born Harlean Harlow Carpenter in Kansas City, Missouri, in 1911. When she was eleven, her parents divorced, and her mother, hoping to get into show business, moved to Hollywood in 1923. After two unsuccessful years pounding the pavement, they returned to Kansas City.

In 1926 Harlow met Charles "Chuck" McGrew, the young scion of a well-to-do family, at Ferry Hall School in Lake Forest, Illinois, and the following year they married and moved to Los Angeles.

Not long after that, Harlow drove a friend to a meeting at Fox Studios, and while waiting for her in the car, she was approached by an executive who told her she should consider trying to get into movies herself. He sent her a letter of recommendation to Central Casting, which provided the studio with most of its extras. On a dare, Harlow signed up with the agency, using her mother's maiden name, Jean Harlow, as her stage name.

Her first film role was portraying a minor character in 1928's *Honor Bound.* The part was so small that her name didn't even appear in the movie's credits. But the camera loved her, and more, larger roles soon followed.

Of course, in those days it wasn't considered entirely respectable to be in the entertainment industry, and she was, after all, the society wife of a wealthy heir. Her husband put his foot down. He told her that her place was in the home and that she would have to choose between him and the movies.

She did.

In 1929, she separated from McGrew and moved in with her mother, who had a new husband and was back in Los Angeles. Within months, Howard Hughes signed young Harlow to a five-year contract. Her first role would be to star in his first talking picture, *Hell's Angels*. It was while shooting the film that the eighteen-year-old Harlow met forty-year-old MGM producer Paul Bern. Their paths would soon cross again.

Hell's Angels premiered at Grauman's Chinese Theatre in May 1930, and while critics were not kind about her performance, audiences loved her. Hughes's publicist, Link Quarberg, came up with a nickname for Harlow—"Platinum Blonde"—and to cement the sobriquet in the public's mind they used it as the title for one of her next films. (She later also became known as the "Blonde Bombshell," another phrase coined just for her.) People couldn't get enough of Harlow. She attracted crowds whenever she made personal appearances, and women across the country dyed their hair to match hers.

By that time Harlow and Bern were having an affair. He convinced Irving Thalberg, the production head of MGM, to buy out Harlow's contract from Hughes, and in 1932 she moved to the fabled studio that was said to have "More Stars Than There Are in the Heavens." Harlow hoped to be one of them.

Now under the guiding eye of a major studio, Harlow's natural talent for lighthearted comedy was nurtured. She was still allowed to be sexy, but she was no longer simply playing wisecracking, brassy blondes.

On July 2, 1932, she and Bern married in the living room of Harlow's home on Club View Drive in Los Angeles, southwest of Beverly Hills. But then, out of the blue, tragedy struck. On September 5, while Harlow was filming *Red Dust* with Clark Gable, Bern was found naked, dead from a gunshot wound, in Harlow's bedroom at his Benedict Canyon mansion on Easton Drive. Police officially ruled it a suicide.

But was it?

Several things seemed suspicious. Two hours had passed between the time the body was discovered and police were called, and when they arrived, several top MGM executives were already on the scene. There were persistent rumors that the site may have been tampered with and that Bern had actually been murdered.

Whether or not Harlow knew anything more about the actual circumstances of Bern's death, she remained mum. That night she'd been staying with her mother, who was by then living at Harlow's Club View address. Distraught and overwhelmed, Harlow is said to have attempted suicide there the next day.

MGM worked feverishly to prevent any scandal over the entire Bern incident. But the studio executives already had their hands full dealing with Harlow: She didn't stay lonely for long. She soon started a none-too-discreet affair with the married boxer Max Baer. To stop the gossip, the vivacious actress was quickly and very publicly married off to a convenient and cooperative cinematographer; the pair quietly divorced less than a year later. Harlow then fell in love and began a two-year romance with MGM leading man William Powell.

By 1937 Harlow was one of the movies' biggest box office draws, and her chemistry on the screen with frequent costar Clark Gable had proved to be particularly magical. They were partnered for yet a sixth film, *Saratoga*, but on May 29, in the middle of shooting, Harlow collapsed on the set.

She went home to recuperate in her new house on North Palm Drive in Beverly Hills. Even though, for a time, she appeared to be improving, her condition was in fact getting much, much worse. Her kidneys were failing. In a time before dialysis, the disease quickly proved fatal, and on June 7, 1937, Jean Harlow died. She was twenty-six.

Over the years her houses went through a succession of owners, until finally in 1966 the Benedict Canyon home fell into the hands of Jay Sebring. And just a few months after that, his girlfriend, Tate, was there, trying to fluff some life into her pillow. She couldn't figure out what was making her so uncomfortable. She turned on her side and pushed her head into the cushion, almost as if she were telling it: *Do your work. Take me to dreamland.*

Then, as she stared into the empty space at the end of the bed, she seemed to catch a small motion in the corner of the darkened room. Something was moving! She tried feverishly to focus her eyes without turning on the light.

It was a man!

But not a flesh-and-blood person: It was a ghost! Its skin seemed to shine dimly from within, making the whole figure a hazy, cold glow.

The phantom paid her no notice. He seemed to be looking for something as he wandered determinedly about the room. But unlike movie ghosts, this one wasn't passing through things. It would bump into a table or a chair, then veer off in another direction, though none of the furniture moved or made any sound.

In fact, Tate realized, there was no sound anywhere. Even the whistling wind had stopped. It was now deathly silent throughout the entire house—except for a faint, incessant, terrified screaming that seemed to be coming from somewhere off in the distance. My God, she suddenly realized: It was her!

Tate jumped out of bed. She had to escape! Bounding past the spectre and out of the bedroom, she raced toward the stairwell. She stopped abruptly at the top of the landing and looked down. There was something sitting, hunched over, at the foot of the carpeted stairs.

She pressed her back against the wall, arms outstretched, and slowly inched her way down toward the living room, never taking her eyes off the unmoving, huddled shape. In a final leap, she lunged past the object and into the center of the room. She turned. Her mouth fell open in horror. It couldn't be!

Was it a man? A woman? She couldn't tell. But there, tied to the newel post at the bottom of the staircase, sat a person, motionless, forced upright. The apparition's head was cocked to one side, eyes wide open, staring emptily into space. It was only then that Tate noticed the gruesome figure was covered with blood, its throat slit deeply from side to side.

This can't be happening! the terrified Tate told herself. She hurried to the liquor cabinet and tore it open. She needed a drink! And another. Hell, she needed the whole bottle.

She stared back at the steps. She hadn't been hallucinating. Whoever or whatever the spectre was, it was still there. Maybe if she could get past it and back up to her bedroom, she reasoned, the spirit up there would be gone. She set out in a sprint. Fortunately for her, the ghost upstairs had wandered into the hall. She jumped into the bed, pulled the covers over her head, and, totally drained, instantly fell dead asleep.

Sebring returned the next day. She told him about her horrifying evening. She was convinced that the restless ghost she had seen was Paul Bern. As for the banshee at the bottom of the stairs, they had no clue as to who it was. But was the apparition actually a prophetic vision of grisly events yet to come?

Before long they had both forgotten the event, or at least put it behind them. Tate flew to London to film *Eye of the Devil*. While there, she met director Roman Polanski, and they fell in love. Surprisingly, not only did Sebring take the news well, but he also became Polanski's friend and remained close to Tate.

Tate and Polanski got married in London in 1968. Polanski introduced Sebring to his friend Wojciech Frykowski and his girlfriend, the coffee heiress Abigail Folger. Frykowski and Folger were invited to stay with Tate at Polanski's place in Benedict Canyon while he was filming in Europe. When he had time, Sebring would drop in and keep them company.

Everything was in place for the macabre, sad finish to their tale. On August 8, 1969, Tate, who was pregnant and just weeks short of delivery, Sebring, Frykowski, and Folger had settled in for a pleasant evening at Polanski's home on Cielo Drive.

Unknown to them, Charlie Manson had sent four members of his "family"—Tex Watson, Pat Krenwinkle, Susan Atkins, and Linda Kasabian—to go to the house (which he had visited when a former occupant lived there) and kill everyone inside. By morning, all of the inhabitants lay dead, as well as another victim: Steve Parent, who was on his way out the driveway after having visited a caretaker on the property. Some of the victims had been shot; Tate had been stabbed sixteen times.

Had the murdered ghost Tate saw three years earlier at Sebring's house actually been a nightmarish omen of her own death by the blade of a knife? It's impossible to say.

And, had the ghost that Tate saw in her bedroom that night been Bern? Perhaps. But at least two other people died in that house between the time Bern lived there and Sebring bought it. For all we know, the spirits Tate saw *could* have been them.

The Bern-Sebring house still stands today, but all's been quiet there for some time. The Polanski residence in which the murders occurred has since been razed, and a new home sits there today. There have been no further reports of hauntings.

The same can't be said for one of Harlow's other homes.

Subsequent owners of her residence on Club View Drive have reported a number of strange phenomena taking place in the two-story house. According to an interview conducted by well-known ghost hunter Hans Holzer, family dogs have whined and growled at invisible presences there, primarily in the upstairs bedroom where Harlow is said to have attempted suicide. Lights have gone on by themselves, the inexplicable scent of perfume has been detected, and at times cold spots are felt in the dining room, kitchen, and bedroom. Occupants have heard soft, disembodied whispers, a woman crying, and footsteps. And now and then, an actual indistinct apparition has appeared.

Harlow was buried in a private, gated sanctuary in the Great Mausoleum in Forest Lawn Memorial Park in Glendale. Although her phantom has never been seen by visitors, some have claimed they felt her spirit's presence.

Perhaps that alone is worth a visit to the cemetery. Harlow's grave site may be the only place that modern ghost hunters have a chance of coming into contact with any of the otherworldly participants in this decades-long dance of death.

Chapter 6
Webb of
Mystery

Oscar-nominated character actor Clifton Webb shared his Beverly Hills home with his mother, whom he adored—and a ghost: that of opera singer Grace Moore. When Webb himself passed away, his phantom also returned to the mansion.

"Mother, is that you?"

Clifton Webb stared out into the courtyard. His white stucco Spanish-style mansion was built in two wings. One paralleled North Rexford Drive, though set back from it; the other cut roughly at a ninety-degree angle, creating a large, open space that had been enclosed for entertaining. There, in the patio, appearing as a faint shadow in the dim light, was the misty form of a woman—not like the one he had seen on so many other occasions. This one was new.

It had to be his mother, Maybelle!

And why wouldn't she return to him? They had been inseparable since the time he was born, way back in 1889, up until her death in 1960. No woman (or, perhaps if what some people have claimed is true, no man) had ever come between them.

When Maybelle passed on—he wasn't sure, but probably at the age of ninety—Webb was inconsolable. He locked her clothes and other personal belongings in her room, keeping it as a memorial, a shrine, a daily reminder of his love for her. Not a day went by that he didn't miss her. And he was as angered as he was amused when his dear friend Nöel Coward tried to cheer him up by quipping, "Clifton, it must be tough to be orphaned at seventy-one."

That's right, Webb realized. He *was* over seventy! Maybe this vision in the courtyard was simply a hallucination. Perhaps he was just seeing things. After all, he wasn't feeling very well these days. The evenings filled with festive parties were a thing of the past. Now he spent his nights just like his days: by himself, seeing no one, carefully cocooned away from the world.

The ghost *had* to be his mother! But was she back to stay? Or had she only come to invite him to Cross Over with her? Either would be welcome.

But then, as if to answer his question, the form grew weaker. It faded, he blinked, and it was gone.

Once more he was alone.

Webb looked around. So much space for one, solitary man. It still surprised him from time to time that he was living in such an opulent Beverly Hills mansion. True, he had appeared in more than twenty films and had three Oscar nominations, but for more than three decades before that he'd been a Broadway baby.

Clifton Webb was born Webb Parmelee Hollenbeck in Beech Grove, Indiana, a small, independent city surrounded by Indianapolis. When he was three, his fiercely independent mother moved to New York City, away from her husband, who would never be a part of the boy's life.

Throughout Webb's youth, Maybelle made sure that he was privately schooled and tutored in theater, voice, painting, and dance. He made his stage debut at the age of seven, amazingly within the hallowed walls of Carnegie Hall as part of the New York Children's Theater group. Tours as an actor, engagements in the opera, and even a turn as a ballroom dancer followed; by nineteen he was working under the stage name Clifton Webb.

Broadway soon beckoned, and he made his debut on the Great White Way in 1913 in *The Purple Road*. Over the next thirty-four years, Webb would appear (and usually star) in an additional twenty-two Broadway shows, including revues, operettas, musicals, and plays such as the original New York production of Coward's ghost-ridden comedy, *Blithe Spirit*. Webb introduced many popular tunes of the day, including George and Ira Gershwin's "I've Got a Crush on You" (*Treasure Island*, 1928), Arthur Schwartz and Howard Dietz's "I Guess I'll Have to Change My Plan" (*The Little Show*, 1929), and Irving Berlin's "Her Easter Bonnet," also known as "Easter Parade" (*As Thousands Cheer*, 1933). His last show on the New York stage, indeed in any legitimate theater, was Coward's 1946 comedy *Present Laughter*.

Webb was in his mid-fifties when his career took a turn he could hardly have expected. Hollywood called.

He had done a few minor film roles in New York, but critics found his performances mannered, fey, and effete. As a result, unlike for other Broadway actors of his generation, the West Coast didn't seem to be in his stars.

At least not right away.

Eventually director Otto Preminger recognized that ineffable something in Webb and, despite studio head Darryl F. Zanuck's disapproval, cast the actor as the nasty, snobbish newspaperman Waldo Lydecker in Twentieth Century Fox's 1944 film classic *Laura*. His supporting role was met with such critical approbation that, lo and behold, overnight Webb was a movie star—with an Academy Award nomination to boot! He received a second Supporting Actor Oscar nomination two years later portraying Elliott Templeton, the wealthy, snooty uncle of the character played by Gene Tierney in *The Razor's Edge*. (Tierney had worked with Webb previously, having portrayed the title role in *Laura*.)

By that time Webb was typecast. If you needed someone who could play pompous, patronizing, condescending, supercilious—you pick the adjective—Clifton Webb was your man. And he didn't disappoint. It was a character he would re-create time and again in a delightful multitude of variations for a film career that lasted almost twenty years.

Over that period he played everything from a regal head-of-household in *Cheaper by the Dozen* (1950) and John Philip Sousa in the 1952 biopic *Stars and Stripes Forever* to an ill-fated passenger on the *Titanic* (1953), a haughty author in *Three Coins in the Fountain* (1954), and a rich antiques collector in *Boy on a Dolphin* (1957).

But his most famous character, the one for which he's probably most remembered, was Mr. Belvedere, a snide author who goes undercover as a "nanny" for three rambunctious children in order to get inside information for a book he's writing. His portrayal of the comedic, uptight babysitter in 1948's *Sitting Pretty* resulted in his third Oscar nomination, this time for Best Actor. It also led to two sequels: *Mr. Belvedere Goes to College* (1949) and *Mr. Belvedere Rings the Bell* (1951).

Standing there all by himself in his empty house, Webb was sure that many people thought he really *was* Mr. Belvedere! Well, maybe they weren't all that wrong. He didn't consider himself arrogant or stuck-up, but he had to admit that he was a bit, well, priggish. He did like things done in a certain way. For instance, he hated tobacco smoke, so cigarettes were just not allowed in his home. If guests didn't like it, they didn't have to come visit.

And why not? It was *his* domain. Webb was familiar with the house long before he bought it, and when he'd heard that actor Gene Lockhart was planning to sell it, he jumped at the chance to own it. Now he had lived there for twenty years. Amazing, Webb thought, how the time had flown by so quickly. He really loved the place. *In fact,* he mused to himself, *maybe I'll never leave.*

Webb was a true believer in the Afterlife and the ability of spirits to return to the land of the living. Hadn't he been very open about it for years, telling friends that he had seen the ghost of his friend Grace Moore in the house a number of times?

Before coming to Hollywood, Moore had already established herself as a Broadway performer and an operatic artist worldwide. Born in Tennessee in 1898, she moved to Washington, D.C., and New York for her music training. She made her Broadway debut in 1913 in the chorus of *The Beggar Student.* By 1933 Moore had appeared in nine shows on the Great White Way, including Jerome Kern's *Hitchy-Koo,* the 1922 and 1923 editions of Irving Berlin's *Music Box Revue* (in the latter of which she introduced the song "What'll I Do?"), and the 1931 Ziegfeld Follies. Her final Broadway show was an operetta, *The DuBarry,* which ran just over two months.

By that time, however, Moore was a star on the concert stage. She made her opera debut with New York's Metropolitan Opera in 1928, singing Mimi in Puccini's *La Bohème.* Also that year she debuted in Paris, and in 1935 she had a command performance at the Royal Opera House in London. In all, Moore spent sixteen seasons with the Met, interspersed with solo concert dates throughout the States and Europe.

(In the early 1950s, the ghost of Frances Alda, the diva soprano, would haunt the old Metropolitan Opera House at the corner of Broadway and Thirty-Ninth Street. Her spirit would remain there, pestering patrons in the parterre until the structure closed its doors in 1966.)

Suitably enough, Moore's first role on film was portraying Jenny Lind (the "Swedish Nightingale" who had first toured the United States in 1850 under the auspices of P. T. Barnum) in the 1930 MGM movie *A Lady's Morals*. Also that year she appeared in MGM's film adaptation of Sigmund Romberg's popular operetta *The New Moon*.

It was four years until she returned to the silver screen, this time for Columbia Pictures. Between 1934 and 1939 she made six movies for the studio, including *One Night of Love*, for which she received an Oscar nomination for Best Actress. Although she failed to win the Academy Award, she was later honored for her concert work by the king of Denmark and received the French Legion of Honor.

At some point during her stay in Hollywood, Moore discovered the mansion on North Rexford Drive in Beverly Hills and made it her West Coast home. (She also kept houses in Connecticut and Cannes, France.) Tragically, she died in a plane crash in Copenhagen in 1947 at the age of forty-eight.

Moore's years in the movies were thought to be pleasant ones. *She must have had many joyful memories attached to this house*, thought Webb. Was it any wonder that her spirit wanted to come back for one more soiree?

At first, after Maybelle's death Webb had turned to séances to try to contact his mother. She'd been as happy in the house as Moore had been. And if that weren't enough for her to want to return, certainly there was her "little Webb," as she endearingly called her son. But it had been no use. Her spirit never came through. His beloved Maybelle had seemed gone for good.

Until that night.

The ghost he had just witnessed in the courtyard was certainly not Moore, but it had definitely been that of a woman. And how many other females would want to return to the house?

Well, well, well, Webb thought. *Mother's back.* A wry smile of contentment crossed his lips as he passed down the hallway, turning out the last of the lights in the corridor. Perhaps he wouldn't be alone after all.

Over the next few years, Webb became more and more of a recluse. He no longer invited in friends for gay evenings of refined frivolity. His health continued to worsen, and on October 13, 1966, at the age of seventy-six, he had a heart attack and died in the comfortable confines of his mansion. His body was entombed in the Hollywood Forever Cemetery.

A year after his death, television producer Douglas S. Cramer married *Los Angeles Times* columnist Joyce Haber, and they moved into Webb's estate. During their years there, reports surfaced that the mansion was indeed haunted, and at one point it was even investigated by famed ghost researcher Hans Holzer.

Before long, a shadowy male spectre began to manifest itself in the patio or the living room, although the tall, gray figure was seen throughout the house. Sometimes merely a voice could be heard, softly muttering, "Well, well, well," Webb's catchphrase, under its breath.

Overnight guests occasionally reported waking up to find an indistinct form hovering in one of the corners of their bedroom or the curtains rustling despite there being neither a fan in the room nor a breeze coming through the window. Or they might be suddenly engulfed in a bubble of cold air.

One room that seemed to be particularly haunted after Webb's death was his personal favorite, which he had dubbed "the Greek Room" because of its decorative motif. Small, personal items set down by visitors there might disappear and later show up in a different part of the house altogether, or the objects would shift without anyone touching them.

Doors would become locked throughout the house, and an invisible force often pushed people (especially women) out of Webb's favorite armchair, which had been left behind. (It was even claimed that the furniture bounced or emitted strange sounds.)

The phantom seemed to be fussy, finicky, and fastidious, just like Webb himself had been in real life. Among other things, it hated cigarettes, and cold gusts would come out of nowhere to suddenly blow out the match if anyone tried to light up. Smokers would see their packs of cigarettes move on the table or fly across the room. For others, individual cigarettes broke in half or the packages sometimes got crushed.

Many, many people who came to the house felt Webb's unseen presence. But even when people weren't aware of him, there were times that their pets would bark or hiss at empty halls or run in terror from certain spots of the home. None would go into the infamous Greek Room.

Unfortunately, modern-day ghost hunters can't check out any of these stories, because the house that Webb occupied has been torn down and replaced with a modern structure. There have been no reports of any sightings or unusual phenomena in the new residence.

But you can't get rid of a determined spirit quite that easily. Apparently Clifton Webb's desire to stick around has simply been transferred to his current "home" at Hollywood Forever Cemetery. His resting place is located in the Sanctuary of Peace area of the Abbey of the Palms Mausoleum, but it's said he doesn't always like to stay inside his crypt. The graveyard might be worth a visit if you're collecting autographs from the Unknown.

Chapter 7

Pretty in
Pink

Rudy Vallee, Ringo Starr, Englebert Humperdinck, and Sylvester Stallone lived in it. But no one had more impact on the house at 1220 Bel Air Drive than Jayne Mansfield. Perhaps that's why her ghost continued to haunt it—and why the house insisted on remaining pink.

He shouldn't have to be doing it again. He'd already painted the entire house twice, from the foundations to the roof, trying to cover over the soft pink coloring for which the mansion had become known. Yet no matter how many times he applied another coat to the surface, the old shade seeped back through.

It wasn't that he didn't know how to paint a house. If he weren't good at his craft, his company wouldn't be one of the top firms servicing residential Beverly Hills and Bel Air. But this place was, well, different. It was almost as if it had a mind of its own.

The house, constructed in a Spanish-Mediterranean style, had been designed by architect G. C. McAllister and built in 1929. It sat on several prime acres in the Holmby Hills section of Beverly Hills, right off Sunset Boulevard. The forty-room mansion was enormous, with seven bedrooms, at least as many bathrooms, a dining room, a library, a bar, and even a wine cellar. In addition, there were rooms for the staff and an adjoining guesthouse. Its first notable owner had been Rudy Vallee, who bought the house around 1932, although he wound up spending very little time there.

The resident who put the home on the map was one of the great screen sirens of the 1950s and early 1960s: Jayne Mansfield.

She was born Vera Jayne Palmer in Bryn Mawr, Pennsylvania, in 1933. After her father's death, her mother remarried and moved the family to Dallas, Texas. In 1950 Jayne married Paul Mansfield and had her first child, Jayne Marie. The young couple moved to Austin, where Jayne enrolled at the University of Texas. Also during this period she won a series of beauty contests. In 1953 she studied at both UCLA and Southern Methodist University, and she performed in her first play onstage.

The following year the young actress insisted on moving back to Los Angeles for her career, and within months of her arrival she was signed by Warner Bros. At first she was given small film roles, all of which showed off her stunning good looks.

In 1955 she headed to Broadway, where she starred for a full thirteen months in the comedy *Will Success Spoil Rock Hunter?* The play opened at the Belasco Theatre before moving nine months later to the Shubert Theatre. Mansfield won a 1956 Theatre World Award for her performance. (The Belasco is believed to be haunted by its founder, David Belasco, but there are no reports of Mansfield encountering the spirit.)

After her run on the Great White Way, Mansfield returned to Hollywood in 1956, signing with Twentieth Century Fox. She won a Golden Globe as New Star of the Year for *The Wayward Bus*; that same year she made the movie version of *Rock Hunter*, which probably remains her most-remembered film role. Her final starring role came in 1957 in the box office nonstarter *Kiss Them for Me.*

During this heady period, Jayne Mansfield not only was one of the most popular actresses in Hollywood, but she also received more press than almost anyone else. In her first year at Fox, more than two thousand photographs of her appeared in newspapers alone.

And what those pix revealed! Mansfield knew how to use her figure, especially her ample breasts, for publicity purposes. (So did her rival sex symbols Marilyn Monroe and Mamie Van Doren; in fact, the press referred to the trio as "the Three Ms.") In 1963 Mansfield was perhaps the first Hollywood actress to go nude in a film for general release, and a series of photos shot on the set of the movie (*Promises! Promises!*) was published in *Playboy.*

One of Mansfield's costars was her new real-life husband, Mickey Hargitay. Mansfield had first seen the Hungarian-born Hargitay when the former Mr. Universe was appearing in Mae West's stage show (which featured several musclemen) at the Latin Quarter in New York City.

Mansfield divorced her first husband on January 8, 1958, and five days later married Hargitay. (He had been divorced since 1956.) Shortly after the wedding they purchased the former Rudy Vallee property, reportedly for a mere $76,000, and the sex kitten immediately set about making it her own.

First and foremost, she decided that the house and the eight-foot walls surrounding it should be painted pink, which she considered her trademark color. To make the walls sparkle in the sun, she had the workers mix crushed sandstone in the paint. The eye-popping color made it absolutely impossible for anyone traveling down Sunset

Boulevard to miss the house, earning it its nickname: the Pink Palace.

To get to the mansion, visitors had to pass through tall, wrought-iron gates, with the initials "JM" swirled into their decorative pattern. Inside the house there was a twelve-foot crystal chandelier, a fountain said to flow with pink champagne, a pink heart-shaped bathtub, and pink fur rugs.

Mansfield had always been quite the self-promoter. To decorate her house, she wrote more than 1,500 furniture makers, builders, and contractors requesting "samples." She made no bones about expecting the pieces to be gratis. It would be worth the donation, she convinced them, to be able to advertise that their products could be found in Mansfield's home. Many of the companies agreed, and she was soon able to fill her house with more than $150,000 worth of furnishings that hadn't cost her a cent!

But of course, the coup de grace at the Mansfield mansion was a pink heart-shaped swimming pool in the backyard. Visitors (and the occasional helicopter hovering overhead) could clearly make out mosaics on the bottom of the pool added by Hargitay spelling "I love you Jaynie." In fact, Hargitay himself did much of the remodeling of the grand mansion. If the house had belonged to anyone else, the eccentric decorations might have seemed gaudy. But somehow it fit in perfectly with the carefully calibrated Mansfield mythos.

The Hargitays had three children together during their five-year marriage: Miklós, Zoltán, and Mariska. They divorced in Mexico in May 1963, but when its legality came into question they briefly reconciled. The following August, Jayne had the divorce officially recognized in the United States as well.

A month later she married film director Matt Cimber, who had previously directed Mansfield and Hargitay in a regional theater production of *Bus Stop*. The marriage lasted two years, long enough for Mansfield to give birth to another son, Tony. Handling the divorce was her lawyer, Sam Brody, who, in the process, became her boyfriend.

By the mid-1960s, Mansfield's film career was more or less over, although she shot some minor movies in Europe. She made several TV appearances, put together a cabaret act with which she headlined in Las Vegas, and began to tour.

Although not in demand on the silver screen, she was still famous, and she could pack a house at nightclubs throughout America. On the fateful evening of June 28, 1967, after finishing up a show at Gus Stevens Supper Club in Biloxi, Mississippi, she got into a car for an overnight trip to New Orleans. She had a TV interview scheduled there for the next morning and twenty-year-old Ronnie Harrison agreed to drive her there in Stevens's 1966 Buick Electra 225 sedan. Sam Brody was seated in the center of the wide front seat; Mansfield was at the passenger-side window. In the backseat, Miklós, Zoltán, and Mariska lay sleeping.

Coming out of a curve on U.S. Highway 90, the car entered an unexpected fog, caused by the low-lying haze of insecticide spraying. Suddenly the rear end of a tractor-trailer, which had slowed in the mist, appeared in the car's headlights. There was barely time to react. The Buick smashed into the truck at full speed, wedging itself underneath the semi's carriage. All three in the front seat of the car were killed instantly from the impact; miraculously, the children survived with only minor injuries. The time of the crash was estimated to be about 2:25 a.m. July 29.

(Despite rumors that persist to this day, Jayne Mansfield was *not* decapitated in the accident. Reporters who descended on the scene photographed a patch of blonde hair in the mangled wreckage, which no doubt prompted the gruesome reports. While it's possible that the hair came from her scalp, it's just as likely that it was merely a wig.)

Mansfield's body was taken to Fairview Cemetery in Pen Argyl, Pennsylvania, close to where she was born, for burial, and a cenotaph commemorating her was placed in the Garden of Legends section of the Hollywood Forever Cemetery.

After Mansfield's death the Pink Palace mansion was owned or leased by a succession of people, including "Mama" Cass Elliott. (And to end another rumor, Elliott did not choke to death on a ham sandwich. She died of a heart attack.)

And then Ringo Starr came into the picture. The legendary Beatles drummer decided that pink wasn't quite his style, so here was the workman trying valiantly to cover up the petulant paint. He knew from experience that pink was a notoriously difficult color to hide, especially by any shade of white.

The housepainter had tried everything: sealants, multiple coats. Still, the pink color always seeped back to the surface. Nothing seemed able to stop it from bleeding through. It was as if something wanted the pink color to stay alive. Was the building somehow bewitched?

When he left it for the last time, the mansion was as white as he could make it. But it turned out to be a losing cause. According to legend, over the next few years it was a never-ending battle to keep the house from returning to its ghostly pink hue.

Then, in 1976 Welsh singer Englebert Humperdinck bought the property. He had met Mansfield in London just weeks before her death, so he thought it was appropriate that the house be restored to its iconic color.

Humperdinck put the house on the market several times throughout the 1990s, and in 2002 he finally sold it to Roland Arnall, the owner of Ameriquest Capital Corporation. The financier already owned the adjoining estate, Owlwood. That twelve-thousand-square-foot Tuscan-style mansion had once been the home of Joseph M. Schenck (an early president of United Artists and longtime chairman of Twentieth Century Fox). Tony Curtis and Sonny and Cher had lived there too. Built in 1936, the house was surrounded by pools, gardens, a tennis court, and guest cottages.

In addition to the Pink Palace, Arnall also bought another property on the cul-de-sac, a smaller seven-bedroom, 8,300-square-foot home once owned by the swimmer-actress Esther Williams. He decided that he'd combine the three properties into one massive estate, and, although the Mansfield and Williams houses had had famous occupants, they were in no way designated historic structures. On November 9, 2002, the Pink Palace was leveled.

Before its final sale, Humperdinck invited Mansfield's children for one last visit so they could remove a keepsake from the home in which they grew up. The sons removed most of a wood fireplace that had been installed by their father. Daughter Mariska Hargitay, a star of television's *Law and Order: Special Victims Unit*, removed an ornamental copper shield from the fireplace in the pool house that her father had engraved "Jaynie—My love will flame for you forever—Mickey." The former bodybuilder chose not to go back. He was quoted as saying, "As far as I'm concerned, the house died when Jayne died."

The house may have deid, but Humperdinck reported several times that he thought Mansfield's ghost had returned to the Pink Palace. He often caught the scent of her favorite perfume—rose petal—throughout the house. And he also saw her apparition, dressed in a long, black dress.

Today, nothing stands on the site of Mansfield's home, so it's impossible to check out the tales of her ghostly materializations for ourselves. But who knows? Mansfield was said to be a firm believer not only in the Afterlife but also in the possibility of communicating with the Other Side. She's thought to have held séances in which she was able to contact her Aunt Kathy, who had Crossed Over fifteen years earlier. Maybe Mansfield's just biding her time until we see her again.

Chapter 8
The Warning

If you got ghost troubles, who ya gonna call? Actually, the ghosts may call you. Elke Sommer, the German-born actress and artist, is convinced that a ghost saved her life by waking her after her house caught fire. Can anyone say otherwise?

The pounding at the door got louder. More insistent.

It had started softly, just barely audible. *If* you were paying attention, you might have heard the gentle thuds.

At first the occupants hadn't even noticed it. They were sound asleep. Besides, the delicate thumping was nothing compared to what they'd been experiencing in their house over the past year. But eventually the rapping became so loud it couldn't be ignored.

"Joe? Do you hear that? Joe! Wake up!" Elke Sommer shook her husband, Joe Hyams. She hardly needed to: He was already wide awake, listening to the sounds at the door as well.

Sommer was born Else Schletz-Ho in Berlin, Germany, the daughter of a Lutheran minister. In 1942 the family moved south to Erlangen, where she entered school, but when her father died in 1954, she was forced to end her studies. She traveled to Great Britain, where she learned English and began to work as an au pair. After returning to Germany, the five-foot-seven blonde decided to try modeling, which led to her entering a beauty contest while on holiday in Italy.

She won! Among those who took notice was the actor-director Vittorio De Sica, who helped her embark on a film career. Her first movie was the Italian release *Uomini e nobi-luomini* (1959), with De Sica as her costar. More films in Italy and then Germany followed, and before long Sommer was not only in demand in films but also an international sex symbol.

In 1961 and 1962 she appeared in almost a dozen more films in Europe before deciding to move to Hollywood. She was soon cast in 1963's *The Victors*. Her starring role that same year opposite Paul Newman in *The Prize* led to her winning the 1964 Golden Globe for New Star of the Year–Actress, sharing the title with Tippi Hedren (*The Birds*) and Ursula Andress (*Dr. No*).

Now, with the incessant pounding on the other side of the bedroom door, Sommer found it ironic that it was her first English-language movie, *Don't Bother to Knock*, in 1961 that led to her coming to America, meeting and marrying the man lying beside her, and eventually being in this very bed in a very haunted house in Beverly Hills.

"Joe! What should we do? How do we stop the racket?"

Joe Hyams was born in Brookline, Massachusetts, in 1923. He left Harvard to enlist in the army in 1942. After seeing action in the South Pacific, earning him a Purple Heart and a Bronze Star, he became a war correspondent for the *Stars and Stripes* military newspaper.

His interest in reporting led, after bachelor's and master's degrees from New York University, to a career in journalism, which began at the *New York Herald Tribune*. In 1951 the paper sent him to Los Angeles to do an article on the emerging issue of illegal immigration. To get a unique angle on the story, he had himself flown into Mexico and joined a group making the dangerous trek across the border. After filing his account, he took a well-earned vacation at the Beverly Hills Hotel.

"Oh, and while you're there, why don't you try to interview a few movie stars?" his editor only half-jokingly suggested.

Lounging by the pool, Hyams struck up a casual conversation with a man who turned out to be Humphrey Bogart's press agent. Hyams and Bogart hit it off, and within a week the young journalist had interviewed not only Bogie but also his friends Lauren Bacall, Katharine Hepburn, Spencer Tracy, and Frank Sinatra.

The paper immediately made Hyams its West Coast bureau chief. He would remain their man in Hollywood for thirteen years.

Covering the Hollywood scene, Hyams naturally met newcomer Sommer. After he interviewed the emerging star for his newspaper in 1964, they started dating seriously while she was in London shooting *A Shot in the Dark*. In November that year, Sommer and Hyams were married in Las Vegas (her first time, his third).

They were both ready to settle down and escape the crazy "madding crowd" that Hollywood could be. They found a secluded home on Benedict Canyon Drive in an area popular with film and television personalities. It was perfect.

Or so they thought. The very first night in their new digs, after retiring for the evening, they were startled to hear banging, crashing noises coming from the first floor. Did they have an intruder?

Cautiously, they cracked the door to the bedroom and strained to hear exactly where the clamor was coming from. Whatever was causing the disturbance seemed to be in the dining room, almost directly underneath them. But oddly, they couldn't make out any footsteps or voices. They realized that they were living pretty far up in the Hollywood Hills, and wooded animals still roamed the lands, especially at night. Had they left a window open, allowing a stray raccoon, a coyote, or even (God forbid) a skunk to crawl inside?

The commotion continued. Louder. Nighttime in the canyons could be deathly still, so the disturbance seemed deafening. It sounded as if anything—everything—that was sitting on a table or a counter or was hanging on a wall was being swept onto the floor. The table and chairs joined in, rattling in place, pounding out a nightmarish rhythm to accompany the sound of breaking glass, smashing ceramics, and scattering cutlery.

And then, without warning, it simply . . . stopped. Complete, utter silence.

They waited. Five minutes. Ten. Nothing. Whatever had been down there was gone.

Elke and Joe shared a nervous glance. Did they dare go downstairs to see what damage had been done—and whether whatever had caused it was still there?

They inched down the staircase and peered through the darkness toward the dining room, hoping their eyes would adjust quickly to let them see if there was any hint of movement. When after a few moments it seemed safe, they snapped on the lights.

The room was empty. That, of course, was a relief. But to their surprise—no, astonishment—nothing, not a single thing in the entire room, was out of place. Despite all the sounds of obvious destruction they had heard emanating from the room, nothing had been disturbed.

All the doors to the outside and all the windows were closed and locked. There seemed to be only one explanation, as hard as it was to believe. Without knowing it, they had bought a haunted house.

Their suspicions were confirmed on subsequent nights when the manifestations continued. At first they usually followed the same routine. But then, just when they were almost becoming accustomed to the spirit, the live-in phantom became bolder. Disembodied voices began to join in the mix of the shifting furniture, smashing glasses, and clinking silverware. It sounded as if an out-of-control dinner party was going on, in full swing, carried out in pitch blackness in the middle of the night. But when the dining room was checked out the next day, nothing in the room had shifted position.

Then, for whatever reason, the spectre began to leave physical evidence that it had been there. Marks were left where furniture had been scraped across the floor. Eventually the couple began to see objects move on their own.

It all seemed to be standard-issue poltergeist activity, more mischievous than menacing, only occasionally bordering on real damage or serious danger to the inhabitants or the property. But unlike most poltergeists, Elke's ghost decided it was time to make himself visible.

Both Sommer and Hyams began to encounter the pale apparition of a middle-age man, dressed in a white shirt, lingering in the dining room. And they weren't the only ones to see him: The spectre also startled guests. In all, the unidentified apparition showed up at least five times between 1964 and 1968.

Finally Sommer and Hyams decided to take action. Elke contacted the parapsychology laboratory that was then at UCLA and got in touch with Thelma Moss, PhD, a paranormal researcher. With Moss's guidance, more than thirty investigators visited the Beverly Hills home over the next several months, and unerringly they independently sensed an invisible entity in one particular corner of the dining room.

Realizing that this would make a fascinating story for its readers, *Life* magazine sent Allan Grant to do a photographic essay of the house. Although he didn't capture any actual phantoms on film, four or five frames on one of the rolls somehow were fogged, as if they had been exposed by a strong but unfocused light source. The surrounding frames weren't affected. The photographer, who was a complete skeptic when it came to the supernatural, was at a loss to explain the anomaly. It had never happened to him before— nor did it ever again.

One of the psychics who visited the home also came up with a dire prediction, which she published in the *Journal of the American Society of Psychical Research*. Within a year, she foretold, a fire would break out in the haunted dining room and any occupants of the house would have to jump out of a second-story window to escape. Though her warning raised some concern, the point of the inquiry hadn't been about what *might* happen; it was about trying to figure out what was *already* happening, so the article was soon forgotten by Sommer and Hyams.

Until eight months later. And this time, unlike all the times before it, the noise wasn't coming from downstairs. The pounding was *upstairs*—on the bedroom door.

Hyams crawled out from under the blankets and eased himself uncertainly across the room. The knocking had become firm, adamant, persistent. He looked over his shoulder. Sommer's face flashed him a worried expression, but he had no choice. Hyams grabbed the doorknob, gave it a twist, and with one firm yank pulled the door open.

No one was there. And as soon as the door was ajar, the knocking immediately stopped.

Hyams, clearly frustrated, was turning back to Sommer when he noticed a heavy, black cloud of smoke billowing up the stairwell. The house was on fire! He groped his way down to the dining room, found it ablaze, and managed to put out the flames.

The next day, newspaper stories gave a full account of the fire and the couple's miraculous escape. Well, not the *full* story. The house's resident spirit and the psychic's ominous forecast didn't make it into that day's paper.

Investigators were able to confirm that the fire had begun in the dining room, but they never determined how it got started. Sommer and Hyams didn't need to be told.

According to several mediums Sommer consulted, the poltergeist had probably set the fire as a prank, just to be playful, but the flames got out of control. When it realized that the couple's lives were in peril, the spook sped up the stairs and hammered on the door to warn them.

Elke and Joe had had enough. They soon moved out of the house, and, amazingly, despite the fact that by that time *everyone* knew the place was haunted, the property had no trouble selling.

It sold again and again and again. Over the next several years, the property is said to have changed hands more than a dozen times. There has never been any public explanation for the rapid turnovers.

Sommer has frequently talked about the haunting in interviews; in fact, she describes the occurrences quite thoroughly in the 1986 documentary *Hollywood Ghost Stories*, and Hyams wrote about the events in a *Saturday Evening Post* article, "The Day I Gave Up the Ghost."

After leaving the *Herald Tribune*, Hyams continued to write about Hollywood for magazines, authored twenty-seven books, and became a well-respected expert in martial arts. He and Sommer divorced in 1981. He later remarried and, in 2005, moved to Colorado. He died in Denver on November 8, 2008, from coronary artery disease at the age of eighty-five.

Throughout the 1960s, Sommer appeared in a series of light comedies, all of which showed off her physical assets to their best advantage, and with her fluent facility in seven languages she also continued to appear in foreign-language films. By the 1980s, much of her acting work was in television, and she remained a popular face on TV talk shows as well. Sommer, too, remarried, in 1993, to hotelier Wolf Walther. She lives in Bel Air, and in recent years she has concentrated on her writing and painting, which has been one of her passions since childhood.

Although Sommer and Hyams ended up living their lives apart, they shared one of the most intense experiences possible during anyone's lifetime: an absolutely unaccountable, undeniable encounter with the Unknown.

Chapter 9

Faster than a
Speeding Bullet

When George Reeves, TV's Superman from the 1950s, was found dead on the floor of his Benedict Canyon home, police ruled it a suicide. Many, including his mother, claimed otherwise. Perhaps we should visit the house and ask his ghost.

"Superman's dead!"

On June 16, 1959, newspaper headlines across the country screamed the impossible. The Man of Steel was no more.

According to police, at some time between 1:30 and 2:00 a.m., a very inebriated George Reeves, who had portrayed both mild-mannered Clark Kent and the caped superhero for six seasons on TV's *Adventures of Superman,* had placed a gun to his own head and pulled the trigger.

Even as millions of fans mourned Reeves's death, parents were at a loss how to explain to their young kids that their hero, a man who could be weakened only by Kryptonite, was able to die.

One of those little boys who simply worshipped the man in tights—let's call him Tommy—just had to see for himself that it was true. He knew where Superman lived because he passed by it all the time. His home was only about a mile down Benedict Canyon.

Yes, in Tommy's heart of hearts he knew it was only an actor playing a role. In fact, his parents reminded him of that every time they drove by the star's home to get to Mulholland Drive. Whenever the boy started to excitedly point out the house, his father reminded him that Mr. Reeves was only a performer pretending to be Superman. His dad was insistent—had made Tommy promise—that he would never sneak up to the house and bother the man. Actors were normal people too (well, kind of, his mother would always add with a gentle laugh), and they deserved their privacy.

Tommy's family lived about two miles up Benedict Canyon from Sunset Boulevard, not quite as high up in the hills as Reeves, but distant enough that they didn't have to deal with the never-ending traffic down below. Both sides of the street were lined with modest (for Beverly Hills, that is) ranch and split-level houses, including the ones in which he and Superman lived.

For the past year, Tommy had religiously watched *Adventures of Superman* every Monday at five o'clock. From 1953 to 1956, the half-hour syndicated show had appeared in prime time, at 8:30 p.m., on KECA there in Los Angeles, too late for his parents to let him stay up to watch. But in 1957 ABC picked it up nationally and, knowing that kids made up the bulk of their audience, moved the program to an afternoon slot.

Tommy loved *Superman*. Whenever the show was about to come on, he would run into the bathroom, grab the largest towel out of the cabinet, tie it around his neck, and race back to his spot on the couch in front of their enormous seventeen-inch Philco TV. You could always tell when Superman was onscreen flying, because Tommy could be seen running around the room, his arms extended straight out in front of him. Sometimes he even believed he could fly, if he tried hard enough. His parents were still mad at him from that time he had snuck up on the roof, yelled, "Up, up, and away," and "flown" off, resulting in a twisted ankle when he unceremoniously crashed to the ground.

But now everyone was saying that the man Tommy idolized, or at least the actor who played him, was dead—*and* that he had killed himself. How could that be true? How could anyone not want to be Superman?

George Reeves had been born George Keefer Brewer in Iowa in 1914, but his parents separated when the boy was less than a year old. His mother, Helen, traveled to California, where she moved in with her sister.

When George's mother remarried, his stepfather, Frank Bessolo, adopted the boy and gave him his last name. He began acting in high school and, after graduation, began to box—until his mother, convinced that her son had movie-star good looks, made him stop.

He enrolled at the theater school of Pasadena Playhouse (today, a very *haunted* theater) and performed in several shows on its main stage. He became a contract player at Warner Bros. studios, where his surname was changed to Reeves. His first big break came when he was loaned out to MGM to appear as one of the Tarleton twins in *Gone with the Wind*. Real critical acclaim didn't come until 1943, however, when he appeared opposite Claudette Colbert, Paulette Goddard, and Veronica Lake in director Mark Sandrich's *So Proudly We Hail*.

By the time of the movie's release, however, the nation was at war. Reeves had been drafted into the army in 1942 and was later moved over to the Army Air Forces. For most of his time in the service, he performed in the Broadway and national tour versions of their show *Winged Victory*, as well as in its movie adaptation.

Throughout it all, Reeves looked forward to returning to Hollywood and working again with Sandrich, who felt the young actor was star material. Unfortunately, the director died in 1945, and this setback for Reeves was coupled with a general downturn in movie production after the war. A few minor roles followed, then two years of live anthology shows on New York television. He came back to Hollywood in 1951 for Fritz Lang's *Rancho Notorious*, in which he played a small supporting role.

While Reeves was there, he was offered the title role in the new Superman movie.

Yes, new, because Reeves was far from the first actor to portray the Man of Steel. Superman had been created as a comic strip character by two teenagers, Jerry Siegel, who wrote the panels, and artist Joe Shuster. At first all the major newspapers syndicates rejected the strip, but the superhero finally saw the light of day in a comic book, *Action Comics*, in 1938.

The character was a huge success, and before long, the Strange Visitor from Another Planet did have his own daily comic strip. In 1940 *The Adventures of Superman* premiered on radio. It ran for eleven years, with actor Bud Collyer portraying the hero. Collyer also voiced Superman in a series of seventeen Max Fleischer cartoons from 1941 to 1943. Superman came to the big screen in two popular live action serials (*Superman*, in 1948, and *Atom Man vs. Superman*, in 1950), played by Kirk Alyn (who, years later, would appear in a cameo as Lois Lane's father in the 1978 Christopher Reeve film version of *Superman*).

Reeves was given the chance to play the Man of Tomorrow in 1951's *Superman and the Mole Men*. The full-length feature would also act as the pilot for a syndicated TV series,

Adventures of Superman, which would start production that same year. (The movie was later edited into a two-part episode that aired late in the first season.)

At first the actor was inclined to turn it down. He thought that few people in America owned TVs, which would limit his visibility; and he was afraid that television was a step down from his (admittedly sluggish) movie career. Also, in comparison to motion pictures, television didn't pay that well, and the actors received a salary only during the weeks of production. As it later turned out, weeks and even months would pass between filming, and his run-of-the-series contract (in which the producers could call him back to work with only thirty days' notice) prevented him from taking any extended out-of-town engagements or committing to a movie with a long shooting schedule.

And he was afraid of being typecast.

But once he accepted the iconic role, George Reeves embraced his time as the Last Son of Krypton. He enjoyed personal appearances, not the least because he received additional income for them. But he also took his position as a role model for children seriously. He stopped smoking and, by Hollywood standards, he became enormously cautious in his private life, the most serious infraction of which was his affair with Toni Mannix, the wife of Eddie Mannix, the general manager of MGM Studios.

Reeves had been married to actress Ellanora Needles, from 1940 to 1949. But by the time he started his series, Reeves was unattached, thirty-seven, six-foot-two, 195 pounds, strikingly handsome, and available. And almost overnight, he had also become famous. Sometime during the first year of shooting *Superman*, Reeves and Mannix became lovers.

(Their association was professional as well. Reeves and Mannix both helped raise money to find a cure for myasthenia gravis, a degenerative muscular disease, perhaps a perfect charity for someone who played the Man of Steel. In 1955 Reeves became the national foundation's chairman.)

After *Superman*'s second season, Reeves, tired of the role and angry over the low salary, was prepared to quit the series. During its first two years, Reeves had been able to squeeze in a few movies, but the experiences were unsatisfying. He could accept only minor roles because he was always working around the *Superman* schedule. He was also increasingly afraid of never being able to escape the superhero character. (Legends persist that Reeves's part in 1953's *From Here to Eternity* had been substantially edited after test audiences recognized him on the screen and yelled out, "Look! It's Superman!"—an accusation always denied by director Fred Zinnemann.)

At the last minute, the producers gave Reeves an enormous raise so he was making, depending on which report you believe, anywhere from $2,500 to $5,000 a week, but, again, he was paid only during the eight weeks or so each year that the show was actually being shot. True, during the 1957 season he was allowed to direct three episodes, which brought in a bit more income, and he appeared in a number of commercials for Kellogg's (the show's sponsor), but for Reeves, *Superman* seemed to be a dead end.

By the spring of 1958, after 104 episodes, it looked as though the show had finally run its course. Reeves greeted the news with a mixture of happiness and regret. He would be free to pursue new roles, but it *was* difficult to give up the security of the salary and fame, as well as the real camaraderie among the actors on the *Superman* set.

By then Reeves and Mannix were no longer seeing each other. In fact, sometime in early 1959 he was engaged to Leonore Lemmon, a thirty-six-year-old socialite from New York who was divorced from her third husband.

According to the trades, he was going to marry Lemmon in Mexico on June 19, then go on to do a number of personal appearances in July in the United States and Australia. As the date approached, things seemed to be looking up for Reeves—that is, if one is to believe that continuing in the role of the Man of Steel would make him happy.

You see, it had been decided that there would be another season of *Superman* in the fall, and plans were well under way. Producers had even promised Reeves that he could direct more episodes. The actor had been reluctant at first to re-don the red cape and blue tights. But his last movie role, in Disney's *Westward Ho the Wagons*, had been way back in 1956, and financing for a science-fiction movie he hoped to direct had fallen through. Once again, he seemed stuck.

Early on the night of June 15, Reeves, Lemmon, and a writer, Richard Condon, went out for dinner and drinks. Reeves and Lemmon argued, and soon after the three returned to the house on Benedict Canyon the actor went upstairs to bed. Around midnight, two friends, William Bliss and Carol Van Ronkel, unexpectedly arrived, and Lemmon decided to entertain. The noise was loud enough that at one point Reeves came downstairs to complain, but he stayed long enough to exchange a few words and have a drink before grumpily going back to bed.

How much time had gone by before it happened? Five minutes? A half hour?

Bam!

All four people in the living room reacted immediately to the sound of the gunshot coming from the second floor. Bliss leaped up the small flight of stairs and into Reeves's bedroom. The actor was lying faceup on the bed, naked. His feet were still on the floor with a 9mm Luger lying between them. A single bullet had blasted through his skull, traveling upward into the ceiling.

Although no suicide note was found, after examining the crime scene and interviewing everyone who was at the party, police eventually declared that Reeves had committed suicide.

Of course, Tommy knew none of that when, just before the end of the summer, he decided to sneak up to Superman's house and see for himself whether his hero was still inside.

He wouldn't go at night: Even he knew that would be too dangerous. Besides, if his parents caught him, they'd kill him. Or at least ground him for life. No, he would get up very, very early and slip out first thing in the morning. He could be back before anyone else in the house was awake.

The week before school was to begin, Tommy slid on his jeans and sneaked out the side door just before six. A light mist still hung in the air, and he shivered involuntarily. Well, the chill would go away soon enough, Tommy thought, as he began to briskly ride his bike up Benedict Canyon. Soon he was passing Clear View Drive as it branched off to the right.

Finally he was there. Superman's house. He looked around, checking whether anyone was watching before he quickly darted up the short driveway to the closed garage doors. He made a quick right, darting down the sidewalk between the low hedge and the front of the house.

Suddenly worried that he might be spotted, Tommy knelt down in front of the living room window. Fear (and the lack of anything to eat before leaving the house) made his stomach start to churn. What was he doing there? Was he nuts?!

Well, if he was going to look inside, he'd better do it quick. The first light was dawning, and he'd soon be visible to anyone walking out to get the morning paper; and besides, he had to get back home before his parents realized he was gone.

Tommy gingerly raised both hands and placed his fingertips on the windowsill. Then, ever so slowly, he stood up and peeked into the room.

It was dark. Quiet. Whoever was living there, *if* anyone was still living in the house, wasn't up yet and moving around. He let his eyes drift from one side of the room to the other. Except for a few pieces of furniture neatly in place, it was empty.

Then, off to one corner, Tommy noticed a faint glow. He turned his gaze to a carpeted staircase that led to the second-level bedrooms. As he stared, a hazy shape began to coalesce about midway up the steps. It was tall—a man.

Then, incredibly, a large triangle began to form in the middle of the iridescent figure's chest. In its center: a large "S." As the phantom came into focus, anyone—especially Tommy—could recognize who it was. Although his caped outline seemed almost gray, not its usual bright red, blue, and yellow, he was unmistakable.

It was Superman!

For what seemed like hours, although it was no doubt only seconds, the spectre appeared to hover there on the stairs. Then, as if it were aware that someone was watching, the ghost slowly turned and looked straight at the boy. Tommy would know that face anywhere: George Reeves.

The actor, in his full Superman outfit, gave Tommy that huge grin that warmed up the TV every Monday night. Then he gave Tommy a conspiratorial wink, just like the one Clark Kent flashed viewers at the end of the episodes in which Lois Lane questioned why he and Superman were never in the room at the same time.

And with that, the spirit glimmered once, twice, and then was gone.

Tommy was not alone in what he saw that morning. Over the years, several subsequent owners of the house claimed that George Reeves's spirit, often clothed in his Superman regalia, would appear to them in the bedroom where the actor died. Visitors have reported seeing Reeves's spectre at other locations inside the home as well and occasionally standing outside.

Even though the television show is long over, the character George Reeves so memorably portrayed for so many years has continued to have a seemingly eternal life. So why shouldn't the actor's ghost?

Controversy has continued to surround Reeves's death to this day, primarily because many people (including the actor's mother) could not accept that the actor, even intoxicated and depressed, would ever kill himself. There were no fingerprints on the gun, not even Reeves's own, but police pointed out that the weapon was so well oiled that it was impossible to lift any prints. Nevertheless, the question persisted: Was Reeves actually a victim of foul play?

Rumors continued to swirl as Helen Bessolo hired a private detective. While the death was being investigated, the planned cremation of Reeves's body was postponed. When it finally took place, conspiracy theorists claimed that it was done to remove any possible evidence of a murder. Reeves's will, last updated in 1956, left his entire estate to Toni Mannix. As a result, some thought his ex-mistress, or perhaps her jealous husband, had something to do with his death. But there was never a shred of evidence against them, and no official accusation was ever made.

Today, the remains of George Reeves lie in a crypt at Mountain View Cemetery and Mausoleum in Altadena, California.

The year 2009 marked fifty years since the death of George Reeves, who for a certain generation will always be the real Superman. Who's to say his ghost won't be around for at least a half century more?

Chapter 10
The Duke
Sets Sail

Larger-than-life film star John Wayne has ridden into the Final Sunset, but he apparently misses his private yacht. He's been known to come aboard from time to time and once, when its engine cut out, even steered it to safety.

Chad started collecting the last of the glassware. He had already cleared the buffet table, the tiny appetizer plates, the stray cocktail napkins. But cups and wineglasses seemed to be everywhere—which would explain why this particular harbor cruise had been so, shall we say, jolly.

Chad knew it was supposed to be a congratulatory cruise for the employees of some business or other—a Friday noon sailing, a few speeches and service awards, followed by the rest of the afternoon off—but Chad, who'd seen his share of corporate events, was surprised by the amount of alcohol that had been consumed that day.

And to think that all of those people were now back on the streets heading home in the middle of rush hour! Thank heavens he still had an hour or more to close down the galley. That would give the people more than enough time to be far away when he got on the freeway.

Hornblower Cruises had been in business for almost thirty years, with boats located in San Francisco, Berkeley, San Diego, Marina Del Rey, and there in Newport Beach. It offered event cruises for everything from weddings, birthdays, and anniversaries to business getaways like the one that just wrapped up. Some of their vessels had dinner and sunset cruises as well as whale-watching excursions. One of their San Francisco ships even offered a lunch cruise that sailed around Alcatraz!

But the yacht Chad happened to be on that day was special. It had once been owned by the Duke himself, John Wayne.

Wayne always loved the sea, and it could be argued that he became an actor only by default when his hoped-for career in the navy never materialized.

He was born Marion Morrison in Winterset, Iowa, but his family moved to California, first to Palmdale, then in 1911 to Glendale. It was there that Wayne got his lifelong nickname. His pet Airedale terrier, named Duke, often walked with Wayne by the local fire station, and one of the men in the precinct started calling the boy "Little Duke." Wayne liked the sound of it, and the first time he received credit in a movie (*Words and Music*) he used the stage name Duke Morrison.

Wayne played football for both his junior and senior high schools in Glendale. After he graduated in 1925, he applied to the U.S. Naval Academy but was turned down. With his dream of a life as a sailor put on hold, Wayne applied to the University of Southern California.

He was accepted and awarded a football scholarship. During his time at USC, Wayne spent a summer working in the prop department of Fox Film Corporation on the recommendation of Tom Mix. (The movie cowboy had appreciated the footballer's getting him tickets to the USC games.)

Then, in 1928, while body surfing at the "Wedge," a spot known for its large, powerful, and unpredictable waves off

Balboa Peninsula in Newport Beach, Wayne injured his left shoulder, making him unable to play for the Trojans. With the loss of his scholarship, the boy was forced to leave the university, and back to the studio he went.

Before long, he met director John Ford, who liked the rugged, athletic, six-foot-four youth and gave him extra work in one of his movies. It was the beginning of a long friendship and a rewarding professional relationship for both of them.

Wayne was soon playing bit parts, then actual roles. He also appeared with his former USC teammates in three movies that had football sequences. But his breakthrough film came in 1930, in a Western called *The Big Trail*. The director, Raoul Walsh, wanted to change the Duke's stage name to Anthony Wayne (after American Revolutionary War hero "Mad" Anthony Wayne—whose ghost, by the way, haunts U.S. Route 322 in Pennsylvania and Storm King Pass outside Cornwall, New York). The head of Fox, Winfield Sheehan, wasn't thrilled with the choice, so Walsh next suggested the young man be called John Wayne. The actor, like so many contract players whose names were changed by the studios, had no part in the decision.

The Duke made a string of mostly forgettable Westerns through the 1930s, but with each one he became more recognizable and his fan base grew. Finally in 1939 he was teamed with John Ford for *Stagecoach*, and his portrayal of the Ringo Kid made Wayne a star. In all, Wayne and Ford wound up making more than twenty films together, including what is referred to as Ford's cavalry trilogy: *Fort Apache* (1948), *She Wore a Yellow Ribbon* (1949), and *Rio Grande* (1950).

Over the war years, Wayne, who had both an age and family deferment from the draft, chose not to enlist. He went on to play a number of military heroes in movies with great gusto, however, and his unbridled patriotism made him a role model to many who were actually in the service.

In his later years, Wayne became an outspoken conservative, including his defense of the war in Vietnam. Through it all, his box office clout never suffered. He was idealized on film as a rough but honest Everyman, who rose to fight against enormous challenges for what was right. His idiosyncratic speech and walk made him instantly recognizable worldwide—as well as a target for comics and impressionists everywhere.

By the 1960s Wayne was not only famous but wealthy as well, and he could afford to indulge his passion for the sea. He bought a nine-thousand-square-foot harbor-front home with its own dock in Newport Beach. And what's a dock without a boat?

When Wayne decided to buy a yacht, he got serious: In 1965 he settled on a 136-foot-long former Canadian navy minesweeper owned by his friend, Seattle lumber magnate Max Wyman, for a reported $110,000. The boat had started life on July 6, 1942, and served admirably in World War II. In fact, when Wayne refitted the ship, he kept the twin solid brass plates in place that the navy had put on the prow. With a top speed of fifteen knots and a cruising speed of eleven knots, it was quite a vessel!

Wayne reconditioned the boat, which was already well appointed, into a true luxury yacht. When he was finished with the *Wild Goose*, as he renamed it, she had three decks, five staterooms to accommodate twelve guests, plus crew quarters for six. It carried two tenders, and, to make sure the chef never ran out of Wayne's favorite New York strip steak, the kitchen had a walk-in freezer.

Today, the top deck (which was once a helicopter pad) has been enclosed to serve as a 150-seat dining room. The center deck features a room with a wood-burning fireplace and the salon that still holds Wayne's personal poker table. The lowest public deck contains the library, a children's stateroom, and Wayne's original bedroom suite. The staterooms are all decorated with rich woods and stylish furniture, and the yacht also has two bars and a full-service galley. The huge vessel—it was the largest in the Newport Beach harbor when it first moored there—was painted white with teak trimming.

Wayne liked to have his celebrity friends onboard, especially Dean Martin, Sammy Davis Jr., and Bob Hope, who were frequent guests. Although he was always gracious with fans and the press, he was at heart a very private man and valued the chance to get away for carefree days with just family.

(Wayne was married three times. He had four children with his first wife, Josephine Alicia Saenz; his second wife was Esperanza Baur. But it was his third wife, Pilar Pallete, and their three children who spent the most time on the yacht.)

By the time Wayne bought the *Wild Goose*, he had already had his first major brush with death. A five-pack-a-day cigarette smoker, Wayne was diagnosed with lung cancer in 1964. On September 16, a large tumor was removed along with his left lung, and he became a champion to cancer victims when he went public with his illness, proclaiming in a December 29 news conference, "I licked the Big C." Beating the odds, he remained cancer-free for twelve years.

It was after his struggle with lung cancer that Wayne and his family moved to Newport Beach. Given a second chance, he spent as much time as possible on his beloved yacht, simply enjoying life. Although he frequently sailed to Catalina Island, just thirty-four miles from Newport Beach, he would also take the *Wild Goose* to Alaska in the summer and Mexico in the winter.

By this time, although he still remained a living legend, his films were not doing as well at the box office as they once had. His last movie, 1976's *The Shootist*, in which he played a gunfighter dying of cancer, was critically one of his best but (perhaps because of its bleak subject matter) had difficulty finding an audience.

Also, by the mid-1970s, Wayne was no longer spending much time onboard the *Wild Goose*. His children had grown and moved out. He'd separated from Pilar in 1973, but they never divorced. And his health was radically declining. He suffered a stroke in 1974, and he had surgery for an enlarged prostate two years later. In April 1978, he had open-heart surgery for a faulty valve and then in early 1979 was operated on for stomach cancer. His last public appearance was on April 9, 1979, when he presented the Academy Award for Best Picture to *The Deer Hunter*—which was ironic given Wayne's unwavering support of the Vietnam conflict.

Two weeks before John Wayne's death he was awarded the Congressional Gold Medal, the highest civilian honor lawmakers can give. It's inscribed simply "John Wayne, American." His family received the medallion in a posthumous ceremony the following March; three months later Jimmy Carter awarded the actor the analogous Presidential Medal of Freedom.

His other honors include a Best Actor Academy Award for his portrayal of the eye-patched, craggy Rooster Cogburn in *True Grit* (1969), as well as two Oscar nominations, one for Best Actor in *Sands of Iwo Jima* (1949, but released 1950) and the other as a producer for Best Picture nominee *The Alamo* (1960). When he placed his footprints, fist print, and signature into wet cement outside (the haunted) Grauman's Chinese Theatre on January 25, 1950, it's said that he made sure the concrete contained grains of sand from the beaches of Iwo Jima.

Wayne died of complications from cancer on June 11, 1979, and was buried at the Pacific View Memorial Park cemetery in Corona del Mar.

When he knew for certain he didn't have long to live, Wayne personally set about finding a new owner for the *Wild Goose*. He wanted to be sure that whoever received it would cherish the yacht as much as he did.

He found such a person in Lynn Hutchins, a Santa Monica lawyer. Wayne's last trip onboard the *Wild Goose* was to Catalina Island on the weekend of April 15, 1979, over Easter. Just two months later, he was gone.

Rumors began to surface almost immediately that the yacht was haunted, and the reports seemed to be confirmed by stories in the Associated Press and the *National Enquirer*. Hutchins claimed that he would regularly hear the heavy footsteps of a spirit walking on the deck overhead. He would also catch the unexplainable sound of invisible beer mugs rattling against one another at the bar. Or there would be a cold spot by the couch that Wayne used to favor.

Hutchins saw the apparition for the first time in August 1979, around four in the morning outside the bathroom next to what had been Wayne's bedroom. He recognized the spectre instantly. The Duke was unmistakable. The spirit was tall, large-framed, and wearing a cowboy hat. Before long, the ghost began to appear at any time, night or day, in the stateroom or in the salon.

Hutchins's wife also confessed to once seeing the phantom standing in the doorway as she stepped out of the shower. Wayne, always a gentleman, discreetly disappeared.

Perhaps most disturbing, the reflection of the Duke's ghost tended to show up in a mirror over the bar in the main salon. Usually the haunting was preceded or at least accompanied by the tinkling of glassware. In fact, the sound was always a pretty good sign that Wayne's spirit was aboard.

Hutchins eventually sold the yacht to the Wild Goose Yacht Corporation, which enclosed the top deck so it could comfortably accommodate a large party for dining. Eventually the boat became part of the Hornblower fleet.

But not before Hutchins had one last unusual experience on the yacht. In 1980, while sailing through Newport Harbor, the yacht's engines unexpectedly cut out. Adrift with no navigational capacity and in such tight quarters, the boat was in severe trouble. But then, to the amazement of the crew, the *Wild Goose* began to move on its own, against the wind and current, until it finally beached itself directly in front of Wayne's old mansion.

The yacht must have looked very different back when Wayne had it, thought Chad as he picked up the last of the dirty glasses from the grand bar. Placing them into a tub to carry down to the galley, he was startled to hear the sound of bottles clinking against one another behind the counter. Not seeing any immediate explanation, Chad wondered what was causing it. The sea was calm; besides, the boat was docked. Slowly his eyes were drawn to a blurry motion in the large mirror above the bar. Standing directly behind him, or so it seemed by looking at his reflection, was a large man wearing western attire, one shoulder slightly higher than the other and arms bent at the elbow.

Something about him looked familiar. Had the guy been at the party? *Everyone was supposed to have left over an hour ago,* thought Chad. He was about to tell the stranger he would have to disembark when a small smile crossed the lips of the solid-seeming apparition. Instantly Chad realized who the phantom was.

A thousand thoughts suddenly streaked through the young man's mind at once. It wasn't possible. It couldn't be . . . John Wayne! He'd been dead for more than a decade.

Chad spun around to get a better look at the spectral guest standing behind him. But when he faced the chair next to where the spirit had seemingly been standing, no one was there! He turned back and looked into the mirror again: The phantom was gone.

So all the stories Chad had heard were true. But he had never believed them, and he certainly never thought he'd ever run into the man himself. *Well, Pilgrim,* Chad thought as he started to wipe down the counter, *better get this old yacht lookin' shipshape.* Turns out it wouldn't be just the captain looking over his shoulder anymore.

Part Two

SPIRITS OF THE SILVER SCREEN

Hollywood has been the movie capital of the world for a hundred years, since D. W. Griffith shot *In Old California* there in 1910, so let's take a closer look at its many haunted movie theaters, playhouses, and film studios.

We'll start our ghost walk at the most famous Hollywood movie palace of all: Grauman's Chinese Theatre. Then traveling east down Hollywood Boulevard, we'll check out four more haunted theaters just a few doors apart: the Vogue and Warner Pacific movie theaters; the Pantages, which presents plays and musicals; and the former Hollywood Palace, which has been used for radio, TV, and theater, and today is a nightclub. Across town, two phantoms appear in the Silent Movie Theatre, which is dedicated to screening classic films from the pre-sound era. Then it's off to the studios. Culver Studios, Paramount, Universal, Raleigh, Occidental, and GMT all have at least one ghost walking around their lots.

There are plenty of spirits to go around. In Hollywood, moguls and minions alike return from the Spirit World to stay in the spotlight.

Chapter 11

He Walks
the Forecourt

Victor Kilian invited the wrong man back to his house. Fellow actor Ramon Novarro met a similar fate. While Kilian's ghost has begun appearing in the forecourt of Grauman's Chinese Theatre, Novarro's spirit stays closer to home.

Way back when, growing up in Allentown, Pennsylvania, Randy knew that after graduation he wanted to become an actor. Maybe Broadway, or someday movies, or TV. But he knew it couldn't happen where he was.

He put off the big move for years—after all, he needed to save up enough money first, right?—until late one February night, trapped in his house by a classic nor'easter blizzard, he caught a rerun of the 1933 classic movie *42nd Street* on TMC. There, in the climax of the film, was producer Julian Marsh telling Peggy Sawyer that it was career suicide to live in Pennsylvania. "Allentown? You going back to Allentown?" he scolds her, setting her up for one of the most famous lines in motion picture history: "Sawyer, you're going out a youngster, but you've got to come back a star!"

Right there and then Randy decided: If he wanted to make it, he had to get out of there. But where to go? New York or Los Angeles? Well, New York was only two hours away. If he didn't get a break right away, it would be all too easy to give up and run back home. But if he threw everything he owned into the back of a car and traveled three thousand miles to the other side of the country, he would have to think twice before dragging it all back and admitting defeat. *And,* he thought as he caught sight of the storm outside the window, *it doesn't snow in L.A.*

A month later he was yet another in a long and endless chain of wannabe stars who chased his dream of fame and fortune to Hollywood. He settled into a bachelor apartment—one room and a bath, a hot plate instead of a stove, a foldout couch for a bed, and no kitchen sink.

He knew he had to find an agent. He also wanted to sign up with an acting coach, then start to spread his name around by getting into a showcase or two. He'd probably need new head shots, too.

But first things first. He wanted to get the lay of the land, see what Hollywood was all about. Walking down Hollywood Boulevard, he was shocked to discover that very little of Old Hollywood was left. The studios had moved out long ago. Most of the hangouts of the stars, like the Brown Derby, were gone. There were still a few: the Pig' N Whistle and Musso & Frank restaurants. But even some of the longtime movie theaters, like the Vogue and the Warner Pacific, were closed and boarded up. At least one landmark was left that he could still visit, and he'd known about it since he was a kid: Grauman's Chinese Theatre.

With the exception of the Hollywood sign itself, there was no more iconic symbol of the city.

In 1918, Sid Grauman, a movie theater entrepreneur, constructed the Million Dollar Theater in downtown Los Angeles. Four years later, he opened the exotic Egyptian Theatre, complete with palm and lotus motifs, in Hollywood itself. By 1925, he had decided to build a Chinese-themed flagship movie palace nearby.

He acquired a long-term lease on property on the north side of Hollywood Boulevard just two blocks west of the Egyptian, and to finance the endeavor he became partners with Douglas Fairbanks, Mary Pickford, and Howard Schenck. (Fairbanks and Pickford would also be central players in building the Hollywood Roosevelt Hotel across the street the following year.)

Meyer and Holler, the same architects who had designed the Egyptian Theatre, were put in charge of the project. Construction of what was to become known as Grauman's Chinese Theatre began in January 1926. Norma Talmadge turned the first shovelful of dirt to break ground; Chinese actress Anna May Wong drove a ceremonial rivet into a girder of steel as part of the festivities.

The ninety-foot-high theater was built to look like a giant red pagoda, with small Chinese-style dragons lining the copper roof. A thirty-foot dragon carved from stone was placed on the front wall over the entrance, and two huge sculptures known as "Heaven Dogs" were positioned to guard the front doors. Forty-foot curved walls flanked a large courtyard. To decorate the interior, actual artifacts including temple bells and small pagodas were imported from China.

On May 18, 1927, the $2 million movie palace opened its doors with the premiere of Cecil B. DeMille's silent screen epic *The King of Kings*, preceded by a live show, *Glories of the Scriptures*, accompanied by a Wurlitzer organ and a sixty-five-piece orchestra. The cinema opened to the public the following day, and the theater has remained the sentimental favorite for Hollywood movie premieres and red-carpet events ever since.

It added another chapter to its Hollywood history when it became the site of the Academy Award ceremonies from 1944 through 1946. In 1968 the theater was officially declared a Historical-Cultural Landmark, requiring its preservation. (Indeed, the theater undergoes a nonstop combination of restoration and renovations, as well as inspections—especially lying as it does in an earthquake zone.)

Standing in the forecourt of the theater, Randy took in dozens upon dozens of movie-star hand- and footprints pressed into the concrete. What a great tradition! Although it may have surprised him—and the four million other people who visit every year—the Chinese Theatre's most famous feature may come from an accident. According to one legend, while the place was being built, Grauman inadvertently stepped into the wet cement that was drying in the courtyard. In one of those inspired moments of creativity, the showman realized that if those footprints belonged to a *famous* person instead of him, people might visit the place just to see and compare them to their own. And while the folks were there, they might buy a ticket to go inside to see a movie. Regardless, the publicity alone was worth its weight in gold.

He naturally turned to his movie-star partners. Officially, Pickford was the first person to immortalize her prints and autograph in cement on April 30, 1927, followed immediately by husband Fairbanks. That first year, eight more stars added their imprints: Norma Talmadge, Norma Shearer, Harold Lloyd, William S. Hart, Tom Mix, Colleen Moore, Gloria Swanson, and Constance Talmadge. Over the years more than two hundred stars have been honored by the request to put their prints and signatures into concrete. Some even added imprints of their trademarks, such as eyeglasses (Harold Lloyd), cigars (George Burns and Groucho Marx), and noses (Bob Hope and Jimmy Durante).

In 1929 Grauman sold his one-third share in the theater to William Fox (who owned the Fox West Coast Theatres) but stayed on as the managing director until his death in 1950. And, of course, his name remained attached to the theater as well. The words Grauman and Chinese Theatre seemed to be inextricably linked.

But then in 1973 the Chinese Theatre was sold to Ted Mann, owner of the Mann Theatres chain and husband of actress Rhonda Fleming. He changed its name to Mann's Chinese Theatre, and it stayed that way until the chain went bankrupt in 2001. The cinema then became the property of a conglomerate owned by Warner Bros. and Paramount Pictures. In a nod to its historic past, the name of the movie palace was officially changed back to Grauman's Chinese Theatre on November 9, 2001 (although the former owner's name remained part of the multiplex next door, Mann's Chinese 6 Theatre).

In 2013 the landmark became the TCL Chinese Theatre after TCL Corporation, an electronics manufacturer from China, acquired naming rights. The main auditorium was also redesigned to create the world's largest IMAX theater.

Looking down at the floor of the courtyard, Randy passed slowly from one autograph to the next. The entire history of American cinema seemed to be at his feet. Like everyone else he paused here and there to match his own feet against the imprints left by the stars. He smiled when he saw that the long-standing tradition was obviously still being continued to include actors of his own generation.

Randy suddenly realized that, amazingly, he was alone. The daytime tourist rush had passed, and now, at dusk, the nighttime onslaught of moviegoers had not yet begun. Even the impersonators—the folks who dressed up like Batman, Wonder Woman, Spider-Man, and the like to be photographed with sightseers—seemed to be taking a break. In the quiet lull of the early evening, he had the forecourt all to himself.

Oh, wait. No, he didn't.

Standing with his back to the movie house, Randy noticed a dark figure, an elderly man, slowly making his way along the sidewalk in front of the courtyard, pacing back and forth from one side to the other. Every so often he would pause, look around as if searching for someone, then lower his head and move on. Randy stood still, entranced. The whole time, the man said nothing but carefully surveyed the faces of the few people who did pass him by.

I wonder what, or who, he's looking for, Randy thought. Of course, maybe he was just waiting for a friend. Everyone knows the Chinese Theatre in Hollywood, so it's a natural meeting place.

The ghostly man seemed to alternately grow frustrated, then become completely at peace. Agitated, then fully serene. Finally the interloper stopped, dead center in front of the forecourt. He turned slowly and directly faced the theater. His sad eyes focused on Randy, meeting his gaze. Slowly Randy realized that he had seen that face before, hundreds of times in old movies and television shows. Who *was* it?

He was just about to speak to the stranger when—and there were no other words to describe it—the man simply faded and then vanished.

At first too stunned to move, Randy then walked over to the spot where the figure had been standing. He looked down. It was one of the few patches of the courtyard without any handwriting or footprints. Randy spun around 360 degrees. The man was completely gone. It was as if he had never been there.

Suddenly, Randy was aware of perhaps a dozen or more people milling around in the courtyard. Had they been there all along but he had been too entranced to notice them?

Puzzled, unsure of what he had witnessed, Randy walked out of the courtyard and turned down Hollywood Boulevard toward his hotel. Like every new hopeful who ever came to Tinseltown, he was sure that, with a little luck, he would be back to the Chinese one day, pressing his own hands into that concrete. But for now . . . well, for now, he needed a drink.

Born in Jersey City, New Jersey, in 1891, Victor Kilian (also seen as Killian) entered vaudeville at the age of eighteen and made his debut on Broadway in *The Good Fellow* in October 1926. While still in New York, he appeared in a few small movie roles, his first being an uncredited bit part in 1929's *Gentlemen of the Press*.

In 1935 he was summoned to the West Coast: With the advent of sound pictures, Hollywood was raiding the theater world for actors who could talk, and Kilian fit the bill. He adapted quickly to the new medium, usually playing a minor part such as a sheriff or a bartender or, now and then, the villain. By the end of the decade, the six-foot-one actor had been in almost fifty films.

While shooting a fight sequence for the 1942 John Wayne movie *Reap the Wild Wind,* an accident blinded him in one eye. It hardly slowed him down. In the years 1942 to 1950 he appeared in an astonishing forty-six more films, though in many of them his roles were so small that the character didn't even have a name. Anyone remember him as the baggage man in *Meet Me in St. Louis* or a gambler in *Duel in the Sun*?

Still, he was working—which came to an abrupt halt in the 1950s with the Hollywood blacklist. "Named" in the

McCarthy congressional hearings, Kilian's film career was finished. Although he did manage five roles in 1951 (for which he wasn't identified in the credits), after that he never appeared in another movie. In all, he had done 127 films.

Although Broadway by and large ignored the pressure from Washington to blacklist actors, writers, and directors, Kilian was not unaffected there either. Even though he had been in a play as recently as 1947, it took until November 1957—six years after his last movie role—to get back on Broadway. At least when he did return, it was in a landmark show: the original production of *Look Homeward, Angel*.

He was cast in plays the two following seasons. His final Broadway show was the 1961 production of *Gideon*. During his time on the Great White Way, Kilian had performed in twenty-six shows.

By then, the blacklist was a thing of the past, and television beckoned. Over the next fifteen years, he appeared in episodes of *Gunsmoke*, *The Brady Bunch*, *The Jeffersons*, and *All in the Family*, among many other shows. Most notably he portrayed "the Fernwood Flasher," the title character's grandfather in the series *Mary Hartman, Mary Hartman*.

Unfortunately, Kilian's wife, Daisy Johnson, was not there to share the resurgence of his popularity. After forty-six years of marriage, she had died in 1961. They did have a son, Victor Kilian Jr., who'd been born in 1916 and had also briefly been an actor in his youth. (He would pass away in 1981.)

At the time of his own death, Kilian Sr. was living alone in a small set of rooms in the Lido Apartments on Yucca Street in Hollywood.

The official account of what happened on the night of March 11, 1979, is that one or more burglars broke into his apartment and beat him to death while robbing him. According to other published reports, though, Kilian had met his killer in a bar near the Chinese Theatre (possibly the one attached to the Hollywood Roosevelt Hotel lobby) and, wanting companionship, had asked the man back to his place to carry on their conversation. Along the way, they naturally passed by the famous forecourt bearing all of the signatures and footprints of the stars. Did Kilian's assailant know at the time who the actor was, and that if it hadn't been for the blacklist cutting his career short, Kilian's prints may well have been enshrined among them? Would it have mattered? Within hours, Kilian was dead. His murder has gone unsolved with no suspects.

The trail may have grown cold for police, but apparently Kilian hasn't stopped trying to find his own killer. As Randy discovered during his disquieting visit to the Chinese, the shadowy figure of Kilian's ghost is said to walk the sidewalk in front of the courtyard. And it has been doing so since around 1982. Perhaps one day the spectre will catch the attacker if he's so foolish as to return to the scene of the crime. And then what?!

Although Kilian's spectre is the one that seems to be encountered most often at the Chinese, several spirits have haunted the interior as well!

Theater staff sometimes saw the lower corner of the main curtain in front of the screen flutter when the place was closed for business or between showtimes, as if a person were behind the drape and running his or her hand along it. Others heard unusual, unidentifiable sounds emanating from back there as well.

Some employees have began to call the spectre that was causing the commotion Fritz. He's said to have been a troubled worker who, according to legend, hanged himself behind the movie screen shortly after the place opened.

But whatever phantom is inside the theater, it may not be staying behind the curtain. There have been rumors of occasional strange sounds and flickering lights in the employees' dressing area as well. A few staff members have seen dark, unidentifiable shapes falling from the ceiling but disappearing before they reach the floor. And if that weren't enough, apparently there's an invisible, foreboding presence in the downstairs ladies' room that makes some patrons and staff uneasy and even unwilling to go down there.

Victor Kilian isn't the only Hollywood star to die violently at the hands of a visitor to his home. Ramon Novarro, one of the silent screen's most romantic leading men, met the same fate.

Born Jose Ramón Gil Samaniegos in Durango, Mexico, in 1899, he fled north with his family during the Mexican Revolution of 1916. A cousin of Dolores del Rio, he started playing extra parts and bit roles in movies in 1917. His first major role was in 1922's *The Prisoner of Zenda*, and it was the movie's director, Rex Ingram, who suggested the actor change his name to Ramon Novarro.

Meanwhile, another "Latin lover" type, Rudolph Valentino, was scorching up the screen. Despite the studios' attempts to cast the two as rivals, they became friends. Both would be immortalized by their larger–than-life images flickering on the silver screen.

Novarro's real breakthrough role was in *Scaramouche* in 1923, and two years later he played the title role in the silent sensation *Ben-Hur*. When Valentino died suddenly in 1926, Novarro had the field all to himself.

The Hollywood heartthrob and matinee idol played opposite the major leading ladies of the day, including Joan Crawford, Greta Garbo, Myrna Loy, and Norma Shearer. Although he did make a successful transition to talking pictures, by 1935 when it came time for MGM to renew Novarro's contract his screen appeal had diminished. The studio did not pick up its option. Fortunately, he had invested wisely enough, so money was not a major concern. His years as a movie star may have ended, but he continued to work sporadically in minor roles on film and television up until the year he died . . . which occurred on the night before Halloween 1968.

Despite his Hollywood image as a Latin ladies' man, Novarro was, in fact, homosexual. On October 30, he invited twenty-two-year-old Paul Ferguson and his seventeen-year-old brother Tom to his Spanish-style home in Laurel Canyon. The evening did not go the way he'd planned.

According to testimony at the men's trial, the brothers thought that Novarro kept a great deal of money at his house, and they began to beat him relentlessly, trying to get him to tell them where it was hidden. Novarro fought back, unsuccessfully. Furniture was toppled over; police later found blood trailing across three separate rooms. Eventually the young men fled, taking off with only $20 they found in a bathrobe. They left the naked actor on the floor of the master bedroom, choking to death in a pool of his own blood.

Obviously Novarro did not go peacefully. As a matter of fact, as is so often the case with people whose lives are cut short by violence, he hasn't gone at all. His disturbed, unseen presence is felt to this day by those who enter his old mansion.

Perhaps his spirit is still unsettled knowing that the men, although convicted, spent little time in jail before being paroled. Around 1989 Paul Ferguson was arrested for raping a woman in Missouri and went back to prison, but to Novarro's ghost, it may seem that the brothers got away with murder.

If there's a lesson to be learned from the brutal deaths of Victor Kilian and Ramon Novarro, it's this: Be careful whom you invite into your house. If it's a stranger, the unfamiliar guest could be your last—at least in this lifetime.

Chapter 12
In Vogue

In 1901 a fire destroyed a school on the site where the Vogue Theatre was built thirty-five years later. Teacher Miss Elizabeth and six of the twenty-five children who died in the blaze are just some of the phantoms that then stalked the movie auditorium.

Wake up, Joe! the man told himself. *You can't afford to lose this job, even if it is for just one week.*

The movie theater had closed up years before, but for some reason the American Film Institute decided to make this rundown fleabag of a movie house into one of the three venues for its July 2001 International Filmfest.

Well, Joe wasn't going to argue with their decision. It was hard enough for him to find work as a projectionist. All the major theaters and chains were union houses. No, he had to keep his mind on what he was doing.

Joe yawned. Why had he stayed up all night to party? He knew he had to be on his toes tonight. Fortunately, it wasn't as if what he had to do was so difficult.

The movie came in several reels, and the first two had to be threaded and looped into their respective projectors before the show began. They would be set so that as the first reel ended, the second projector would automatically start up. Then Joe would have to remove the first reel and replace it with the third reel. And so on until the movie was finished.

Originally, long before Joe started in the business, the length of a reel was standardized at a thousand feet, which takes about eleven minutes to run, slightly longer for silent-film stock. Thus, the early "two-reelers" would have run from twenty to twenty-four minutes, because the actual amount of film on any given reel might vary slightly.

As lengthier movies were being shot, technology improved, allowing projectors to be constructed to accept larger spools. The standard length of a reel was doubled to around two thousand feet. Thus, today, the average movie with a running time of an hour-and-a-half to two hours would be a five-reeler. That meant that reels would have to be switched three times as the film progressed so that the movie would continue without a hitch.

Joe double-checked. Everything was in place. He dimmed the house lights and the first reel started up. It was 8 p.m. The second reel would kick in around 8:30. He had plenty of time to sit back and relax.

Joe awoke with a start. What time was it? How long had he been asleep? And what was that damn sound? That flap, flap, flapping, off in the semidarkness?

He looked sharply to his right and realized to his horror that the reel on the second projector was finished, and the loose end of the film was fluttering on the spinning spool.

But why was no one down in the auditorium yelling for him to start the third reel? Why wasn't the theater manager banging at his door?

He peered out through the small window toward the far-away screen. The movie was still playing. He jumped up and ran over to the first projector. Sure enough, the initial reel had been removed: There it was, sitting on the table against the wall. The third reel had been mounted and threaded onto the first projector and then started when the second reel finished. But how was that possible? The projector booth had been locked. Who had switched out the first reel?

After that evening's event, the movie theater would again stand vacant for years before it was finally turned into a nightclub. But at the time, Joe had no clue as to who his unseen helper might have been. If he had asked around, though, he might have heard the tales of ghosts that supposedly haunted the building.

In its early days, Hollywood was little more than a collection of small houses among the orchards and fields that lay at the foot of the Santa Monica Mountains. Its dirt-packed main street was known as Prospect Avenue, not by the name we know it today—Hollywood Boulevard.

According to the modern ghost legend, a four-room schoolhouse known as Prospect Elementary was built on the plot of land that the Vogue would one day occupy. In fact, the school's playground was situated where the auditorium section of the cinema stood.

In 1901 the schoolhouse caught fire, trapping most everyone inside. When the flames and smoke had cleared, twenty-five children and their teacher, Miss Elizabeth, lay dead in the ashes.

The site held too many sad memories to build another school there, so a textile factory was built in its place. It, too, burned to the ground just a few years later.

But Hollywood was growing by leaps and bounds, and the property was too valuable to sit vacant for long. In 1936 the Vogue Theatre was opened on the spot. As opposed to Grauman's Chinese and Egyptian Theatres, the two magnificent movie palaces along that same stretch of Hollywood Boulevard, the Vogue was more modest, designed to hold just eight hundred patrons. There was no large courtyard in front, just a traditional marquee overhanging the sidewalk and only a small lobby with a meager refreshment stand.

(The majestic El Capitan Theatre, today Disney's flagship cinema in Hollywood and catty-cornered across the street from the Chinese, started out as a legitimate playhouse. It wasn't converted into a cinema until 1942, after which, for more than forty years, it became the Paramount Theater.)

According to urban legend, the building has at least two ghosts of its own. One is a man who committed suicide in the balcony. The other is a manager who also died in the theater. His face supposedly used to appear in a high window behind the ticket booth in the alcove or outside lobby under the marquee. So many people were frightened by the spooky visage that management finally covered over the glass.

The fortunes of Hollywood noticeably declined in the 1970s, and the area in which the Vogue found itself became rather seedy. Although the Chinese Theatre and, to a lesser extent, the Cinerama Dome down on Sunset Boulevard were still considered prime locations in which to premiere a picture, as movie audiences began to prefer the convenience of suburban multiplexes, the Vogue and most of the other movie theaters along Hollywood Boulevard became second-run houses, fighting hard to stay alive.

Finally, in the spring of 1992, the Vogue was forced to close its doors. For five years it remained vacant, unused, except for vagrants who were able to sneak inside to escape the elements.

Then in spring 1997 the International Society for Paranormal Research was looking for a new headquarters and a place to hold seminars. The Vogue, which by then had a reputation for being haunted, seemed ideal.

The ISPR was founded in Los Angeles in 1972 by parapsychologist Dr. Larry Montz. His mission was to move psychic research out of the laboratory environment and to put together teams with both scientists and clairvoyants. They would work together out in the field, doing practical, on-site investigations.

In the 1990s the ISPR moved to New Orleans to start a six-year study of paranormal activity in the Big Easy. To assist them in their work, ISPR members started a bold, unprecedented project: They would allow interested novices who had no previous experience in ghost research to take part in their paranormal investigations. The undertaking became known as Ghost Expeditions. Even while the ISPR was centered in the French Quarter, Ghost Expeditions were also set up in England and Los Angeles.

When the organization transferred to the Vogue in the mid-1990s, Montz and his staff were surprised to discover that hauntings were active and ongoing in the venue, so they shifted course to set up a long-term study of the theater.

They began to gather information from former staff members and patrons, and before long they heard more than four thousand first-person experiences. Among the most startling incidents was one screening during which about thirty-five out of the six hundred moviegoers packed into the theater saw a little girl skipping rope up and down an aisle. Many even complained to the management about her. The employees didn't quite know what to say. They were well aware of the youngster who had disturbed the patrons. But how could they explain to people that they were seeing the ghost of someone who had died more than seventy-five years before?

The ISPR, including Montz's associate Daena Smoller, started its own observations. And what did the investigators encounter? Objects that moved on their own. Theater seats lifting up and lowering by themselves. Personal items traveling from one place to another. Yellow orbs of light appearing in photographs. Unusual scents and unidentifiable noises in the auditorium.

There was even the rare manifestation of a ghost— sometimes a full apparition, sometimes only partial. One of them, a male phantom, actually shoved a festivalgoer to one side on the staircase to the balcony.

Eventually the team felt that they could identify nine separate entities that were trapped in limbo inside the Vogue. Six of the earthbound spirits were children, all of whom had died in the schoolhouse fire. The chattiest was Annabelle, an amiable little girl. The others were a girl named Jennifer and two young boys, both named Michael, as well as fraternal twins, Peter and Pamela.

Then there were the three adults. The one who had been there the longest was the teacher, Miss Elizabeth. The other two were of more recent vintage, having both passed over in the 1980s. One, named Danny, was occasionally employed by the theater for maintenance and died from drug use when he was about thirty. Perhaps he was happiest at the cinema; at any rate, he chose it to be his home for eternity.

But it was the last spectre that our fictional hero, Joe, would have been most interested in that night. For about forty years a German immigrant named Fritz was the Vogue's ever-present projectionist, having begun there when the cinema opened in 1936. Fritz was so dedicated that he died of natural causes while at his post in the projection booth during a matinee screening.

Normally Fritz stayed very low-key unless someone wasn't doing his or her job properly or patrons started to damage or abuse his beloved theater in any way. Then he might get a bit irritated and, well, make his presence known. Other times he might lend a friendly, helping hand around the theater, including in the projection booth.

In 2001, as the ISPR was winding down its research, its members decided that they should try to "clear" the theater—the term "exorcise" seems so vulgar—by helping the remaining seven spirits, including Fritz, move on to the Next Plane. (They claimed to have helped the twins Cross Over in 1998.) On December 23, after a cleansing ceremony, the ISPR announced that the theater was free of ethereal inhabitants.

The ISPR then closed up shop in Los Angeles and relocated back to New Orleans, unfortunately also ending their Ghost Expeditions in Hollywood.

All of this makes for a great ghost story, but recent scholarship has shown that there was never a schoolhouse standing on the site of the Vogue Theatre. There was an elementary school located about six blocks east at Prospect (now Hollywood) and Ivar in 1901, but at the time there were thirty-seven students, not the twenty-five that supposedly perished. Also, there was no teacher by the name of Miss Elizabeth and, perhaps most important, the schoolhouse never burned down. Another elementary school about a mile further east, the Los Feliz School at the corner of Hollywood Boulevard and New Hampshire Avenue, was destroyed by fire—perhaps by arson—in 1914. How or whether either of these schools became the basis for the Vogue's ghost legends is unknown.

In 2010, the interior of the defunct theater was completely renovated, and it became a nightspot by the name of supperclub Los Angeles, the sixth venue of an international franchise that began in Amsterdam. Visitors to the event space would never recognize its origin as a modest cinema, and there have been no reports of modern hauntings within its doors.

Chapter 13

Warner
at Work

Sam Warner, one of the brothers who founded the Warner Bros. studio, was said to have cursed their flagship movie theater, now called the Pacific Theater, when it wasn't completed in time for the premiere of The Jazz Singer. *Is that why he still haunts its empty corridors?*

The theater had to be finished. It just had to!

Sam Warner had put not just his personal reputation on the line. The future of his entire company was probably at stake.

Warner Bros. Pictures was in financial trouble when Sam finally convinced his brothers that the future lay in talking movies. This new theater on Hollywood Boulevard was going to be their flagship movie palace, and it was where they would—God willing—be premiering their next picture, the first feature-length movie to feature synchronized sound: *The Jazz Singer*.

It had been an amazing twenty-three-year journey to get this far.

The Warners—Sam, his elder brothers, Harry and Albert, and his younger brother, Jack—were sons of Polish Jewish immigrants, four of eleven children. After living for a time in Baltimore and Ontario, Canada, the family settled in Youngstown, Ohio. There, in the early 1900s, Sam was the first Warner to enter "show business" by (with a partner) renting the town's Old Grand Opera House to present a summer season of vaudeville and kinescopes.

After working for a time as a projectionist, Sam persuaded the family to help him purchase an old Kinetoscope projector. Along with Albert, he traveled the carnival and fair circuit throughout Ohio and western Pennsylvania showing *The Great Train Robbery* to amazed locals.

A single season of receipts was enough to convince brother Harry that a living could be made in exhibiting motion pictures. Together, around 1907, the three brothers converted an old building in New Castle, Pennsylvania, just seventeen miles east of Youngstown, into the Cascade Movie Palace. (The brothers would have been astounded to know that the theater is still standing today, restored and reopened for use in 2006.) Its success led them to add another theater in Youngstown, the Bijou, to begin their "chain."

They quickly realized that distribution was key to their success in the motion picture business, so in 1907 they relocated to Pittsburgh, opened the Duquesne Amusement Company there, and then added a branch office in Norfolk. It was at the Virginia location that Jack officially joined his brothers in the movie trade.

The next step seemed logical. To make *real* money, they not only had to distribute and exhibit the movies, but they also had to make the product. In 1910 they helped finance Carl Laemmle and his Independent Motion Picture Company. Two years later, they formed their own production company, Warner Features. Harry and Albert stayed in New York to handle business on the East Coast, Jack went to San Francisco, and Sam traveled to Hollywood.

Their first movie was 1918's *My Four Years in Germany*, based on a popular antiwar novel. With the money it earned, they opened production offices in Culver City, then later, in 1919, relocated to Sunset Boulevard in Hollywood. (The main colonial-style office building, with its long row of tall columns, still faces Sunset today and is part of Sunset Bronson Studios. The Warner Bros. studio has long since moved onto the old First National Studios lot in Burbank.)

On April 4, 1923, the company officially incorporated as Warner Bros. Pictures Inc. They soon had a big success with *The Gold Diggers*, followed by a series of films with Rin Tin Tin—their first big box office star—as well as John Barrymore. During this period, they were also home to producer Darryl Zanuck and director Ernst Lubitsch.

Then, in 1925 Sam Warner came up with the idea of adding synchronized sound to their movies, using technology created by Western Electric's Bell Laboratories. This was very early science: The music would not be laid on a separate "sound track" on the film itself the way it's done today, by what was first known as the Movietone system. Rather, the Warners' Vitaphone system relied on the sound that was recorded on a disc being played back while the film was projected on the screen.

Eldest brother Harry at first rejected the idea but was eventually persuaded to give it a try in a number of short movies that would be shown before main features. But he insisted that sound be used only for background music and special effects noises, not for the actors' speaking. At first, even Sam didn't advocate recording the actors' voices. The proposed use of sound was to be able to dispense with the expensive orchestras that were being hired to play along with the films in the major movie houses.

In 1926 eight short subjects with sound were produced to be shown in front of the silent feature *Don Juan*. (One of them featured the singing of Broadway sensation Al Jolson, who worked in minstrel-style blackface.) Although the shorts attracted a lot of attention, *Don Juan* was not a success, and the company almost went into bankruptcy. Something bold had to be done!

Sam was more convinced than ever that "sound" was the wave of the future. He convinced his brothers to acquire the rights to *The Jazz Singer*, the story of a cantor's son who must choose between following his father's profession and becoming a singer on the stage. George Jessel had played the title role on Broadway, and he was the Warners's first choice for the movie. But Jessel turned them down because they rewrote the ending. In the play, the son returned to the synagogue; in the film, his choice is the Great White Way.

So Jack turned to Al Jolson, Broadway's biggest star—often referred to at the time as "the world's greatest entertainer." The plan was to produce *The Jazz Singer* as a silent movie, interspersed with musical sequences in which viewers would hear Jolson singing the songs. But it turned out to be more than that. During the film, short spoken dialogues led into the songs, and Jolson interspersed many of his tunes with jokes and exclamations, such as his trademark "Wait a minute, you ain't heard nothing yet."

(As history would prove, Sam was right. Once audiences saw *The Jazz Singer*, there was no turning back. And it finally established Warner Bros. as a major studio to be reckoned with.)

For now, all Sam had to do was get the theater ready in time.

The movie would have its premiere right in the heart of Hollywood. The theater's design was by G. Albert Lansburgh, who had already created the Orpheum Theatre in downtown Los Angeles and the Wiltern Theatre on Wilshire Boulevard. The auditorium would be placed within a four-story office building with two entrances to the theater's lobby: a main entry on Hollywood Boulevard and another on Wilcox Avenue, which bordered on the west.

It's hard to overstate the glorious decor. The lobby was a potpourri of styles—Renaissance Revival, Rococo, Spanish Baroque, and a little Moorish thrown in for good measure—all of which seemed to somehow blend together in perfect harmony. Garden landscapes separated by Italian archways were painted on the walls of the 2,756-seat auditorium. Rather than have a dull, uninteresting asbestos fire-safety curtain drop between shows, famous area artist John B. Smeraldi filled the curtain with pictures of peacocks and blossoming trees, all painted on gold leaf.

But the pièce de résistance, what would become the trademark image of the theater, was a pair of twin radio masts, or signal towers, that would be added later to the rooftop.

But things were not running smoothly. A few problems were to be expected in any new project, but it seemed to Sam that everything was going wrong. There were the usual construction delays, but Sam was most concerned that putting in the new sound equipment was taking much too long. He had taken personal responsibility for its installation.

Sam was there around the clock, skipping meals and sleep, pressing his crew, pressing *himself* to get everything ready in time. The newspapers would be there. The heads of the other studios would be there. And they would all marvel at the film, crowning Warner Bros. the king of the talkies.

"Damn you," Sam cried out to nobody and everything as he stood in the empty lobby. "When will I be done with you?"

As the date of the premiere approached, it became obvious to the brothers that their new theater in Hollywood would not be ready in time. Even Sam reluctantly had to agree. It was decided that *The Jazz Singer* should have its debut at their Warner Theatre in Manhattan. Though he was disappointed, Sam planned to make the trip. But the state of his health intervened.

In September 1926 Sam had begun having nosebleeds, incapacitating headaches, and dizzying vertigo. He turned out to be suffering from a severe sinus infection, which, in the era before antibiotics, developed into an acute mastoid infection.

The Jazz Singer opened on schedule in New York on October 6, 1927, ushering in an era of sound movies that changed Hollywood forever. But none of the Warner brothers was in a mood to celebrate.

Sam's condition had deteriorated rapidly, complicated by pneumonia. The day before the movie opened, Sam suffered a cerebral hemorrhage while being operated on to remove diseased cells from his brain. He died at the age of forty. Devastated, his brothers hurried back to Los Angeles for the funeral. He was buried in the Home of Peace Cemetery in East Los Angeles.

The Warner Brothers Theater, as its name officially read on the first night program, finally opened six months later, on April 26, 1928, with a minor film, *Glorious Betsy*. Jolson gamely acted as host for the evening's ceremonies, and as part of the event a plaque dedicated to Sam Warner was hung in the lobby.

It's a pity that Sam wasn't there to enjoy it. Or was he?

For many years the movie palace was one of the top theaters in Hollywood. Between 1953 and 1964 it became the Warner Cinerama Theatre, premiering *This Is Cinerama* (which played an amazing 133 weeks), followed by the handful of movies made in the panoramic three-strip, three-screen process. The last, *How the West Was Won*, played there for ninety-three weeks in 1963 and 1964. The cinema was also the site for the world premiere of 1968's *2001: A Space Odyssey*, which ran an also astounding eighty weeks.

It was during this final run that the theater was sold to the Pacific Theatres chain and was renamed the Hollywood Pacific Theatre. In 1978 the grand movie palace was broken into three separate, smaller theaters. The main auditorium was reduced to 1,250 seats, and the balcony level was converted into two 550-seat houses. As a result, the theater acquired the unofficial, inelegant moniker of the Pacific 1-2-3.

What's amazing is that, through it all, Sam Warner has apparently never left the building.

Ever since the cinema opened, people have reported seeing his frustrated ghost pacing back and forth in the lobby where he was said to have cursed the theater. In the 1970s two members of a night cleaning detail saw the phantom walk the entire length of the foyer, stop at the elevator, push a button, wait for the lift to arrive, and then step inside just before the doors closed. In fact, until it was put out of operation by the 1994 earthquake, the elevator often seemed to have its own mind, changing floors without being called—at least, not by any living patrons.

Sam's spectre has also been spied upstairs in his old offices, but more often these days he remains invisible. Nevertheless, night watchmen on the ground floor hear him moving around overhead—footsteps, chairs being dragged across the floor, doors slamming, and random rappings.

Are the stories correct? Is Sam Warner's spirit really trapped in the theater, still feverishly trying to prepare it for the first showing of *The Jazz Singer*?

No one can say.

The Pacific was damaged during the Northridge earthquake in January 1994, and the construction of the Los Angeles subway directly under the theater also disrupted the movies. The theater was closed for safety reasons on August 15, 1994.

Although the structure's interior usually can't be visited by the general public, it has been used to house occasional special events. For about four years, starting from 2002, it became the USC Entertainment Technology Center Digital Cinema Lab to test new digital projection systems.

Given Sam Warner's interest in new technology, it's little wonder that his spirit seemed to be especially active during their tenure. He loved to play tricks with their electronic gadgets and tools. He'd make other high-tech toys, such as cell phones and PDAs, disappear. Or he might simply move the objects around so they turned up in completely different areas than where they were left. Sometimes he'd replace them with similar but different items.

For a few years beginning in 2008, the lobby was used for Sunday church services. Hollywood is currently undergoing major revitalization, so at some point the movie palace may reopen its doors to the general public.

So if they do resurrect the old theater, now designated a Historic Landmark, will you have a prayer of seeing Sam's ghost? Chances are good. You can be sure he'll be there in spirit for the grand reopening.

Ready for a few, quick, related ghost stories?

Some people think Al Jolson's spectre has also returned, but not to the old Warner Theatre in Manhattan or any of the Broadway houses in which he starred. Instead, the apparition of a man wearing period clothing has been seen in the balconies and under the stage at the Royal Alexandra Theatre in Toronto. Because the phantom first appeared during the run of the bio-play *Jolson*—and because the great entertainer *did* play the theater while he was alive—many believe that the nightshade is "Jolie" himself.

One of the great Warner Bros. stars, especially in the 1930s and early 1940s, was handsome, athletic Errol Flynn. The six-foot-two swashbuckler (a mantle he inherited from silent-screen star Douglas Fairbanks) made ladies swoon (and made men want to be him) in a series of Warner costume dramas, including *Captain Blood* (1935), *The Charge of the Light Brigade* (1936), *The Adventures of Robin Hood* (1938), *The Private Lives of Elizabeth and Essex* (1939), *The Sea Hawk* (1940), and *They Died with Their Boots On* (1941).

His private life was anything but. He was notorious for his fast living and sexual escapades. His acquittal following a 1943 statutory rape trial led to the creation of the catchphrase "In like Flynn." Many an orgiastic party took place at his eleven-and-a-half-acre crestline estate just off Mulholland Drive in the Hollywood Hills. Flynn even had two-way mirrors and peepholes installed throughout the house so he could eavesdrop on guests making love in the various bedrooms.

Some of his friends were just as incorrigible. For example, according to Flynn's memoirs, *My Wicked, Wicked Ways*, after John Barrymore's death the film director Raoul Walsh stole the Great Profile's corpse from the funeral home where it was being prepared for burial. He snuck it into Flynn's house, propped up the body in a chair, and just waited for Flynn, drunk from a night on the town, to return and discover it.

In the 1970s there were numerous reports that Barrymore's old Bella Vista estate in Beverly Hills was filled with spirits. The seven-thousand–square-foot mansion, in Spanish-Mediterranean decor, was attached by a private cable car to lower-level gardens, guesthouses, a pool, and a cabana.

Among the phenomena that took place in the house were phantom footsteps, the ringing of a nonexistent telephone, and the cries of a spectral baby. Some claim it's also haunted by the ghost of a workman who was killed in an accident on the cable car as well as the apparitions of all three Barrymores: John, brother Lionel, and sister Ethel.

Screenwriter Gene Fowler acquired John Barrymore's cuckoo clock as a keepsake after the actor's death, even though the timepiece had been broken for several years at that point. It was a few *more* years until Fowler decided to reset the clock to the hour of Barrymore's death, 10:20, as a tribute to his friend. When he pulled out the clock, he discovered that its hands were already pointing at that time!

But back to Flynn. He died of a heart attack in 1959, only fifty years old, his early death no doubt hastened by his opium use, hard drinking, and chain smoking. He's buried in the Garden of Everlasting Peace at Forest Lawn Memorial Park in Glendale, but according to subsequent owners of his house, he never really moved out.

According to neighbors, spectral lights and noises of ghostly, nighttime parties continued in his hilltop home for years, especially in August. The house was later owned by country-and-western star Stuart Hamblen, who sold the property to singer-actor Rick Nelson.

In their essential book *Hollywood Haunted*, Laurie Jacobson and Marc Wanamaker tell how both Nelson and his daughter, Tracy, encountered ghosts in the old Flynn house. They were sure that one of them, the figure of a man that appeared in the dining room late at night, was Flynn. On separate occasions, they both heard what sounded like burglars ransacking the house. But when they thought it was safe to go investigate, they discovered that nothing in the rooms had been disturbed. Doors to unoccupied rooms sometimes locked from the inside. Tracy also occasionally felt the presence of a female spirit in her part of the house. She would catch the scent of inexpensive perfume. The toilet would flush or the shower might start on its own. Was one of Flynn's ex-lovers in the house?

There's also a ghostly link between Rick Nelson and his father, Ozzie. The Nelson family (Ozzie, Harriet, David, and Ricky) was known by generations of Americans from their show *The Adventures of Ozzie and Harriet*, which started on radio and moved to television. While on the radio (from 1944 to 1952), the sons' characters were voiced by actors, but when the show moved to TV, the boys appeared as themselves, literally growing up in front of America.

Throughout, the Nelsons lived on Camino Palmero, a side street off Hollywood Boulevard, just a few blocks west of Grauman's Chinese Theatre. Ozzie died in 1975 at the age of sixty-nine. Harriet stayed in the house, living alone, for five more years, selling it in 1980. Its new owner was convinced that Ozzie, who was deeply attached to the home, was still there. Although his ghost was never seen, doors would open and shut by themselves, and light switches and water faucets turned on and off without being touched. If not Ozzie, who?

And finally, comedienne-actress Carol Burnett talks fondly about her time as an usher at the Warner Brothers Theater back in the 1940s. When she received a star on the Hollywood Walk of Fame, it was placed right in front of the movie palace.

Burnett graduated from Hollywood High School in 1951. The building opened in 1905, and its theater is said to be haunted by at least three ghosts: a young boy named Toby who shot himself in the school's theater after his girlfriend left him; a girl wearing white who hanged herself from one of the catwalks over the stage because she flunked a class; and a teacher dressed in gray who haunts the green room (the actors' backstage lounge and reception area). The campus may also be haunted by the spirit of a former janitor, and it may be these or other phantoms that cause unusual sounds throughout the school grounds as well as making classroom doors open by themselves.

It's said that there are at most only six degrees of separation between any two people, that with no more than five introductions any person can be linked to anyone else. In Hollywood, it seems the Spirit World is connected even closer than that.

Chapter 14

Playing
the Palace

Formerly a playhouse, then a TV and concert venue called the Hollywood Palace, Avalon nightclub is haunted by all sorts of ghostly phenomena, from apparitions and light orbs to unexplainable electrical outages. Some date back to the 1920s; some are of more recent vintage. All have the talent to terrify.

Now what? The night watchman had seen more than his share of unusual goings-on in the old theater, but it had been quiet the past couple of months. Was it all about to start up again?

Fred had been warned before he was hired that some people thought the place was haunted, but he decided that being able to face the unexpected was a natural part of his job as a guard—even if that usually took the form of a human intruder, most often a vagrant looking for a warm night indoors, not some visitor from the Beyond.

His first encounter the other night, well, it had been almost creepy enough to make him quit. Had the house ghosts been testing him?

It had been about 2:30 a.m., magic time for spooks, long after the building had been secured for the night, and he was making his appointed rounds. On the third floor, while passing a room that had been set aside as a comedy club during a recent makeover, he heard piano music coming from the other side of the closed, locked door. Whoever was playing was no amateur. The person knew exactly what he or she was doing: The song was bluesy, jazzy, bewitching, all at once. Maybe some musician who had performed in the main room that night wandered upstairs, somehow found the door open, started playing, and simply lost track of time. Still, the performer wasn't supposed to be there.

After hours the building was darkened but he always left himself enough illumination to safely navigate without tripping over things or falling down the stairs. This night, however, Fred looked down and saw a shaft of light coming out from under the door. The bright beam clearly meant all the lights were turned on inside the other room.

Even though he didn't think he had anything to fear, Fred slipped his key into the door quietly. He liked the element of surprise. It gave him that extra split second to anticipate and prepare for whatever move the violator might make.

He turned the knob slowly, then threw the door wide open. Instantly all the lights in the room went out. The place was pitch black. Instinctively he ran his hand along the wall and surprisingly found a light switch. He flipped it on. The room was empty!

Cautiously, even before stepping all the way inside, he swept the room with his eyes, from one side to the other. Nope, no one was there. There didn't even seem to be any place someone could hide. And even if there were, no one could have gotten away from the piano that quickly.

Fred strode over to the piano. Its cover was open, the keyboard exposed, and the bench pulled out. Not pushed to one side, as the seat would have been if someone had suddenly jumped up and dashed away. No, just far enough for someone to sit at the keys and doodle.

Although somehow he knew he wouldn't find anyone, the watchman examined every square inch of the room. He walked around all of the seats and small tables, then checked the windows. Whoever, or whatever, was in the room had simply disappeared.

That was when Fred stopped taking chances. He decided that not only did he need some sort of companionship in the empty, cavernous building at night but he also needed someone who was more, uh—he thought the correct phrase was "sensitive"—to ghosts than he was. That's why Fred now brought along a German shepherd. He'd read somewhere that animals can pick up the presence of invisible spectres in a room.

Apparently some animals freak out when they come into contact with spectral entities. They'll run out of a room, hiss or bark, or refuse to go down a seemingly empty corridor. *But this guy is fearless,* thought Fred, looking down at his canine companion: He must have been bred to confront the Unknown. The dog almost strutted around the vacant play-house, sniffing here and there, as if to say, "Come on, Spirit World, I dare you. Bring it on."

What Fred didn't know was that, despite the name that might be on the deed, the spirits really owned the building.

The theater began its life as the Hollywood Playhouse, a legitimate stage for plays and musicals. Built with a Span-ish Colonial Revival facade by architects Gogarty and Weyl, the three-story, 33,000-square-foot structure was on Vine Street just a few doors north of Hollywood Boulevard. The playhouse premiered its first show, the long-forgotten *Alias, The Deacon*, with veteran Broadway and film actor Berton Churchill on January 24, 1927.

It didn't turn out to be the most fortuitous time to hold a grand opening, however. Just two years later the Great Depression hit, and playgoing became an unaffordable luxury for many. But President Franklin Roosevelt recognized the need for the arts to be part of a successful recovery program for the country, and government-funded shows under the Works Progress Administration were sent out on tour. During the years its productions were presented at the Hollywood Playhouse, the venue became known as the WPA Federal Theatre.

In the 1940s the place was converted into a radio studio, and for many years the CBS Radio Network used it to broadcast its West Coast shows, such as comedienne Fanny Brice's *Baby Snooks* and, in her pre-television years, Lucille Ball's *My Favorite Husband*.

In 1942 the playhouse was dubbed the El Capitan Theatre—not to be confused with the movie theater across the street from Grauman's Chinese Theatre. (At the time, *that* movie palace was known as the Paramount Theater.)

From then until 1949, the El Capitan housed *Ken Murray's Blackouts*, a variety-revue-burlesque show that kept audiences laughing through the war years and beyond, for an incredible 3,844 performances.

In the 1950s the theater was refitted for television. Among the many shows that came out of the El Capitan were Groucho Marx's *You Bet Your Life* and, for a time, *The Lawrence Welk Show*. On September 23, 1952, a special set was erected on the stage from which Richard Nixon telecast his famous "Checkers" speech in a desperate attempt to keep his political career alive.

In 1963 *The Jerry Lewis Show* began to broadcast a variety show from the theater. With high hopes for the TV program, the playhouse was renamed the Jerry Lewis Theatre. Such optimism was short-lived, however; the series lasted only three months.

Lewis's show was replaced by an hourlong variety show for ABC. Once again, the name of the playhouse was changed to match that of the television show: *The Hollywood Palace*.

The show first aired on January 4, 1964, and ran successfully for just over six years. As opposed to *The Ed Sullivan Show*, in which the titular host appeared every week, *The Hollywood Palace* changed hosts every episode (although the season premiere was always hosted by Bing Crosby). The show had a few firsts, including the U.S. television debut of the Rolling Stones and the first national network appearance of the Jackson 5.

The theater was also used to tape daytime television. In the mid-1960s it was the home to such favorites as *The Newlywed Game* and *The Dating Game*, among many others. It was an occasional concert venue as well. In fact, the Beatles' first West Coast appearance was at the Hollywood Palace, just before their two performances at the Hollywood Bowl.

After *The Hollywood Palace* went off the air, ABC continued to operate the theater as a studio for several years. The last tenant in the mid-1970s was Merv Griffin. When he opened his own studio farther down Vine, south of Hollywood Boulevard, the Hollywood Palace was closed.

And so it remained until 1978, when ABC sold the theater to a businessman, Dennis Lidtke, who transformed the playhouse-studio into a concert venue and dance club. To mark the transition, he shortened its name to simply the Palace. Although the building continued to change ownership over the years, it's remained a nightspot for music ever since. (For example, the Ramones played their final concert

there on August 6, 1996.) At the same time, it's been available for special events such as awards shows, corporate
functions, film premieres, and studio parties. Even political
rallies have been held there. At one, President Bill Clinton
outlined his "Don't ask, don't tell" policy regarding homo-
sexuals in the military.

The theater's most recent makeover came in September
2002, when Hollywood Entertainment Partners purchased
the property and upgraded the facilities. Now known as
Avalon, it's one of the hottest clubs in Hollywood.

Today the main level has a lobby that filters into a dance
floor, lined with tables, bars, and DJ booths. It was near
the large stage that Fred noticed the disturbance that night
back in the 1990s. What it turned out to be amazed even
Fred, who by then had come to believe that the place was
indeed a playhouse for phantoms.

As Fred crossed the room he saw a man in a tuxedo
standing by the right front corner of the platform. At first,
the stranger seemed to be studying the watchman and the
canine in casual amusement. Fred stared back, hoping to
recognize the interloper. But it slowly dawned on him, much
to his bewilderment, that the person, apparition, whatever
it was, didn't have a face. Sure, it had a head; it seemed to
have a ring of hair over the scalp. But where the face should
be, there was nothing but a translucent emptiness.

The phantom turned away from the guard and looked
over toward the far end of the stage. He began to move
slowly, deliberately, from one side of the platform to the
other. Even as Fred rushed toward the spectre, the guard
desperately tried to take in everything he could about the
man: his frame, stature, walk—anything that might help
him identify the guy later.

Then it struck him: The man seemed to be unusually short, or, to be more precise, shortened. His body had no feet. Rather, his legs met the stage at the middle of his shins. It was as if the stage were the surface of a pool of water, and the man was walking through it up to his calves.

Just as Fred was about to intercept the spectre at the left side of the stage, the apparition faded into the darkness. The mysterious stranger was gone. The dog rushed past the guard, leaped onto the stage, and stood, suddenly still, sniffing the floor at the spot where the peculiar figure had vanished.

Fred wouldn't find out until years later, long after he had left the Palace, that back until the playhouse was converted into a television studio, the original stage had been much lower. The spectre he had seen wasn't melting through the floorboards: He was simply walking on the stage at the level it had been when the man was alive.

What Fred encountered during his time as a night watchman was only the tip of the iceberg. There are other ghosts in the Palace. Many others.

An unseen female phantom seems to be happiest in the lobby on the second floor that overlooks the dance floor. She wears a flowery perfume and will tap passersby on the shoulder just to get their attention.

And she's not alone up there. For years theatergoers on the second floor have complained about the disembodied voices of a male and female loudly talking and laughing throughout the shows. They've also been heard near the seats and bar area on the main floor.

Another vocal spectre is that of a little girl who's heard sobbing in a stall in the women's restroom in the downstairs lobby. When it's reported, the staff always duti-fully searches the toilet, but they've yet to find the elusive crying youngster.

One of the ways in which paranormal researchers hunt for ghosts is with an electromagnometer or some similar device that perceives the presence or changes in fields of energy because it's believed that ghosts emit or tamper with electrical auras. If that theory is true, it might explain why the theater's stage lights, musical amplifiers, and other elec-trical equipment sometimes go nuts.

Surges of energy might also explain why adding machines and calculators back in the 1990s would some-times unexplainably go haywire. They would also print out combinations of numbers that almost appeared to be words and sentences. (Are the Palace ghosts trying to contact us using some sort of coded message?) At least two people have seen papers slide out from under the door of the unoccu-pied, locked accounting manager's office.

So-called "cold spots" in the theater not caused by drafts, air-conditioning, or other ventilation, are thought by many to be evidence of a ghostly presence. One other-wise unaccountable icy spot can be found over the back-stage staircase on the south side of the theater. Another is often felt in the front of the balcony.

Then there are actual manifestations. Shimmering blue orbs have been seen wafting through the air on the main floor. More than one person has had unidentifiable streaks of light show up in photographs, visible only in the prints after the film was developed but not seen at the time the picture was shot.

Dark, indistinct forms have been spotted all around the club, often in the balcony lobby. On at least one occasion, a watchman saw a large, cubelike mass hovering over the empty stage.

Many of the apparitions are much more distinct. A man in a tuxedo has been seen sitting at one of the tables on the main floor; another (or perhaps the same man, because his face has never been discernible) shows up in the lobby. A different unknown male, always dressed in a hat, most often appears in a hallway down in the basement. Those who have run across him have reported feeling a kind of negative, though not evil, force coming from him. A similar uncomfortable presence has been sensed on the north stairwell leading down to the basement; whether it's the man in the hat is unknown.

Two people who have been seen clearly are a well-dressed elderly couple (affectionately known as Hank and Mary) who show up in the north side of the balcony from time to time, always dressed for an elegant evening out on the town. The problem is, their clothing dates to the early 1930s. They're so engrossed with each other that they seldom see when someone is coming close to them, but they always vanish before they can be touched.

At least three other spirits have been given names: Harry, an electrician, and Emily, a chorus girl, date from the time of Ken Murray's *Blackouts*. Emily has never been seen, but her heels are heard backstage, clacking in the south corridor on the second floor. Harry has appeared all over the building and is a bit of a prankster; he likes to hide tools and tie ropes into knots. The third apparition is thought to be a stagehand named Whit, who's usually encountered on the catwalk in the fly gallery over the stage.

And the manifestations and sightings go on. And on. But don't worry: There's no need to rush to see them. Whether the theater's called the Playhouse, the Palace, or the Avalon, the ghosts that have collected within its walls over the past ninety years don't seem to be going anywhere soon.

Chapter 15

The Hughes
Haunting

The ghost of former owner Howard Hughes still walks the hallways and visits his old office on the second floor of the Pantages Theatre, while the phantom of a woman can be heard singing in the balcony. And they may have company!

Can a theater be haunted by unhappy memories of its owners? If so, no playhouse has a better right to be full of phantoms than the Pantages Theatre on Hollywood Boulevard, owned at different times by two of the most famous, but ultimately unfulfilled, men of the mid-twentieth century: Alexander Pantages and Howard Hughes.

Pantages was born in Greece in 1867. He ran away from his family at the age of nine during a trip to Cairo and after working on merchant ships and, later, the Panama Canal, he made his way to San Francisco. He did anything to stay afloat—first waiting tables, then turning to boxing. But like so many others with visions of easy money in their heads, in 1897 he raced to the Yukon Territory in the great Klondike Gold Rush.

He never discovered gold, but he did meet a soul mate: testy, talented performer and dance hall hostess Kate Rockwell, nicknamed "Klondike Kate," with whom he became partners in a small revue and burlesque house, the Orpheum.

The two had a rocky relationship and split in 1902. Pantages traveled to Seattle, where he opened a vaudeville and movie house called the Crystal Theater. By that time Rockwell had moved to Vancouver, where she had opened a tiny movie theater of her own. She later relocated to eastern Oregon, where she quietly lived out the rest of her life.

(Her ghost is now said to have returned to the Klondike, haunting one of the other playhouses she owned there, the Palace Grand Theatre. It still stands today, or at least an exact replica of it does.)

Meanwhile, in 1904, Pantages had set up a second theater in Seattle: The first playhouse he named after himself, the Pantages. He knew his stuff. By 1920 he owned about thirty theaters outright and managed or controlled the booking in around sixty more. With almost a hundred theaters at his disposal, he was able to create the Pantages circuit, with which he could offer exclusive, long-term contracts to vaudeville acts.

He moved to downtown Los Angeles around 1920 and quickly opened a theater and offices at Seventh and Hill Streets. Pantages became involved with the film industry, partnering with Famous Players, which was then part of Paramount Pictures, to have product for his theater chain.

Back in New York, David Sarnoff and Joseph P. Kennedy had taken control of Keith-Albee-Orpheum, a rival vaudeville circuit that dominated theaters east of the Mississippi. In 1928 they changed the company's name to Radio Keith Orpheum, or RKO. (Radio was added to the mix because Sarnoff was also the main shareholder of Radio Corporation of America, or RCA.) They tried to buy out Pantages, but he turned them down.

Meanwhile, Pantages longed for a playhouse in the center of the entertainment industry: Hollywood. On June 4, 1930, he threw open the doors to an Art Deco masterpiece, named (like so many others) the Pantages Theatre, right on Hollywood Boulevard near the intersection with Vine.

It was designed by Pantages's favorite Seattle architect, B. Marcus Priteca. Originally planned as a twelve-story building, only the two lower, theater levels were ever built due to the 1929 stock market crash. But what *was* constructed was grandiose. Upon entering, patrons were awed by the vast carpeted lobby, domed gilded ceiling, chandeliers, and two immense side staircases that led to upper balconies. But the richness and grandeur didn't stop there. It extended into the auditorium itself to cover every square inch of the interior.

At first, live entertainers performed between films. But vaudeville was dying, and after just two years, the theater was used primarily as a movie house.

Not only were things going poorly for Pantages professionally, but his personal life was also in shambles. In 1929 he was accused of rape by a seventeen-year-old dancer named Eunice Pringle. Pantages was found guilty in his first trial but won acquittal on appeal. By then, however, he was broke. He was forced to sell his complete chain, including his beloved theater in Hollywood, to RKO for much less than it had originally offered. His life was shattered. He died in 1936 and was buried in Forest Lawn Memorial Park in Glendale.

You might think that with his intense, spiritual connection to his namesake theater that it would be Alexander Pantages who haunts the playhouse. But no!

Howard Hughes was, to say the least, a complex man. Born in 1905, he took over the Hughes Tool Company at the age of nineteen following his father's death. By that time the younger Hughes had studied engineering and math and already taken flying lessons.

He moved to Los Angeles, and by 1927 he was producing and directing films, including *The Front Page* (1931), *Hell's Angels* (1930), *Scarface* (1932), and *The Outlaw* (1943). Divorced from his first wife, the dapper Hughes dated a succession of Hollywood beauties, including Bette Davis, Ava Gardner, Olivia de Havilland, Katharine Hepburn, and Gene Tierney.

Also during this period, he was consumed by his passion for aviation. In 1932 he had set up Hughes Aircraft Company as a division of his tool corporation. Five years later he set a transcontinental airspeed record in his H-1 Racer (now in the Smithsonian's National Air and Space Museum), and the year after that he set another record by flying around the world (with a crew of four) in just three days. In 1939 he became the major stockholder of TWA, and by the end of World War II Hughes Aircraft was a major defense contractor for the U.S. government.

By the late 1950s Hughes had begun his well-known descent into probable madness that only ended with his death on April 5, 1976. But in 1949, when he bought a majority interest in RKO and, with it, acquired the Pantages, Hughes was still in his prime. He moved his offices into the two rooms on the second floor that were originally used by Pantages himself and for several years conducted all of his business out of them.

For a decade, from 1949 to 1959, the theater hosted the Academy Awards. In 1965 it was bought by Pacific Theaters. (Three years later the company would also pick up the Warner Brothers Theater, just a few blocks west.) The Pantages closed in January 1977 for renovations, and when it reopened it was no longer a cinema. With the Nederlander Organization as a new partner, the venue became a premier legitimate theater and has operated as a playhouse

ever since, mostly presenting road companies of Broadway musicals and now and then a major concert. In 2000 Disney took out a long-term lease to present a sit-down production of *The Lion King*, and as part of the deal the theater had a $10 million restoration, returning it to the magnificent splendor of its opening night sixty years earlier. Later, after a nearly two-year run, *Wicked* departed in January 2009, allowing the theater to once again become a home for touring productions.

Beginning in the 1980s, people working in Howard Hughes's former offices on the second floor have sometimes felt an uncomfortable, unseen presence in their midst. It's usually accompanied by a sudden cold breeze, not caused by any ventilation or air-conditioning. Others have heard clacking noises that sound like the brass handles that were on old file-cabinet drawers. Doorknobs turn; desk drawers open and close. Now and then the scent of a cigar will waft through the smoke-free offices. And ever since intruders vandalized the area around 1990, security guards have heard unexplainable bangs and thumps coming from the area. Perhaps most disconcerting, an apparition has also been spotted. It's a tall man, in standard business attire. Most people are convinced that the ghost is that of the reclusive Hughes.

The mogul's ghost has also been seen sitting in the back of the theater's mezzanine. Back in the day, Hughes had a doorway cut between his offices and the upper level of the auditorium. When he wanted to be alone to think, he apparently would stroll over and sit in the empty house.

And he's not alone in the theater. According to legend, back in 1932 a woman died in the mezzanine during one of the movies. (Other sources say it was during the performance of a musical.) The cause of her death is unknown.

Beginning shortly after the theater break-in occurred, the unknown female's voice has been heard, quietly singing away at all hours of the day and night. Supposedly her dulcet tones were even picked up by a microphone during a live performance in 1994, merrily singing along with the cast.

And there may even be a third, unknown spirit in the playhouse. Within the past decade or so, one of the women from the wardrobe department decided to leave through the auditorium instead of using the stage door. As she was walking up the aisle, all the lights in the house suddenly cut out. Before she had time to become disoriented in the dark, she felt a gentle hand take hold of her elbow. The invisible Samaritan escorted her safely to a side exit. Some think the ghostly guide was Howard Hughes; some say it was Alexander Pantages. The truth will probably never be known.

Whoever the Pantages entities are, they're evidently theater lovers, because they show no sign of allowing death to be their final curtain. Obviously, they're going to keep giving encore performances—whether we want them to take another bow or not.

The building that holds the Pantages Theater is huge, taking up the better part of a city block. Several unrelated businesses have storefronts as part of the structure along Hollywood Boulevard. To the immediate left of the theater entranceway (when facing the marquee) is a dive bar known as the Frolic Room. Also known as Bob's Frolic Room, the watering hole was established in 1934, replacing Halgreen's Fountain Café. Rumor has it that in the post–World War II era the hangout was, for a time, secretly a gay bar.

The Frolic Room has its own ghost: the image of an anonymous man who appears in the mirror that hangs behind the bar. Folks staring into the reflective surface will turn to look at the man standing behind them, only to find no one there.

Some think the ghostly male figure may be Howard Hughes. After all, when he owned the Pantages, Hughes micro-managed all parts of the building. He's even said to have installed the neon sign that still stands outside the Frolic Room's door. Also, it's claimed that when the Academy Awards were being held at the Pantages, Hughes would use the Frolic Room as his own private lounge. Maybe he's still stopping by for a nightcap.

Chapter 16
Without a
Word

It's not what you hear; it's what you see that counts. The ghosts of two former owners still like screening their favorite early-film classics at the old Silent Movie Theatre in Hollywood's Fairfax district.

"Can I help you?"

Laurence Austin, the owner of the Silent Movie Theatre, was cleaning up in the lobby as the intense nineteen-year-old approached. The young man obviously was not there to watch the screening of the obscure comedy short starring Larry Semon in the auditorium. Austin knew that cinephiles were a mixed bag, but to his practiced eyes the guy somehow just didn't fit in with the usual crowd that entered the place. He was there for something else.

Christian Rodriguez knew that actions spoke louder than words, and he was in a hurry. He nervously reached into his pocket and pulled out a small revolver. He pointed it at the aging proprietor with the universal signal that says, "This is a stickup. Give me all your cash."

There wouldn't be much. There were few patrons on the other side of the lobby doors. Even when the place was packed, there weren't all that many people. The theater sat only 158, and tonight it wasn't even half full.

But cold steel can be very convincing. Austin raised his hands slightly, palms open, to show that he wasn't hiding anything. He walked calmly to the box that held the evening's receipts, opened it, and turned it so the intruder could see how meager his takings would be.

No sense doing anything rash, he figured. No reason to get hurt. At most, there were three, four hundred dollars in the till. The young man barely looked down into the box as he scooped up the loose bills, then stuffed them into his pocket. Odd, thought Austin, the guy didn't seem to be all that interested in how much money he'd be making in the heist.

A flash of panic crossed the boy's brow as he continued pointing the gun at the old man's chest. *He has his money,* thought Austin. *Why hasn't he darted out the door?*

It was only then that the truth dawned on him. The kid wasn't really there to rob him. That was just a cover, the money a bonus. He was there to . . .

Those watching the silent movie were startled by the gun blast. (There was certainly nothing on the screen that called for such a sound effect.) By the time someone thought to go out to ask Austin if he knew what was going on, the owner was dead, his blood spreading across the lobby floor, and the assailant was long gone.

In 1942, fifteen years after *The Jazz Singer* had forever changed the face of movies, John Hampton opened the doors to the late Art Deco–style Silent Movie Theatre on Fairfax Avenue in what is today West Hollywood. Although he enjoyed modern films and certainly would never expect, or want, a return to the days of nontalking movies, the cinema of the silent era was still his passion.

Along with his wife, Dorothy, Hampton amassed a treasure of thousands of silent movies, from one-reel shorts to full features. He had copies of many of the masterpieces—films by Charlie Chaplin, Buster Keaton, Mack Sennett, D. W. Griffith—but he also had an eclectic mix of little-known movies featuring forgotten actors.

Sure, some of the stuff was mundane and in a logical world probably didn't deserve to be preserved, but it didn't matter to Hampton. It was the genre that entranced him, and to him all of its output was gold. He loved the actors' wide-eyed expressions, their exaggerated movements, the flickering title cards that gave barely adequate approximations of what the characters were feverishly mouthing on the screen.

His movie theater was never a real moneymaker. It had been born out of a desire to share the joy of watching the timeless pieces of celluloid with fellow enthusiasts. Occasionally, old-timers (including those who had actually worked on the films) came to see them the way they should be seen: projected onto a giant screen. And over the years, as the place became an institution, it attracted a young breed of cineaste who appreciated the films as an art form.

Unfortunately, the pioneers of filmmaking who had a vested interest in keeping their work intact were mostly gone. And the postwar studios didn't share Hampton's enthusiasm. They only wanted to look forward and were allowing the old movies in their vaults to deteriorate or disappear.

Though not a professional preservationist, Hampton knew that silent-era film stock was brittle and fragile, so he did what he could to keep his own movies from crumbling into dust. He personally tried to restore some of the films by bathing them in vats of chemicals he kept in an old tub above the theater and at accommodating film-processing labs around the city.

But in those days, even though it was known that the chemicals could be deadly if they were ingested or even inhaled, few realized that long-term exposure to them could also lead to dire consequences. At the end of the 1970s, Hampton broke the news to his stunned admirers: He had developed cancer, probably as a result of handling the toxic chemicals for so many years. The theater was closed, and in 1990, Hampton died.

The cinema, which had been the only movie theater in the country dedicated solely to screening a regular slate of silent films, sat shuttered for twelve years before Laurence Austin bought it in 1991.

It was January 17, 1997, when Austin's attacker entered the lobby and took his life. A police investigation revealed that his death was no bungled burglary. Instead, James Van Sickle, the theater's projectionist and Austin's live-in partner, had hired Rodriguez to kill the older man to inherit his estate, estimated to be worth about $1 million. Both Van Sickle and Rodriguez were found guilty of murder and sentenced to life in prison.

Upon Austin's death, the movie house was closed, and it went up for sale in March 1998. Once again it seemed that the theater had come to the end of the road. But fate had other plans. Charlie Lustman, a silent-film aficionado, was passing by when something told him he had to buy the place. Deciding that the tradition of screening silent flicks deserved to be continued, he reopened the theater to much fanfare in late 1999.

Despite an initial burst of interest, however, audiences dwindled over the years, and to supplement its income the theater was rented out for parties, concerts, wedding and bar mitzvah receptions, and the occasional private screening. By early 2006, special events had become the house's primary money-earner, and silent movies were being screened only on holiday weekends.

In June 2006 Lustman decided to sell the theater to two brothers, Sammy and Dan Harkham (only twenty-five and twenty-four years old, respectively, at the time), and they asked Hadrian Belove to help return the Silent Movie Theatre to its glory days.

The brothers owned Family, a boutique bookstore, and Belove was proprietor of an eclectic, independent West Los Angeles video rental store called Cinefile. Together, under the umbrella name Cinefamily, they decided to expand the Silent Movie Theatre's mission as a revival house to include worthy but seldom seen films from the sound era, although silent movies (especially rarities) would remain a vital part of the programming formula.

To prove their dedication to the project, Cinefamily spent almost $1 million installing a new screen and sound system, spacing out the seats to provide more legroom, replacing the floors, putting in a state-of-the-art projection booth, and upgrading the concessions stand. The marquee outside was restored to its Art Deco splendor, and the second floor was renovated into an art gallery and café/coffeehouse. A digital Yamaha keyboard was acquired to back the silent movies, and tickets were offered both for individual sale and on a subscription basis.

What they may not have counted on were the ghosts.

Why had Lustman, seemingly on a whim, purchased the theater, and why did he decide to reopen it, of all nights, on Halloween? At first, his reason might seem surprising. He claimed, "John Hampton, the original owner, spoke out to me while I was riding by one day."

Had Hampton's ghost actually called out to him from beyond the grave? No one knows for sure. But one thing is certain. Hampton's spirit was no stranger to the place. And neither was Austin's.

During Lustman's tenure, Hampton's phantom regularly appeared in the upstairs lounge that was once his and Dorothy's apartment. Austin's spectre also showed up, but when he manifested, it was usually to employees in the lobby after the theater had closed for the night.

Will the hauntings continue now that new owners have taken over and fewer silent films are being shown? It's probably too soon to tell. But there's no reason to believe that Hampton and Austin aren't planning to stick around for a "second feature." When it comes to a love of movies, even the Spirit World is probably one big happy Cinefamily.

Chapter 17
The Man in the
Bowler Hat

Was it an illness or an accident that felled studio producer Thomas Ince? Regardless, his spirit seems to have found no rest. Neither have the phantoms of Lon Chaney, Bela Lugosi, and a host of Hollywood's workaday actors and crew members that continue to haunt its many studios.

As the shots rang out across the deck, time stood still. Everyone froze in place. Up until then, the cruise had been idyllic, a perfect getaway. How could there be gunfire out here on the yacht, miles away from the hubbub of Los Angeles?

William Randolph Hearst, the newspaper magnate, barreled up onto the top deck from down below, his face red with fury, firing his handgun as he ran. Where was that no-good son of a . . .

Suddenly one of the shots hit its mark—although not the target Hearst had intended. With a heavy thud, Thomas Ince dropped to the floor, fatally wounded.

Hearst stopped cold. *Oh my God,* his mind raced. *What have I done?* But already he was calculating how to cover up the crime.

It had all started out with what was supposed to be a relaxing party on his twenty-eight-foot yacht, the *Oneida,* as a belated forty-third-birthday present for his friend, movie producer Thomas Ince. Of course, with Hearst it was always hard to separate business from pleasure. He was also hoping to move his Cosmopolitan Productions film company into Ince's studios, and he thought that a tranquil cruise would be just the place to negotiate the deal.

Against Hearst's better judgment, he had also asked Charlie Chaplin along. For some time Hearst had believed that his lover Marion Davies and Chaplin were secretly seeing each other behind his back, and he had even had detectives tail the couple to confirm his suspicions. The thought of the two together drove him jealously insane. But Davies had pleaded with Hearst to invite the comedian, so he finally acquiesced.

But he couldn't show his displeasure to the other guests. Not William Randolph Hearst. He was the head of the most powerful newspaper syndicate in the world and controlled a major media empire. He had to present himself as cool, collected, in command of any situation. If there were any truth to the stories about Davies and Chaplin, well, he would deal with that another time. But for today he would just play nice. Not only would it show how magnanimous he was if, as he assumed, others onboard had heard the rumors as well. But also, what did he have to lose? Nothing could happen out at sea. The yacht, though sizeable, was small enough that even if so much as a flirtatious glance passed between the two, he would be able to catch it.

Hearst had no room to talk, of course. He was a married man, and his involvement with Davies was the worst-kept secret in Hollywood. In fact, he had been more or less living with Davies full-time since 1919. His wife, Millicent, had carved out an independent life for herself as part of New York society, but she would never divorce him.

For her part, Davies was sweet and sincere, if only a minor talent. What Hearst privately thought of her work as an actress is unknown, but he promoted her endlessly and had pretty much set up Cosmopolitan to produce starring vehicles for Davies. (She wound up appearing in twenty-nine silent movies and seventeen talkies with the company.)

Davies was also a brilliant hostess—at the beach house that Hearst built for her, on the *Oneida,* and, years later, at her twenty-seven-room mansion in Beverly Hills.

Thomas H. Ince, the guest of honor on the cruise, was born in Newport, Rhode Island, in 1882. He had been an actor, screenwriter, director, and producer before single-handedly revolutionizing the film industry. For all intents and purposes, he was the first to insist on a "shooting script," as they've become known, that breaks down every scene, shows whether they would be shot as interiors or exteriors, tells which actors would appear, and so on. Ince's innovation allowed him to streamline production to get more product at lower costs.

He had started as an actor and director in 1910 for Carl Laemmle's Independent Motion Picture Company (or IMP) before moving on to the New York Motion Picture Company. Ince was placed in charge of the company's Bison division to make Westerns. To facilitate production in 1912, Ince purchased 460 acres of land and leased an additional 18,000 acres in Santa Ynez canyon between Santa Monica and Malibu on which to shoot panoramic vistas. He built standing sets and populated the camp with members of the Miller Bros. 101 Ranch and Wild West Show so he had a regular company of rough-and-tumble cowpokes to appear in his films. He also began to work with William S. Hart, making him the first true star in cowboy movies.

In 1915 Ince became partners with fellow film pioneers D. W. Griffith and Mack Sennett to found the Triangle Motion Picture Company in Culver City, California, to produce, distribute, and exhibit their own films—one of the first studios to control their own product from start to finish.

Three years later he broke away from the others, purchased property from Harry Culver, and opened his own Thomas H. Ince Studios. His offices, built in 1919 and situated at the studio entrance, were housed in a white, colonial-style building resembling Mount Vernon. Meanwhile, Triangle evolved into Sam Goldwyn Studios; in 1924 it would become Metro Goldwyn Mayer Studios.

Even though the party on the yacht that fateful week was in Ince's honor, the noted producer had missed the boat when it sailed from its harbor in San Pedro on November 15, 1924, because he was attending the premiere of one of his movies, *The Mirage*. He didn't catch up with the yacht until the next day when it reached San Diego.

Now here it was, four days later. The morning had started uneventfully enough, but there was a strange quiet in the air. Hearst couldn't put his finger on it, but something just didn't feel quite right. He looked around the deck and mentally started ticking off the guests.

Where was Davies . . . and Chaplin? Hearst quietly descended the narrow stairs to the lower deck and sought out Marion's cabin at the end of the hall. He gently began to turn the knob. It was unlocked. Hearst paused for just a moment, unsure as to whether he wanted to see what might be on the other side. But he had to know! He threw the door open and strode into the center of the cabin. He took in the entire stateroom in a single glance.

There they were—in each other's arms.

Chaplin knew there was no denying what was going on. He didn't even try. He darted for the door. If Hearst had put out his arm, he might have caught the Little Tramp, but he was too busy pulling out his revolver.

Marion gasped, knowing how fierce Hearst's temper could be. He gave her a withering look, a mixture of disgust and despair. But he couldn't really blame her for succumbing. Chaplin's reputation for seducing women was legendary.

Hearst turned back to the door. The interloper was gone. Well, he'd fix that lowlife! He lunged out the cabin and ran after Chaplin.

Was Hearst really planning to kill the movie star? Or was he just hoping to scare him so much that he would never dare come near his saintly Davies again? It's hard to say. But shoot he did. And with the gunfire, Hearst felled his unintended victim: Thomas Ince.

Or so the most famous version of the story, of which there are several, goes.

Regardless of what really took place, Hearst couldn't afford a scandal. It was bad enough that he was married and carrying on an affair. Middle America was fed up with the many tales of debauchery coming out of Hollywood. And as luck would have it, Hearst's own newspapers were partly responsible. They had fanned those flames by printing "yellow journalism" accounts of the Fatty Arbuckle trial for the rape and murder of the young actress Virginia Rappe.

There's no way of telling what Hearst promised the people onboard to keep quiet about what happened that day. But it is speculated that the meteoric rise of gossip columnist Louella Parsons, who was one of the guests, was the result of a guarantee of lifelong employment by the Hearst syndicate.

It was reported to the press that Ince had fallen sick onboard the yacht. On the morning of November 17, Ince, unconscious but still alive, was transferred off the boat in San Diego and taken to his home in Hollywood. He died there on November 19.

An early headline in the *Los Angeles Times* actually reported that Ince had been shot, but the story was retracted by the evening edition. Hearst's own papers reported that Ince had taken ill at the newspaperman's ranch, but that story, too, was changed when it was proven that Ince was aboard the boat.

Matters were complicated by Chaplin's secretary, who claimed to have seen a bullet wound in Ince's head as he was removed from the yacht. Finally, the district attorney in San Diego felt compelled to do an official investigation of the matter, but when his first witness, a Hearst employee named Dr. Daniel Goodman who had been on the yacht, testified that Ince had complained of chest pains, the DA quickly wrapped up the case and ruled that the movie producer had died of a heart attack caused by acute indigestion or possibly ptomaine poisoning.

Perhaps Hearst had nothing to do with Ince's death. But he wasn't known for his altruism, yet not long after Ince's funeral (which Hearst did not attend), he set up a trust fund for Ince's widow. He also paid to have Ince's home torn down and replaced with a magnificent mansion, which became known as the Chateau Elysée. (The building still stands, operating today as the Celebrity Centre for the Church of Scientology.) Conspiracy theorists note that Ince was cremated, which would have destroyed any evidence of a shooting if another inquiry were ordered later.

The memory of what happened to Ince on the *Oneida* haunted Hearst for the rest of his life.

Apparently the studios Ince built are haunted as well.

After Ince's death, Cecil B. DeMille bought his studios, and over the years the property has been sold many times and undergone a number of different names, including Pathe, DeMille, RKO-Pathe, Selznick, Desilu-Culver, and Laird International Studios, but they are most often simply referred to as Culver Studios. The three-story office modeled after George Washington's home is still standing and used as an administration building to this very day.

Several classic movies were filmed on the "back forty" of the lot, including the 1927 *King of Kings*, the original *King Kong*, and much of *Gone with the Wind*, as well as many iconic television shows including *Batman*, *Lassie*, and *The Untouchables*.

Ironically, Orson Welles's thinly disguised indictment of William Randolph Hearst, *Citizen Kane*, was also filmed at the studios. (Welles himself, wearing a cape, is said to haunt a bakery called Sweet Lady Jane in West Hollywood that he often visited when he was alive. At times, even when he's not visible, the scent of his favorite brandy and cigars float through the air.)

Beginning around 1988, when the main Culver Studios offices were being remodeled, Ince's ghost, wearing his distinct bowler hat, began to appear in the building. Most often he's seen climbing the stairs heading toward what was his private screening room. He's also been spotted on the catwalks above several of the soundstages, especially Stages 1–4. If the apparition sees someone, it'll merely frown, then turn and walk through the nearest wall.

They say there's no place like home, and apparently Ince isn't fond of people fiddling with his. According to a crew member, on at least one occasion the spectre spoke, saying, "I don't like what you're doing to my studio."

Over the years other unidentified spirits have been spied around the lot at night, including a female form that manifests on the third floor of the main building. As she vanishes, she's always accompanied by a blast of cold air.

But foremost among all the spectres at the studio is the guy who started it all, the unlucky birthday boy, the man of the midnight hour, Thomas H. Ince.

The Culver Studios are far from the only haunted movie studios in Hollywood. In fact, most of them seem to have at least one resident spirit. Should we take a quick survey?

In the 1930s and 1940s, Universal Studios produced a string of classic horror movies, including *Frankenstein*, *Dracula*, *The Mummy*, and *The Wolfman*. Preceding them all was the 1925 Universal thriller *The Phantom of the Opera*, starring Lon Chaney.

Stage 28 was built on the back lot in 1923 specifically to hold the gigantic sets required to realistically depict the interior of the grandiose opera house and its labyrinthine underground lair. The soundstage is still in use today. Dozens of employees and guests, from set designers to security guards—even people who don't know the stage's history—have spotted the ghost of a man wearing a black cape scurrying high overhead on the catwalks. Legend has it that they're seeing the ghost of the original Phantom, "the Man of a Thousand Faces," Lon Chaney himself. Even when he doesn't materialize, doors sometimes open and shut at will. Lights also turn on and off, seemingly on their own. Shades of crashing chandeliers!

For many years, Chaney's recognizable ghost was seen sitting on the bench at a bus stop on the northeast corner of Hollywood and Vine. Before making it big, Chaney used to wait there to catch the bus to Universal Studios to act in minor roles. It was said that after becoming famous, Chaney would sometimes have his limousine driver stop at the bench, and the star would offer up-and-coming actors a lift to the studio. Sightings apparently ceased after the original bench was replaced with a kiosk-style bus shelter. The bus stop has since been moved to the northwest corner of the intersection.

Fellow Universal star Bela Lugosi, who was never able to shake off his indelible image as Dracula, has returned to haunt the land of the living, too, but not the studios. Instead, he walks Hollywood Boulevard, which he used to love to stroll late in life, happily greeting fans.

Lugosi passed away of a heart attack in 1956 at the age of seventy-three. By that time, he was broke, all but forgotten, and had been in and out of treatment for drug addiction. There have been reports, though, that his postmortem presence is also felt in the small Hollywood apartment where he was living at the time of his death. Strange noises are heard there, and pets sometimes refuse to walk up the stairs.

Lugosi's body was prepared for burial at the W. M. Strothers Mortuary, the so-called Mortuary of the Stars because of all its celebrity clients. At the time there was an agreement with the Chamber of Commerce that funeral processions would avoid Hollywood Boulevard on their way to the cemetery so as not to upset tourists and hurt local businesses, but according to an apocryphal story, the driver of Lugosi's hearse felt control of the wheel being yanked from his hands. He was forced to turn onto the fabled street, perhaps by the actor's spirit, so that Lugosi could take one last trek down his beloved Hollywood Boulevard.

At the request of his son, Bela Lugosi Jr., and fifth wife, Lillian, Lugosi was buried in one of the famous Dracula capes he had worn on tour. Although filmdom's most famous vampire apparently doesn't like to stay in his coffin, he's interred at Holy Cross Cemetery in Culver City.

But back to the movie studios. Hollywood is dotted with facilities lesser known to the general public. Raleigh Studios began in 1914 when Adolph Zukor bought a horse barn in which he could shoot a silent film with Mary Pickford for his Famous Players Film Company. The property grew and has operated under many owners over the years, making it one of the oldest (if not *the* oldest) continually operating movie studios in the United States. It took the name Raleigh Studios in 1979 and operates today as an independent studio, unaffiliated with any of the majors, with nine soundstages available for rental usage.

Reports began to surface as early as the 1920s that the Raleigh lot was haunted. One area in particular, Stage 5, built in 1926, is especially active. According to studio folklore, at some point (it's said around the 1940s) an electrician on the catwalk above the soundstage accidentally fell thirty-five feet to his death.

From time to time, crew members report hearing his disembodied voice echoing from the catwalk. It's thought that his spirit might be what causes one of the large overhead work lamps to swing back and forth, seemingly on its own. The lights also will turn themselves on, sometimes repeatedly, after workmen have shut the place down and locked up for the night.

The hallways behind Stage 5 are home to a translucent, spectral lady wearing a ball gown. She's been caught, only in the nighttime, walking down the corridors and passing through the walls into adjacent dressing rooms and offices.

A crewman locking up Stage 2 one night felt what he described as a blast of wind passing right through him. And somehow a grip who fell from a twenty-foot scaffold inexplicably escaped injury when, just before crashing to the floor, he felt himself being caught by some invisible force, and then being lowered gently down to the ground.

Other areas are haunted as well. The spectre of a costumed female apparition has been seen walking through a crew commissary that resembles a Mexican cantina. (It was originally built as an outdoor movie set.) The building next door was once used as the wardrobe department, so it's thought that the spirit was an actress who crossed through the area on her way from the fitting rooms to the soundstages.

And speaking of clothing, the corridors of one of the buildings that once contained dressing rooms (now converted into office space) is haunted by a male phantom. He's dressed as a stagehand and, when spotted, will stop, stare, then vanish into thin air.

GMT Studios in Culver City, also available for rental, has seven soundstages, four floor-to-ceiling cycloramas (curved walls that can be painted to provide background panoramic scenes), and three standing sets: a police station, a courthouse, and a prison (left over from Clint Eastwood's *Escape from Alcatraz*). The studio is haunted by the ghost of a twenty-five- to thirty-year-old woman wearing a green dress. Staff have also heard the distinct sounds of creaking and cracking wood, although no damaged woodwork is ever found, and unexplained streaks of light and unidentifiable noises have shown up on both still photos and videotape shot on the soundstages.

At haunted Occidental Studios there are the usual doors that open or slam shut as well as the ethereal sounds of voices, laughing, and metal banging on pipes. There's also a bewitched second-story corridor behind a soundstage and the stairwell that leads up to it from the ground floor. It's the home of the apparition of a floating female ghost. So many strange goings-on have happened on the lot that the place has acquired the nickname "Accidental Studios."

Finally there's Paramount, the only major studio still located in Hollywood.

Paramount Pictures can trace its origins back to 1912, when Adolph Zukor, a New York nickelodeon owner, obtained the American distribution rights to *Queen Elizabeth*, a four-reel movie starring the French actress Sarah Bernhardt. Zukor went on to found the Famous Players Film Company to produce movies. In 1916 it merged with the Jesse L. Lasky Company and Paramount Pictures Corporation, a national distribution firm, to form the Famous Players–Lasky Corporation. The result was Paramount Pictures, which constructed its first soundstages on Marathon Avenue between Melrose Avenue and Santa Monica Boulevard in Hollywood.

Those few buildings were the humble beginnings of a studio behemoth that today has more than thirty production and service departments, thirty soundstages, and nine exterior full-time standing sets.

And many of those facilities are haunted.

Some say it's because the studio is located next to Hollywood Forever Cemetery, where several Paramount stars and bigwigs are spending eternity. In fact, Stages 29 through 32 are just on the other side of the graveyard's south wall. Stages 31 and 32, as well as the catwalks of Studio 5 for some reason, are particularly prone to haunted activity. The most frequent phenomena come in the form of disembodied phantom footsteps, heard by security personnel on their rounds as they check the deserted soundstages at night.

Numerous men have witnessed the apparition of a woman reeking of a flowery perfume on the top floors of the studio's Hart building. Items left on desks there are sometimes found scattered on the floor the next morning. Doors seemingly shut on their own, windows become locked, and invisible fingers tap visitors on the shoulder. Some believe the unidentified spectre may be Lucille Ball, because her Desilu Studios were once located in the Hart building. (There have been reports that the redheaded comedienne may also haunt her old house on North Roxbury Drive in Beverly Hills.)

Supposedly, on December 30, 1993, at least four security guards were dispatched to find intruders in both the Chevalier and Ball buildings in the back lot. Even though someone was momentarily spotted in one of the structures, and unexplained lights shone from the other, no one was ever found—at least, no one living.

Nor was that the only time a spectre has appeared in the Ball building. A female phantom passed by two employees working late one night on the second floor. They didn't recognize her, so when the men turned to ask the stranger who she was, the spirit had disappeared.

Perhaps the most famous ghost to haunt Paramount is Rudolph Valentino, who, despite having appeared in earlier films, truly became a star from the studio's 1921 release *The Sheik*. He apparently still turns up from time to time in Paramount's old wardrobe department, floating among the period costumes. Valentino, of course, now resides just over the wall in Hollywood Forever Cemetery.

There are many entrances into Paramount Pictures, but the gate closest to the graveyard wall is located at the northeast corner of the studio at Lemon Grove Avenue and North Wilton Place. Night guards at the pedestrian walk there have been spooked for years by apparitions dressed in early- or mid-twentieth-century clothing as they either nonchalantly stroll through the admission gate or, more disturbingly, pass right through the high cemetery wall. Sometimes they simply poke their heads through, take a look around, and then pop back into the cemetery.

One final story: A watchman assigned to one of the prop department storage buildings located next to the graveyard was surprised by an usual discovery. That particular structure housed the monumental plaster props, those weighing three to four hundred pounds, and they were positioned in precise, numbered spaces so they could be easily catalogued and retrieved. One morning the guard walked in to find all of the props had been slid together into a tight bunch in the center of the room.

The workman didn't find the practical joke amusing. He had to move them all back, and they were heavy! When the same thing happened the next day, he decided to find out who was pulling the prank. That night he hid with a friend in the warehouse. Around two or three in the morning, the men heard scraping sounds as the hefty props were being dragged across the concrete floor. They snapped on all of the lights to catch their prey, but instead they got the shock of their lives. The statues were moving around by themselves! The men fled from the building in holy terror, never to return.

Today many of the Hollywood studios offer tours, Universal and Paramount among them. If amateur ghost hunters take one, they might be able to catch some of these haunted happenings for themselves. Of course, there's never a guarantee that they'll spot a ghost, but in the land of illusion, anything is possible.

Part Three

HOLLYWEIRD ON LOCATION

Everyone wants to see the famous sites that put Hollywood on the map. Fortunately, many of the landmarks are open to the public or can be entered by pulling a few strings. Visitors may even glimpse some of the ghosts haunting these legendary attractions.

First off: the Hollywood sign, said to be revisited by the unhappy ingenue who jumped to her death from the iconic billboard. Then a visit to a couple of the city's spacious parks. Griffith Park seems to carry a curse from its days as a Spanish rancho. And after dark, the ruins of a razed mansion come to life on a walking trail in Runyon Canyon.

Two nightclubs, the Comedy Store and the Magic Castle, play host to ghosts within their walls. And phantoms feel right at home when they're staying at the Roosevelt or Knickerbocker Hotels.

But the Hollywood hauntings don't stop there. Just before the final credits roll, we'll visit the most haunted graveyard in all filmdom: Hollywood Forever Cemetery.

Chapter 18
Hollywoodland

Millions have been lured to Tinseltown by those fifty-foot letters on the hill: HOLLYWOOD. *And some, like twenty-four-year-old Peg Entwistle, have never escaped from under their shadow, even after death.*

One more rung.

Just one rung.

Teetering there, a thousand feet above the city, Peg Entwistle was thoroughly exhausted. But she knew better than to stop or to look down. Stare straight ahead and climb—one slow, agonizing step at a time.

From her vantage point, Peg was privy to a unique view of the fifty-foot-tall, thirty-foot-wide letters mounted high on the slope of Mount Lee. On that balmy autumn day in 1932, climbing the workman's ladder that had been left propped up against the backside of the giant "H," Entwistle could see the reality behind the illusion: the telephone poles and wooden framework that held up the huge pieces of sheet metal.

But she could no longer make out all thirteen letters that could be seen by everyone in the city far below: HOLLYWOODLAND.

They're just like the movie sets, she thought. *Facades with nothing behind them.* Peg was used to playing make-believe: After all, she had been in eleven Broadway plays, and numerous shows at school before that. Now she'd just finished her first—and, as it would turn out, her last—film, a minor role, barely larger than a walk-on. But somehow, in the middle of a vast movie soundstage, the flats that substituted for the walls of rooms and the fronts of buildings seemed even more artificial than the ones used in the theater.

The trip west; the movie. It had all seemed so promising. Then everything had turned out so wrong. But was that enough to resort to this act of desperation? Was there really nothing worth living for?

Peg had been born Millicent Lilian Entwistle a brief twenty-four years earlier in Wales. Her parents, Robert and Emily, both English, raised Peg in the posh West Kensington area of London. Her mother died when Peg was just two years old, and in 1912 her father traveled to America to work as a stage manager for impresario Charles Frohman. Two years after that, her father married again, and before long Peg had two little brothers.

But then in 1921, when she was thirteen, her stepmother died of meningitis. The following year her father was struck and killed by a car in a hit-and-run accident. Peg and her brothers were immediately adopted by her uncle Charles and aunt Jane.

Growing up, Peg was fascinated with the theater, and in 1924 she was enrolled at Henry Jewett's Repertory in Boston. She showed immediate promise under the guidance of director Blanche Yurka, and in 1925 she was given the role of Hedvig in Yurka's production of Ibsen's *The Wild Duck*.

(A girl in the audience at one of the shows said years later it was seeing Entwistle's performance that made her want to be an actress. Her name was Bette Davis.)

That same year, actor-producer Walter Hampden, who was a friend and employer of her uncle, put Peg in his

Broadway production of *Hamlet*. It was an uncredited role, a glorified extra, but her presence was strong enough to draw the attention of the members of the famed New York Theatre Guild. She was accepted into their acting program—the youngest ever—and in June 1926 she made her official debut on the Great White Way.

Over the next six years, Peg appeared in ten more Broadway shows, often getting better notices than the plays themselves. Between runs she toured with Theatre Guild productions.

Her last Broadway show, a revival of J. M. Barrie's *Alice-Sit-By-the-Fire*, closed early due to its star, Laurette Taylor, missing performances, but Entwistle was immediately brought to Los Angeles by producers Edward Belasco and Homer Curran to appear in a new play, *The Mad Hopes*, which would star Billie Burke and feature an up-and-coming actor named Humphrey Bogart.

That had been only four months ago. Now at the very top of the ladder, balancing herself against the huge "H," Peg couldn't believe how bright her prospects had been. It seemed like a lifetime ago.

The play had been a hit, with many of the reviews specifically praising her work. Three days after it closed, she was at her uncle's house on Beachwood Drive, located just below the HOLLYWOODLAND sign, when the call came: A major studio wanted her to make a screen test.

Within days the blonde, blue-eyed ingenue had shot an audition reel and was signed for a one-picture deal by RKO Studios. Entwistle was sure the role was going to pave her way to fame and fortune. The film was called *Thirteen Women*, and it would star Irene Dunne, Myrna Loy, and Ricardo Cortez (whom Paramount was promoting—unsuccessfully—as their next Rudolph Valentino).

At last! Entwistle had felt certain that she was fated to be a star. All of her dreams would come true!

It was all right that it wasn't a starring role. After all, that's how her theater career had started out. But fate wasn't on her side. Though not a disaster, the movie was a disappointment for the studio. Test audiences weren't impressed, and in an attempt to salvage the film, whole scenes were cut, all but eliminating Entwistle's already short screen time.

Then RKO decided not to offer her another contract. Entwistle was devastated.

She had come so far. For nothing. And now it had come to this. On September 16, with no offers of work for stage or screen in sight, with her career seemingly at a dead end, Peg scribbled a note for her aunt and uncle and tucked it into her purse. She slowly, painstakingly made her way up Beachwood Drive, up through the brush at the foot of Mount Lee, up to the base of the HOLLYWOODLAND sign.

Almost in a trance, she removed her coat and shoes, set them down along with her pocketbook, and then began to climb the caretaker's ladder. No one was there to see her. No one was there to stop her. One last look at the City of Broken Dreams. And she jumped.

Two days later a hiker on the trails at the top of the hillside spotted the jacket and handbag. Puzzled, she picked them up and looked around. Where had they come from? Then, in horror, her eyes caught a crumple of bright color in the darkened brush. A hundred feet down in a gully at the base of the cliff lay the lifeless body of a young woman.

The hiker hurriedly picked up the jacket, shoes, and purse, then raced down the trail to her car. She knew she had to tell somebody, but she didn't want to get involved. After circling the Hollywood police station a few times to make sure no one was watching, she crept up to the front steps and gently set down the stranger's things. She then drove a few blocks and placed a call to the central police division to report what she had discovered and where to find the girl's possessions.

When detectives opened the pocketbook, they found the note, which read:

I'm afraid I'm a coward. I am sorry for everything. If I had done this thing a long time ago it would have saved a lot of pain. P.E.

It was two more days before Peg's uncle made the connection between his niece being missing and the person the *Los Angeles Herald Examiner* had dubbed "the Hollywood Sign Girl." Entwistle had told him she was upset about having been dropped by the studio, so she was going to walk to a local drugstore to buy some books and then meet up with friends to console herself. He hadn't been worried about her absence until he recognized the initials at the end of the note.

An autopsy was performed. Peg had not been drinking, so she knew what she was doing when she flung herself off the sign. She had died of internal bleeding, technically from multiple fractures of the pelvis. Her funeral was held at the W. M. Strothers Mortuary, where she was cremated. Her ashes were buried in her father's grave back in Glendale, Ohio.

Entwistle had thrown away her life because she believed her career was over. But in a cruel twist of fate, just a day or two after Peg died, a letter arrived at her uncle's door. It was from the Beverly Hills Playhouse, offering her the lead role in a play in which, ironically, just before the final curtain her character would commit suicide.

To this day, Peg Entwistle, more famous in death than in life, is the only known person to have committed suicide by jumping off the HOLLYWOOD sign. And she's returned.

"Greg! Take a look through these binoculars. Do you see her?"

Amy handed the glasses to her boyfriend. They were on their first visit to Hollywood, and, needless to say, getting a photo of the famous sign was high on their list of things to do.

Sure, Amy had wanted to match her own hands and feet with those immortalized in concrete outside the Chinese Theatre. She walked back and forth on Hollywood Boulevard, checking out the stars' names on the sidewalk. And Greg had dutifully driven her all over Beverly Hills as she faithfully clutched her "Map to the Stars' Homes." But to Amy, it was the sign up there on the hill that meant Hollywood.

She knew all about its history. The sign wasn't put up by the City of Hollywood itself. It had been erected in 1923 to advertise a real estate development called Hollywoodland. In fact, that's what the sign had originally read.

The developers Woodruff and Shoults (whose principal investors included Harry Chandler, owner of the *Los Angeles Times*) asked Thomas Fisk Goff to design the logo and had his firm, the Crescent Sign Company, erect the thirteen massive letters. Four thousand lightbulbs were set into the wood and sheet metal letters, which, when illuminated, allowed the sign to be seen at night throughout the city.

It was never intended to be permanent. Originally, the Hollywoodland syndicate planned to take down the letters as soon as its last lot was sold. But it soon occurred to them that they owned the land on which the sign stood. Why spend the money to have it removed?

For many years the sign had an official caretaker, Albert Kothe, who kept a shack behind the first "L." But maintenance was ended in 1939. As lightbulbs had burned out, they were never replaced. Letters weren't repainted. Before long the entire sign began to deteriorate.

In 1945 the moribund development company gave the sign, along with acres of land surrounding it, to the Los Angeles City Recreation and Parks Commission. Of course, at that time the sign, still boasting all thirteen letters, was considered nothing more than an advertising billboard, and an unsightly one at that, so the city made no plans for its upkeep.

According to some accounts, sometime in the 1940s Kothe, driving along the ridge of Mount Lee, perhaps on a drunken binge, lost control of his 1928 Ford Model A, which flew off the road and crashed through the letter "H." Others say it was natural wear and tear, including a 1949 windstorm, that caused the "H" to fall over. Regardless, it was clear that many of the letters were starting to fall apart.

The Parks Commission was set to tear down the sign when the Hollywood Chamber of Commerce, anxious to preserve its historical identity separate from the City of Los Angeles (into which it had been incorporated) offered to take the white elephant off the department's hands. They promised to restore it, albeit without reinstalling electric lights, as long as they were allowed to eliminate the last four letters.

Thus, the towering symbol of Hollywood was born.

By the early 1970s, the sign was once again in terrible shape. A frantic campaign in 1973 mustered enough funds to reinforce the letters, but it soon became obvious that if the landmark was going to survive, the letters would have to be replaced.

The project began in earnest in 1978 when an auction was held allowing people to sponsor the replacement of individual letters. The first to donate was rock star Alice Cooper, who paid $27,777 for the second "O" and dedicated it to the memory of Groucho Marx, who had died just the year before.

The new letters of Australian steel were made shorter than the originals, only forty-five feet tall, and they varied from thirty-one to thirty-nine feet wide. The refurbished sign was unveiled in all its glory on November 14, 1978.

Walking along Hollywood Boulevard, Amy and Greg had been able to catch glimpses of the sign, but they had never been able to get a clear view to take a good photo. Finally, one of the costumed Spider-Man impersonators they ran into on the sidewalk—yes, there were competing Spider-Men at different spots on Hollywood Boulevard that day, one fat, one thin, neither very convincing—told Amy she should go up onto the lookout built into the new shopping center, Hollywood & Highland. The complex, attached to the Dolby Theatre, where the Academy Awards are held, has an open, second-story bridge that allows tourists to get a perfect shot of the Hollywood sign, high above any telephone wires or buildings.

As Amy stood there, staring at the sign, she was sure there had to be a way to get closer. In fact, as she looked through her binoculars, it seemed that there was a walking trail from down in the valley right up to the base of the letters. Wouldn't it be neat to touch them?

No, you're not allowed to walk up there anymore, she was told as she wistfully shared her dream with a stranger standing next to her. In fact, in 2000 the Los Angeles Police Department had installed motion detectors and closed-circuit cameras that were activated if anyone got within fifty yards of them.

But you *could* get close.

All you had to do was drive east on Franklin Avenue from Highland, then turn left, north, on Beachwood Drive. Pass between the stone pillars, and you'd be in the area that was known as Hollywoodland.

Hollywoodland! It still exists?

Continue on Beachwood, her newfound friend said, turn left on Ledgewood Drive, then right onto Deronda Drive. As you twist and turn along the narrow roads into the hills, the sign will loom ever nearer. Go all the way up until you come to a dead end in a cul-de-sac, and you're as close as you can get, legally, at least by car. Somewhere near the top, the Samaritan suggested, Amy would be able to get the view she was seeking.

The stranger even offered a way to remember the directions: BLD. Just like the BLT sandwich. Only different. Beachwood, Ledgewood, Deronda. BLD.

Minutes later, Amy and Greg were parked on an open stretch of Deronda, just a couple hundred yards from where the road stopped. Amy raised her binoculars and followed the path of the forbidden trail across the ravine from where she stood. It was almost completely overgrown, with sections hidden by bushes, as it wended its way ever higher until it reached the "D," then moved horizontally along the base of the letters. For the first time she could plainly see that as the trail neared the sign, the track was no longer a real pathway but a crevice in the sandy soil that had been eroded by rainfall over the years. Any climb up to the peak from that direction, even if it were allowed, would be treacherous indeed.

She trained the binoculars on the five-hundred-foot television tower at the top of Mount Lee, then began a slow sweep of the letters themselves, from right to left. She could clearly make out rivets holding the metal to the support frames. Now it became obvious why the sign didn't seem to be level from certain angles: The letters were forced to follow the uneven terrain. D, O, O, W, Y, L, L, O . . . wait! Something was moving!

There! On the top of the "H." Was that—a girl?

She adjusted the binoculars, focusing them onto the very top edge of the letter. Definitely it was a young woman, her face masked by windswept blonde hair. Barefoot. And she looked like she was about to jump!

"Greg! Look! At the top of the 'H.'"

She threw the glasses at her boyfriend, and he placed them up to his eyes. Nothing. There was nobody there. What was she talking about?

"What? Where? I don't see anything."

Amy snatched back the binoculars and frantically pressed them against her eyes. The girl—whoever she was—was gone. Had she fallen? Amy slowly scanned the base of the letters, then looked down into the canyon below. The dry Santa Ana wind blew against her face, and she caught a faint scent of gardenia in the air. The mysterious woman had disappeared.

Amy continued to peer at the hillside for what seemed like hours, until finally Greg pointed to the horizon. The sun had started its slow descent over the hills to the west. It was time to go.

To this day, local residents and sightseers regularly report seeing a spectral girl making her way through the scrub along the trail leading up Mount Lee. Occasionally they even glimpse the apparition standing at the top of the "H," and police have been dispatched to mount a search.

Often when the spirit is seen there's an overpowering odor of gardenias, known to be the scent of Peg Entwistle's favorite perfume, even if the flowers aren't in bloom.

Now and then the ghost appears on Beachwood Drive in the area where Entwistle used to live, silent, resigned, making her way in the direction of the hill.

Regardless of the circumstances, almost as soon as the vision appears, in the blink of an eye it vanishes.

If you see the sad spirit of Peg Entwistle, don't bother calling out or trying to stop her. It's no use. It's a path "the Hollywood Sign Girl" is doomed to repeat for eternity.

Chapter 19

The Curse of
Dona Petranilla

Griffith Park is one of the largest urban parks in the entire United States—more than four thousand acres. Cutthroats, crooks, and curses are all part of its storied past. Is it any wonder that almost a half dozen ghosts might make it their home as well?

Standing at the lookout point beside the dome of the observatory, Matt could see all the way from the mountains to the east down to the coast far to the west. The sky was so clear that it seemed the skyscrapers of downtown were at his fingertips.

It didn't often look like this, to be sure. An early December rain the night before had washed the Los Angeles skies, leaving them cloudless and powder blue the next morning, and a light breeze blew in from the ocean. The sun had actually peaked the thermometer at 72, but now, midafternoon, it had settled down to a comfortable 65. No wonder people moved to L.A.!

Matt had lived in Hollywood for thirty years. That first year and a half he was like a kid in a candy shop, visiting all those places he had always heard about but thought he'd never get a chance to see. Disneyland, Universal Studios, the Hollywood sign. Driving around Beverly Hills and Bel Air. Television tapings; studio tours. He even tried out for *Jeopardy!*

But the thing that really blew him away was that you could actually see stars. Not like the ones up here in the planetarium. Movie stars. TV stars. You could just bump into them.

Well, not every day, of course. But sometimes. Matt recalled the time he was leaving a Denny's on Sunset when a stretch limo pulled up outside, a tinted window rolled down, and he saw Little Richard give his chauffeur a roll of bills to dart inside for some coffee!

More often Matt would see celebrities at some event—on a red carpet somewhere or at the Q&A after the screening of a film. There were book signings, and there was always someone getting a star on the Walk of Fame.

And if you had any kind of nightlife, you were bound to run into them. To paraphrase Cyndi Lauper, stars "just wanna have fun" too! Matt still remembered the time he was sitting in a little theater on La Cienega when, just as the lights went down, Barbra Streisand slipped into the empty seat across the aisle from him. Barbra Streisand!

Funny how you start to take stuff like that for granted. And in an odd way, that's why Matt was there that day. In January 2002, Griffith Observatory, which had stood guard on Mount Hollywood since 1935, closed its doors. Not only was a major renovation needed simply to keep the landmark in operating condition, but a complete technical overhaul was necessary to bring it into the twenty-first century. Four years passed before it opened its doors again to the public, and then, when it did, the demand to revisit was so great that, for months, it was necessary to make reservations in advance. Parking wasn't allowed up at the summit; visitors had to take a shuttle bus from down below.

It was then that Matt realized he hadn't been to the observatory since he had gone in 1986 to peer through the giant Zeiss telescope to view Halley's Comet. *Surely the place deserved another visit by now.*

The observatory was on the grounds of Griffith Park, which covers more than four thousand acres at the eastern end of the Santa Monica Mountains. Matt remembered being amazed that it was such an enormous, open public space, covered by chaparral and miles of hiking trails, in a city of almost four million people.

Tongva or Gabrieleno Indians populated the area when Spaniards first came through in 1769. It was a mere twelve years later that Jose Vicente Feliz acted as a military escort for eleven Mexican families that came into the area and founded the pueblo of Los Angeles on September 4, 1781.

Six years later the governor of the territory appointed Feliz, in effect, the town's city manager, which included the duties of judge, enforcer of the law, and liaison with the local Native American tribes. When Feliz retired around 1800, the Spanish crown granted him 6,647 acres for his services. That land made up the original Rancho Los Feliz, which stretched from the tiny pueblo north, following the Los Angeles River basin.

By 1860 Don Jose Antonio Feliz, a descendant—okay, he was the brother-in-law of the widow of one of Vicente's sons—inherited the property. The ranchero never married, but for solace he lived with his sister, Soledad, and his niece, Dona Petranilla. The girl, around eighteen at the time, was the daughter of Feliz's brother Juan Leon and had been orphaned when she was just a toddler.

When Don Feliz contracted smallpox in 1863, he sent Petranilla away for her own safety. As it became obvious that Feliz was on his deathbed, Don Antonio Coronel, a successful merchant and rancher (not to mention a Los Angeles city council member and former mayor), and Don Innocante, a lawyer, arrived to discuss the preparation of a will.

When Feliz died shortly thereafter—surprise, surprise!— Coronel somehow got the ranch. Soledad received some of the furniture and a few other family items. Petranilla's son—she was married by that time—got some horses. But Petranilla, nothing.

The heirs disputed the will, claiming that Don Feliz never actually agreed to, much less signed, the new will. They took their case all the way to the California Supreme Court, but with powerful forces aligned against them, the family didn't have a chance. The judge sided with Coronel.

Soledad seemed to accept her fate. But everyone was unprepared for the wrath of Petranilla. According to Major Horace Bell, a nineteenth-century author and newspaper publisher who first popularized the legend, Petranilla laid a curse on Don Coronel, his lawyers, and the presiding judge, all future generations who would come to own the property, and the land itself.

Over the years, Innocante was shot and killed in a dispute, and the judge, too, died an untimely death. As for the ranch, the river flooded it in the winter; drought scorched the earth in the summer; and fires burned the brush in between. Cattle died; grapes withered on the vine.

Coronel sold the property to multimillionaire James Lick, whose massive landownings at one point included the entire island of Catalina off the Los Angeles coast. Eventually much of the Feliz ranch fell to Colonel Griffith Jenkins Griffith, who had been born in Wales and came to America in 1865.

Griffith made his fortune in California gold mine speculation. He moved to Los Angeles in 1882, bought 4,071 acres of the old Rancho Los Feliz, and opened, oddly enough, an ostrich farm. (The rest of the property stayed in the Lick family, and a portion of it, known as the Lick Tract, became part of Hollywood.)

At first Griffith had hopes to subdivide the property into smaller parcels, but the plans went awry. Nothing he tried to do with the land seemed to turn a profit.

He didn't attract a lot of sympathy. He insisted that people call him Colonel, even though he had never been in the military. (He had used his wealth and influence to get the California Guard to give him the honorary title.) In 1884 he had forced the city to buy water rights if they wanted to use the river that passed through his property. Plus, he was a raging alcoholic, arrogant, and just plain unpleasant to be around.

So on December 16, 1896, Griffith amazed officials and the public alike when he gave 3,015 acres, approximately five square miles, of his property to the city as a Christmas gift. His only condition was that it "be made a place of recreation and rest for the masses, a resort for the rank and file, for the plain people." Wary, but with the public good in mind, the city reluctantly accepted it.

Enemies say Griffith did it for a tax break or as a feeble attempt to restore his good name. Others say it was because he began to believe the curse and just wanted to rid himself of the land. And some claim he was frightened into it because he had been visited by Don Feliz's ghost.

Had he really seen a spirit? There was no way of knowing.

But even after Griffith's bequest, the curse seemed to haunt him. And it seemed personal! At first only his close acquaintances seemed to notice. But soon it became apparent to everyone: Little by little, Griffith was losing his mind.

A pious Protestant, Griffith somehow took it into his head that his wife, Christina, a Catholic, was in cahoots with the church—including the pope himself—to kill him and steal his property. He was so convinced that often when his wife wasn't looking he would surreptitiously switch their plates at dinner to avoid eating the food he'd been served, for fear of being poisoned.

Finally, in 1903, during an alcoholic bender while staying at the Arcadia Hotel in Santa Monica, the magnate shot his wife in the head. She survived, even though she had to jump through a window and plummet two stories onto the roof of a veranda to escape. She broke her leg in the fall and was permanently blinded in one eye. Found guilty of attempted murder, Griffith was sentenced to two years in San Quentin prison and served one before being released.

Griffith was always considered a mean, calculating, and formidable foe. But upon his release he was a social pariah. And so he remained until his death of liver failure on July 7, 1919. He was buried in what is today the Hollywood Forever Cemetery, but almost no one attended the service.

His will, however, left the city the rest of his Los Feliz land and $700,000 to erect an amphitheater and observatory in his namesake park. He had proposed their construction while he was alive, but the city, aware that he was trying to buy back respectability, refused the money. After his death and with some misgivings, they did take the funds, which resulted in the construction of the Greek Theatre in 1929 and, six years later, the Griffith Observatory.

As Matt walked to his car, he passed the bronze bust of James Dean, placed there because the observatory featured prominently in the actor's 1955 movie *Rebel Without a Cause*. Four of the film's stars—Natalie Wood, Sal Mineo,

Nick Adams, and of course Dean himself—had early, unnatural deaths. (Dean's ghost is said to haunt his grave in Fairmount, Indiana; and the sound of his crashing car is still heard near the stretch of highway in Cholame, California, where he died in a grisly accident.)

Rebel was one of the few movies in which Griffith Park is identified. But it has appeared in dozens of films, starting with the mother of them all, 1915's *Birth of a Nation*, directed by D. W. Griffith (who, surprisingly, was no direct relation to Griffith J. Griffith). In fact, the very tunnel Matt was driving through as he left the observatory and crossed from East Observatory Avenue to Vermont Canyon Road stood in for the entrance to Toontown in 1988's *Who Framed Roger Rabbit?*

What the heck, Matt thought. While he was there, he might as well check out the rest of the park. He drove past the Greek Theatre, down Vermont, and then turned left onto Los Feliz Boulevard. In just over a mile, he turned left again into the main entrance at Crystal Springs Drive. Before long he was at the park headquarters and visitor center, part of which was the original abode built by the Feliz family back in the 1830s.

The afternoon sun had dipped far enough that there, on the other side of the park, the road was already cast in shadows. As Matt passed the merry-go-round, he noticed that the road split just up ahead. As he slowed at the intersection, he saw an intriguing sign. Off to the left, down Griffith Park Drive, was the old zoo parking area. There was an *old* zoo? Was there anything still standing there?

He had only ever visited the current zoo, which had opened two miles down the road in 1966. But the original zoo had been built back in 1912. Matt decided to take a look.

Parking by the picnic area, he walked the paved path and up a short flight of stairs. There, to his amazement, stood the remains of walls, grottoes, and fenced animal enclosures that were built by relief workers from the WPA back in the 1930s.

The ruins were nestled into the lush mountain hillside, and hiking paths branched off in all directions. Just ahead Matt could make out a bridle trail, but the path was empty. There were stables located at the north and south entrances to the park, and by this late in the day all of the riders had no doubt made their way back.

Matt was alone; it seemed unearthly quiet, so much so that it was almost impossible to believe that just on the other side of that grove of trees behind him was the Golden State Freeway. The sky overhead had turned an indigo blue, with a halo of orange rimming the crest of the mountains. And there, directly in front of him, high overhead jutting out of the side of the hill, was an outgrowth of rock that seemed to glow in the last rays of the sun.

Matt recognized it immediately. The bare reddish sandstone stood in complete contrast to the dark foliage and brush covering the rest of the hillside leading up to it. Towering in the air at 1,056 feet, the layered, domelike mound resembled a giant, upside-down hornet's nest. No wonder early settlers gave it the fanciful name Bee Rock.

He stared at the formation, wishing he had enough time to walk the trail to its peak. There on top, a small protective barrier had been put in place to prevent hikers from getting too close to the edge and slipping over. But was someone standing up there, leaning on the fence? No backpacker should be up there this late in the day.

Matt squinted. He couldn't make out a face. The figure was silhouetted by the sun, but it was standing on the wrong side of the barricade, erect, arms outstretched, feet firm, unafraid. Suddenly a bloodcurdling howl, more unsettling than that of any coyote, pierced the silence. It was coming from the creature up on Bee Rock. Then, as the last trace of the wail echoed in the wind, the banshee vanished.

A sudden chill came over Matt. He stood in place for a long time staring up at the peak. Had there actually been someone up there? Or was what he had seen just an illusion, a figment of his imagination?

Well, he couldn't think about that now. It was getting dark, and there were signs posted throughout the park telling visitors that the roads closed at sundown. The mystery would have to wait. It had been two decades since his last visit to Griffith Park. What difference would another day or two make?

Tales that the park is haunted date back to the late nineteenth century. In 1884 during a particularly ferocious storm, ranch hands saw a ghostly figure gliding over the grounds, cursing it. Was it Dona Petranilla? She's been known to appear, dressed all in white, floating over the pathways and even inside the old Feliz adobe that's now part of the park's ranger station.

After Coronel's death in 1894, ranchers camping in the area where the golf course and zoo are located today began to see his ghost roaming the valley late at night. Or they would hear his voice echoing in a mournful cry from the hilltops. It's said that he still appears from time to time on moonlit evenings up on Bee Rock or rides the mountainous pathways.

Another mounted stallion gallops over the trails. Some think the phantom rider is Griffith J. Griffith. Others say it's really the spectre of Dona Petranilla.

And don't forget: The famous Hollywood sign, haunted by the spirit of actress Peg Entwistle, is also found within the borders of Griffith Park.

There have been comparatively few reports of apparitions in recent times. But then, the hiking trails close at sunset, the park itself at ten—long before some ghosts like to come out of hiding. Who knows how many wraiths walk the grounds at night but there's just no one there to see them?

As for the curse on Griffith Park, does it still exist? In 1933 a brushfire swept through the canyons near the old zoo, trapping firemen in one of the gullies. By the time rescuers were finally able to make it in, 29 were dead and 150 more were injured. In April 2006 Los Angeles County's Acute Communicable Disease Control Unit issued a warning that a recent park visitor had come down with bubonic plague. Then in May 2007 a fire charred more than eight hundred acres before it was contained, fortunately this time with no loss of life. Perhaps the curse of Dona Petranilla didn't end with the death of Griffith J. Griffith after all.

Chapter 20

The Phantom
of The Pines

Sometimes ghosts from the past are just having too much fun to leave. Such is the case in one of Hollywood's favorite parks. Hikers beware: You might run into the spectres that still party at the now-ruined mansion once known as The Pines in Runyon Canyon.

It was about time he went.

When Anthony took his first look at the apartment he wound up renting on Fuller, his landlord used the nearby park as a selling point.

"And it's just a couple of blocks to the canyon. If you jog or want to walk your dog—well, you don't have a dog, but if you *did* have a dog—it's a great place to let him run without a leash."

And, indeed, over the past month Anthony had seen what seemed to be an endless stream of people and pets making their way, dawn to dusk, up the grade to where Fuller dead-ended at the gates to the park.

Anthony had never been much for exercise, and just the thought of jogging was enough to give him shin splints. As for the free-range dogs: Who cleaned up after them in the park? Or was he supposed to just be careful where he stepped?

Nevertheless, curiosity finally had gotten the better of him, and realizing he had nothing better to do that afternoon, he decided that now was as good a time as any to figure out what the big deal was about.

The gorge was near the eastern end of the Santa Monica Mountains, which stretch for forty miles all the way from Hollywood out to the Pacific, forming the barrier between the Los Angles Basin and the San Fernando Valley. In pre-European times, Tongva Native Americans most probably occupied the area. It became known as "No Man's Canyons" to the early settlers, and in 1867 the federal government gave the 160 acres now known as Runyon Canyon to a color-ful character named "Greek George" Caralambo in appreciation for his help with the army's short-lived Camel Corps. (Caralambo's company transported supplies from Saint Louis to Los Angeles—believe it or not—by camels.)

From 1874 to 1919, Alfredo Solano, a successful civil engineer and community leader, owned the property. Then it passed into the hands of Carman Runyon, a retired busi-nessman from back east, who bought the property to ride and hunt. He renamed the cleft in the Hollywood Hills after himself.

Already huffing and puffing, Anthony approached the large gates at the top of Fuller. As he made his way across Franklin Avenue, the road started to climb at a steep angle. By the time he had passed Hillside, the last cross street before the main gate, he felt as if he were on a StairMaster. Man, he was out of shape!

The gates, locked shut, were held in place by stone pil-lars, but there to his left was a narrow pedestrian entrance-way. He barely noticed the vendor standing there selling bananas and energy bars; but at the last moment he decided that perhaps he should buy a bottle of water. Who knew how much steeper the road would become?

Because it *was* a road. A driveway. In 1929, while film-ing the movie *Song O' My Heart*, Irish tenor John McCormack visited Runyon's "cabin" and was captivated by the rustic setting. He bought the place the following year and replaced the lodge with a mansion, which he named San Patrizio (after Ireland's patron saint, Patrick).

The canyon was already filled with a mix of pine and deciduous trees (including sumac and oak), sagebrush, toyon, yarrow, and prickly pear cactus, but to set them off McCormack added palms to line the driveway up the house and built terraced gardens into the western hillside.

The singer played host to a series of stars, including John Barrymore, Basil Rathbone, and Will Rogers, and a few, such as Charles Boyer and Janet Gaynor, wound up leasing the property during McCormack's long concert tours. The tenor made his last series of personal appearances in the United States in 1937 and then moved back to England.

George Huntington Hartford II, who was a philanthropist and heir to the A&P grocery chain, bought the grounds in 1942. He moved into the house and gave it a new name: The Pines. He expanded the place to include guesthouses, a pool, and tennis court. But after he was unable to get permits to develop the canyon into a country club (even though it was to be designed by Frank Lloyd Wright), Hartford lost interest in the property and offered to give it to the city. Incredibly, he was turned down.

In 1964 Hartford sold the estate to Jules Berman, who hoped to build luxury homes in the canyon. He tore down the mansion and the outlying buildings, and in 1972 a fire swept through the gorge and consumed anything that remained standing, down to the foundations. Finally, in 1984 the City of Los Angeles and the Santa Monica Mountains Conservancy bought Runyon Canyon Park for use by the public.

That was just over thirty years ago, but to Anthony it might just as well have been a century. To the casual observer, there was no evidence that anything other than the wide, open spaces and hiking trails had ever existed on the site.

Just on the other side of the first set of gates, Anthony's eyes fell on a large green field, encircled by a low wire fence covered with vines. Eighty-five years earlier it had been landscaped as the broad front lawn of San Patrizio. Now in the mornings the space was filled with folks practicing yoga, both devotees and new enthusiasts alike. Passing by the expanse in the late afternoon, Anthony spied only a half dozen people as they stretched and flexed.

Suddenly he was jolted as a small terrier jumped up against his right leg. Where had that come from?

Anthony looked around and suddenly realized there were dogs everywhere. Lots and lots and *lots* of dogs. And none of them seemed to be on leashes, even though they were still required in the lower section of the park. Anthony frowned. He guessed the owners must think that the restriction posted on the front gate was merely a suggestion rather than a law.

Out of nowhere, a young man in his mid-twenties, suntanned, open-shirted, wearing DKNY shades and too much bling to be a nobody, suddenly appeared. He quickly began to apologize, beaming a forgive-him-for-anything smile. Although Anthony couldn't immediately place the stranger, he knew he should recognize that oddly familiar face. Was he one of those endless number of reality TV stars Anthony should know but never did?

"Sorry, dude. She doesn't usually jump up like that. Buffy, stop that! Come over here!"

And with that, the man and his dog trotted off along the length of the yoga meadow. Where were they headed? If the guy really was a celebrity out for an anonymous run, maybe he was heading toward the southwestern, less-traveled entrance off Vista. From there he could dart out into a tinted-window SUV without being stopped for an autograph.

No, he seemed to be turning toward the trail that rose up the western lip of the canyon. Well, Anthony mused, a pretty-boy actor has to keep his body in shape. That trail led all the way up to Mulholland Drive, the serpentine, narrow road following the crest line of the mountains at the top of the canyon. The walk up to Mulholland would certainly give the actor's legs a workout.

Anthony had been told he would have a good chance of seeing a celebrity walking a pooch through this particular park because they felt safe from the paparazzi on the steep jogging paths.

As the stranger disappeared from sight, Anthony felt a mixture of shame, guilt, and pride at having to admit he didn't know the names or recognize half the people who appeared on TV or in movies these days. They all seemed to be interchangeable, not like the stars of the Golden Age of Hollywood. To be a true celebrity, shouldn't the person have to have done something worth celebrating? Or was it enough these days just to be famous for being famous?

He looked up to the top of the canyon. Far overhead, as high as one could climb on the western slope, was the lookout known as Inspiration Point. To the right, not quite as far up but equally daunting to get to, was the eastern summit known as Clouds Rest. On a clear day, from up there it was possible to see all the way across the cityscape of

Hollywood and downtown Los Angeles to the ocean. As much as Anthony liked the thought of standing up there to look out over the panorama, he knew his body's limitations. There was no way, in his condition, that he could make it to the top and back without giving himself a stroke or a heart attack. Oh, well. Another time, another life.

But he could make it up to the head of the canyon, along what eons ago would have been the riverbed flowing through the gorge. He took a swig from his water bottle and slowly started out, consciously pacing himself as he went.

Strange. Just past the exercise yard to his left were five concrete steps, a small staircase leading to nowhere in the middle of the brush. Behind them was a long, low, concrete platform on top of which was, yes, an unaccompanied dog lolling in the sun. The canine perked up at Anthony's presence, raised his head, then realized the interloper wasn't his master. The dog scooted off under the trees, heading toward the short dirt trail beyond. No doubt his owner was hiking back there somewhere.

These must be the ruins of the old McCormack and Hartford place, thought Anthony. Sure enough, as he clambered over the old foundations, he spied the remains of the terraced walls along the hill. Back in the 1930s, before all the nondescript apartment buildings had been built in the area, the place would have been a magnificent sight.

As he approached a second, smaller gate—the one beyond which dogs really *were* allowed to run free— Anthony noted the shell of another small building. All that was left were the four low walls. No telling what it might have been.

But behind it, partially obscured by a tall tree, stood a chimney up against the western ridge. As Anthony made his way through the tall weeds and bramble, he noticed that the area beneath the shade of the tree had been trampled down, and litter lay all around the trunk. Was this a hangout for kids, or maybe the homeless, after curfew supposedly closed the park? Despite the sunrise-to-sunset rule, there was no way to prevent people from coming into the park at night and camping out there—unless they happened to be caught by one of the infrequent park patrols.

Standing at the base of the chimney, Anthony inspected the garish spray-painted graffiti that decorated its bricks. All around it were the foundations of the original structure that had no doubt been built for guests or perhaps a groundskeeper.

Anthony carefully made his way back to the main drag that wended its way up through the center of the canyon. As he walked farther along the trail, which had turned to dirt, he noticed that the high walls of the gorge were closing in tighter. The sun was already going down, and the western wall of the canyon and the lower half of the eastern ridge were already covered in shadow. Still, he had about an hour until, technically, he was supposed to be out of the park, so Anthony trudged on.

At the end of the canyon there was a small clearing behind a circle of trees, backed by an almost vertical cliff. A trail branched to the left; after an almost perpendicular assault it would join the paved path high on the west ridge. Instead, Anthony chose the well-trampled path that, after a hairpin turn, rose at about a forty-five degree angle. As he entered the park, he had seen a park bench up there on a level promontory. Even though Anthony knew there was no way he would be continuing up to the top of the mountain, he wanted to make it as far as the bench.

The walk was harder than it looked. As he made his way up, a steady stream of hikers was already starting down before closing time. Halfway to the vista point, Anthony paused by the old fenced-in tennis court: Considering its age and when it was last used, it was in much better shape than he would have suspected.

He finally reached the short backless bench and collapsed on it. Man, he had to diet! But the view was stunning. A light drizzle the day before had cleared most of the smog out of the air, and the skyscrapers in downtown Los Angeles, seven miles from Hollywood, seemed to be only blocks away. (There were still days when it was so smoggy—hazy, the officials like to say—that the buildings couldn't even be seen from there.) The sky was already that shade of layered blue, red, and orange that was unique to Southern California as the sun dipped down toward the Pacific. Anthony couldn't see past the tall buildings of Century City to the west, but he knew that if he went just a little higher, certainly if he were up at Clouds Rest, that the sea would be clearly visible. Maybe he *could* make it a bit farther . . .

He turned and looked up to the top of the ridge. Who was he trying to kid? Not only did the trail look ominously treacherous, but there was even a sign warning hikers that "only the physically fit"—those were the words it used—should attempt the climb. It was just as well: It was already getting dark. It was time to go.

As he stood, stiffly, Anthony's eyes took in one last sweep across the horizon. His legs were already telling him he wouldn't be coming back anytime soon.

As he started down the hill, he was surprised to discover that he seemed to be alone. Ever since he had entered the park, hikers and dogs—an *endless* supply of dogs—passed by him. Now the trail was empty. Well, it *was* past five. But still . . .

Making his way through the upper gate, Anthony felt a light, cold breeze blow against his face. Unconsciously, he looked to the right as he caught a flash of movement among the brush. It was getting very dark now; by rights, he, like everyone else, should be out of the park. But he focused on the ruins of the old staircase he had investigated on his way in.

A tall, dapper man, dressed in smart, midcentury attire, was sitting on the steps. He seemed to stare straight at Anthony, but then, without a word, he stood, turned, walked up the short set of stairs—and disappeared! He didn't jump off the back of the platform onto the ground, as Anthony had done earlier. He didn't hide behind a bush. He simply vanished.

Then, through the silence of the early evening, Anthony caught the soft strains of music. And voices. It was the sound of a party! And the noise was coming from the empty foundations just a few hundred feet away.

Anthony's feet remained glued to the spot. The air seemed to shimmer as multicolored orbs began to twinkle, some twenty, thirty feet high above the deserted concrete platform. It was as if—impossible!—as if the lights were shining down on him from the second-story windows of an invisible building. Then, slowly, the ghostly walls of an old mansion began to form in the wavering aether.

"Hey! Mister! Are you okay?"

The shout assaulted Anthony's senses. He shook his head and blinked. When he opened his eyes, just as suddenly as it had appeared, the vision, the hallucination, the whatever he had experienced, was gone.

Anthony turned toward the outer gate and saw the man he had met earlier in the day making his way back along the path beside the yoga court. He must have finished the hiking loop and come up from behind. Buffy ran out from under the man's legs and scampered, panting, up to Anthony, who bent down and tousled her hair.

"Boy, am I glad to see you, girl!"

And this time Anthony meant it. Dogs. People. Anything that was living and breathing!

"Just wanted to make sure you were okay," the man called over his shoulder as he gestured for Buffy and passed through the gap next to the locked gate. "You looked like you'd just seen a ghost."

Though Anthony didn't realize it at the time, maybe—no, probably—he had.

In 1907, years before the movie industry took root in Southern California, wealthy Omaha, Nebraska, banker Gurdon Wattles purchased property on North Curson Avenue in the Hollywood (now West Hollywood) district of Los Angeles to build a winter home. Eventually the estate, which he called Jualita, encompassed forty-nine acres. Besides the two-story, Mission Revival mansion—sources differ as to the number of bedrooms and baths—the grounds also held a Japanese garden, an Italian Rose garden, a Spanish garden, a palm court, and orchards. Wattles would open the gardens to the public one or two days a week, making it one of Hollywood's first tourist attractions.

Wattles died in 1932, but his wife and son remained on the property, despite losing much of the family fortune during the Depression. Gurdon Wallace Wattles Jr. sold the estate to the City of Los Angeles in 1965, and it was put under the Department of Recreation and Parks. While some of the gardens were maintained, others were transformed into an open park. Supervision was lax due to budget restraints, and the grounds, especially the Japanese area, were vandalized in the 1980s and 1990s. Much of the restoration has been through the volunteer work of the Hollywood Heritage organization. Today the former estate is separated into three main areas: the Wattles Mansion, Wattles Gardens, and Wattles Park. The property borders the western edge of Runyon Canyon Park.

A ghostly "Woman in White" has been seen strolling through the Wattles grounds at night. An apparition described as a little old lady—who may or may not be the same woman seen outside in the gardens—has been spotted by visitors inside the mansion, especially near an upstairs bathroom. (Some think it's Wattles's first wife, who died shortly after the house was built. Wattles later remarried a younger woman.) People living nearby have heard the disembodied screams of an unknown woman. They've also been startled by the sound of an unseen horse galloping through the park and gardens.

Chapter 21

From Here
to Eternity

The Hollywood Roosevelt played host to the first Oscar ceremonies and has been a home away from home for a galaxy of stars. The hotel has become a haunted habitat by some of its most famous guests, including Montgomery Clift and Marilyn Monroe.

Javier didn't know what to expect. He'd worked reception at other hotels before, and his supervisor had stood by during the first day or two he was here, but this was the first time he would be alone behind the desk.

During the day, there would be several people on duty, but he'd been moved to the night shift. There wasn't a lot of traffic this time of the morning. The Dakota restaurant had stopped serving at eleven, the Tropicana bar out by the pool had closed up at two, and there was no performance that night in Teddy's Lounge, once the vaunted Cinegrill show-room off the main lobby. Normally there were a few hangers-on in the elegant two-story lobby, late-night couples nestled into the black leather divans, or people making small talk at the Library Bar; but tonight even they were empty.

Suddenly a loud ringing snapped Javier to attention. It had been so quiet all night that he hadn't expected a phone call to break his reverie.

"Hello, front desk. May I help you?"

"Yes," came the annoyed voice from 932. "Could you send security, or the concierge, anyone, up here to the ninth floor to stop the racket? Someone's out in the hall or in one of the rooms next to me playing a freakin' trumpet! It's been keeping me up all night."

Javier's service training raced through his head. What was that acronym he was supposed to remember? Right: LAST. Listen. Apologize. Satisfy. Thank.

Well, he had listened to the problem. "Yes, I'm sorry, sir. I'll send someone up immediately. Tha—" But before he had a chance to offer his appreciation for the customer's "choosing the Roosevelt," the irritated guest had slammed down the receiver.

The hotel guard made a perfunctory visit to the ninth floor, but he knew he wouldn't find anything. He'd worked there too long and been called up to investigate too often. There wouldn't be any disturbance once he got to the hallway. It would be deathly quiet. The kid behind the front desk was new, so he hadn't heard.

The place was haunted.

The Hotel Roosevelt was intended from its very beginning to draw the movers and shakers of Hollywood. Planned and financed by a syndicate that included Hollywood luminaries Douglas Fairbanks, Mary Pickford, and Louis B. Mayer, and named after President Theodore Roosevelt, the new landmark opened its doors on May 15, 1927.

At the time, the Spanish-style, twelve-story, 302-room edifice cost an astronomical $2.5 million to complete— almost $27 million in today's dollars. Among those who attended its grand opening were Clara Bow, Charlie Chaplin, Greta Garbo, Harold Lloyd, Gloria Swanson, and Will Rogers.

Located less than a block west and just across the street from Grauman's Chinese Theatre, the hotel was the perfect place to hold the very first Academy Awards. Incredible as it may seem today, that ceremony, which was held in the hotel's ballroom, the Blossom Room, on May 16, 1929, lasted all of twelve minutes. The awards, given for films that were released between August 1927 and July 1928, were presented by Fairbanks (who was president of the Academy of Motion Picture Arts and Sciences at the time) and director William C. de Mille who acted as co-masters of ceremonies.

It was no mass media event, just a simple banquet for fewer than 250 people. And there wasn't a lot of suspense: Although the thirteen categories had multiple nominees, the Academy had announced all of the winners the previous February. In fact, the very first person to win an Oscar wasn't in the Blossom Room that night. Emil Jannings, who was named Best Actor for his performances in *The Last Command* and *The Way of All Flesh,* had to return to his home in Germany, so he was given his award early.

Over the years a veritable Who's Who of Hollywood has passed through the Roosevelt's doors, and many of Tinseltown's brightest stars have temporarily resided there at one time or another. Among them was Montgomery Clift, who stayed in Room 928 for three months while he was shooting his role as Private Robert E. Lee Prewitt in the 1953 movie *From Here to Eternity.*

In the film he plays a sensitive—but then, didn't he always?—young soldier who is pressured by his captain to join the company's boxing club. When he refuses, his superior makes his life a living hell. He later snaps, killing a sergeant to avenge a friend, and he ends up being shot by a sentry during the attack on Pearl Harbor.

Edward Montgomery Clift had been born in Omaha, Nebraska, in October 1920. His early acting career was on Broadway before making his first movie, *Red River*, in 1948. Roles in *The Search* and *A Place in the Sun* (both of which garnered him Academy Award nominations for Best Actor) soon followed.

While at the Actors Studio in New York, Clift had studied the Stanislavski Method (commonly referred to as simply "the Method"), which trains the actor to draw on his or her own life and experiences to re-create emotions during performances. As a result, Clift felt it imperative that he actually learn how to play a bugle for his role as Prewitt so that his handling of the instrument would seem natural.

While living at the Roosevelt Hotel, he could often be heard practicing the horn behind the closed door of Room 928. And from time to time, other guests would catch him pacing the corridor on the ninth floor outside his room, script in hand, as he rehearsed his lines. His hard work earned him yet a fourth Oscar nomination for Best Actor.

In 1956, while shooting *Raintree County*, Clift accidentally crashed his car into a telephone pole, suffering internal injuries. Although he also badly damaged his face, it was ultimately decided not to perform plastic surgery. Pain from the collision endured, and it led to an addiction to pills and alcohol that lasted the rest of his life.

Clift's career, though plagued with substance abuse, lasted ten more years, including such notable films as *The Young Lions*, *Suddenly Last Summer*, *Wild River*, and *The Misfits*. He received another Oscar nomination, this time for Supporting Actor, for his short though outstanding role in 1961's *Judgment at Nuremberg*.

Clift died of a heart attack in his town house on East Sixty-First Street in New York City sometime before dawn on July 23, 1966. He was forty-five.

The actor received a star on the Hollywood Walk of Fame, and apparently he still takes up residence just nine blocks away in and around his old room at the Hollywood Roosevelt Hotel.

Over the years, dozens of guests on the ninth floor have insistently phoned the front desk, demanding that someone come up and stop whoever was playing a trumpet in the hallway. Usually the sound could be traced directly to Suite 928—even when the room wasn't occupied. The calls to the receptionist have been frequent enough that longtime staff know the disturbance is being caused by the ghost of Montgomery Clift.

At least one guest who's stayed in Room 928 has reported being touched by the invisible hands of an unseen entity. Others have seen shadowy forms pacing the hallway outside the room or felt a cold breeze pass by as they walked down the corridor.

Montgomery Clift is far from the only spectre that lingers on at the Hollywood Roosevelt. Among the paranormal presences is the apparition of a once-unknown starlet who lived there from time to time for almost two years while waiting for her big break: Clift's later *Misfits* costar Marilyn Monroe.

Accounts vary as to which room she actually stayed in. Some say it was Room 229; others claim it was Suite 1200 or even poolside in Cabana 246. Perhaps it was all of them at one time or another. Or none of them. That's how legends go. But everyone agrees that one of her first modeling jobs was shot on the diving board (since replaced) at the pool behind the hotel's main tower.

It seems that ever since her tragic death in 1962, her translucent form has been seen lounging next to the pool, usually around dusk. Her most famous appearances, however, take place in her haunted mirror!

That's right: *in* a mirror.

According to the version of the tale that's told most often, around 1985 a maid was cleaning the room (whichever one it may have been) that the actress always asked for when she stayed at the hotel. While polishing the room's full-length mirror, the housekeeper noticed that someone—a beautiful blonde woman—was standing behind her, fixing her makeup. She turned and, to her surprise, found no one there. She faced the mirror again, and the image of the ethereal stranger (whom she now recognized to be Monroe) was back! Again, the attendant spun around to an empty room.

Clearly alarmed, she soon shared her experience with the rest of the cleaning staff, and before long it was common knowledge among the hotel's employees: The mirror was haunted!

Another version of the account says that the mirror was not in Monroe's favorite room but in a manager's office—or that the manager moved it there once the rumors started. Regardless, the story soon leaked out to the public at large, and curiosity seekers began visiting the hotel hoping to see the mirror.

For several years the hotel hung the Marilyn Monroe mirror by the elevators on the lower level near the rear entrance. Tongue firmly in cheek, hotel management placed two large posters of Monroe on adjacent walls so that, if you stood just right, you could see a reflection of the artwork in the mirror's surface. The mirror was relocated to the mezzanine above the lobby for a few years, but it was later placed in storage. Its current whereabouts are uncertain.

(Marilyn's ghost has appeared in at least four other locations. She's been spotted on the sidewalk outside the Brentwood house where she died from an apparent overdose of sleeping pills. Her spirit also occasionally hovers near her crypt in Westwood Memorial Cemetery. And in the past, folks ran across her in the ladies' restroom by the downstairs bar in the Knickerbocker Hotel.) Farther afield, she materialized at the Cal Neva Resort & Casino, located on the shore of Lake Tahoe. (See Appendix D.)

But back to the Hotel Roosevelt. People are still trying to figure out what causes a cold spot in the Blossom Room.

Intense and unexplainable temperature changes have long been associated with paranormal activity, and one phenomenon that draws particular attention to ghost investigators is what's known as a "cold spot," a small area several degrees cooler than its surroundings. Many believe they are either the spirits themselves or portals between the Spirit World and our own.

The Roosevelt's cold spot is a thirty-inch-diameter column of chilly air in the ballroom. Even when the doors and windows are closed and there is no air-conditioning or other ventilation turned on, the paranormal pillar is a very noticeable ten degrees cooler than anywhere else in the room.

Many staff members, including a former catering manager, have seen an unearthly man in black haunting the Blossom Room, usually standing near the wall farthest from the doors. More often the spirit's uneasy presence is merely felt by those who pass through the empty room alone.

These are only a few of the bizarre occurrences at the Roosevelt that have been reported over the years. Guests have also heard disembodied voices and found themselves dead-bolted out of their own rooms. Hotel operators receive calls from locked rooms that they know to be vacant, and phone handsets are lifted from their receivers in empty rooms. At least one guest has seen a spectral woman brushing her hair at the foot of her bed. Others have seen the ghastly phantom of a man whose throat had been slit from ear to ear.

The apparition of an unidentified man in a white suit has shown up in several of the corridors and along the mezzanine railing. The spirit of Broadway (and occasional film) actress Ethel Merman has been sighted relaxing by the pool, and watchmen have spied an unknown spectre taking an early-morning plunge. Ghosts have also been seen on security monitors, though none has ever been recorded on tape.

Visitors have heard invisible children playing in the hallway outside their rooms, and one in particular, a phantom girl of about five who's been dubbed Caroline, has been spied cavorting around the fountain in the lobby in the wee hours of the morning. She's usually wearing ponytails and dressed in blue jeans and a pink coat.

Residents have also said that they've felt strong energy fields in the penthouse suite on the twelfth floor that was once occupied by Clark Gable and Carole Lombard. Some claim they've even seen the actress's ghost.

The hotel, like Hollywood itself, lost much of its glitz and glamour in the 1960s and '70s. In an attempt to make it look contemporary, much of the unique decor was removed, covered, or painted over. But in the mid-1980s, it had a major, $35 million overhaul by the Radisson chain, restoring the grand lady to her former glory. Since its renovation, several cabarets and dance clubs have come and gone in the hotel as Hollywood has begun heating up again after dark. Today the Hollywood Roosevelt is owned by Thompson

Hotels, which operates almost a dozen luxury properties in the United States and Canada.

Although a new generation of stars, clubbers, and celebrities has flocked to the Roosevelt, apparently some of its early residents are still staying on. If there had been only one or two ghost sightings over the years, it might be easy to discount them as simply products of the imagination. But can hundreds of such encounters be ignored?

When you vacation in Hollywood, why not book yourself into the city's most haunted hotel? If you dare, book yourself onto the ninth floor. But be careful: That stranger staying next door may be there on holiday from the Spirit World.

Chapter 22
Knickerbocker Holiday

On the tenth anniversary of Harry Houdini's death, his widow, Bess, conducted a séance on the roof of the Knickerbocker Hotel in an attempt to contact the late showman. Several famous Hollywood personalities have died in the hotel. And the lobby bar also has a supernatural claim to fame: It was visited by the ghosts of Rudolph Valentino and Marilyn Monroe.

If ever a place deserved to be haunted, it's the Knickerbocker Hotel. When it was constructed as a luxury apartment complex on Ivar Avenue in 1925, the eleven-story, three-hundred-room building was the tallest structure in Hollywood. The Spanish Colonial Revival edifice was soon converted into a hotel, however, and over the years many of Tinseltown's greats and near greats have called it their temporary home.

Rick Nelson went there to introduce himself to the Jordanaires, Elvis Presley's backup group, and they later often recorded together. It's said that William Faulkner began his eighteen-year affair there with Meta Carpenter, a Twentieth Century Fox script girl. Milton Berle, Larry Fine (of the Three Stooges), Laurel and Hardy, Jerry Lee Lewis, Presley himself, Frank Sinatra, Barbara Stanwyck, Lana Turner, and Mae West are just a few of the other stars who once lodged there, happily.

For four of its famous patrons, however, the Knickerbocker was not quite so welcoming.

One of the hotel's more colorful guests was 1930s actress Frances Farmer. In January 1943 she was staying at the Knickerbocker while filming *No Escape* when a studio hairdresser filed assault charges against her. That, coupled with her skipping out on bail from a DUI charge, led police to arrest her at the hotel. She put up quite a struggle and had to be dragged from her room half-naked through the hotel lobby. Stays in a series of sanitariums followed, as did an attempt at a comeback; but by 1964 Farmer's alcoholism made her unemployable. She died from esophageal cancer in 1970.

Irene Gibbons, who went simply by Irene, was one of MGM's top costume designers when her marriage fell apart in 1962. Disconsolate, on November 15, 1962, she moved into a room on the fourteenth floor at the Knickerbocker under a fake name. She attempted suicide by slashing her wrists, but when that didn't work, she threw herself from the bathroom window.

She died, of course, but her body never hit the ground below. Instead, she crashed onto the wide canopy over the entrance, and her corpse wasn't found until later that night. She knew her death would cause questions, so in her suicide note she apologized to those she left behind: "I'm sorry. This is the best way. Get someone very good to design and be happy. I love you all. Irene."

William Frawley, born in Burlington, Iowa, in 1887, had his start in show business on the vaudeville stage, first with his brother Paul, then later with his wife on the Keith and Orpheum circuits. He performed in ten plays on the Great White Way before moving to Hollywood for Paramount in 1932.

With a perfect character-actor face and demeanor, Frawley had appeared in more than a hundred movies before

Lucille Ball tapped him in 1951 to play her neighbor and landlord Fred Mertz in television's *I Love Lucy*.

After *Lucy* ended in 1960, Frawley became part of the cast of another TV classic, *My Three Sons*. He played the housekeeper Michael Francis "Bub" O'Casey for five years before poor health forced him into retirement. He spent his last years living alone in a bachelor apartment at the Knickerbocker. He was walking home after catching a movie on Hollywood Boulevard on March 3, 1966, when he suffered a heart attack on the sidewalk (some say the stairs) in front of the hotel. He was brought into the lobby, but attempts to revive him were unsuccessful. He was taken to Hollywood Receiving Hospital, where he was pronounced dead.

At one time there was no bigger name in Hollywood than D. W. Griffith. A rundown of the director's credits would be a history of early Tinseltown itself. Born in 1875 in LaGrange, Kentucky, he traveled to New York at the age of eighteen to pursue a career in the theater. But life had other plans. Instead, he agreed to first act, then direct in that new medium, motion pictures, for the Edison Company. He next moved to the American Mutoscope and Biograph Company (or simply Biograph), for which he would eventually direct over 450 short subjects. It was while in Los Angeles filming a Western for Biograph that he decided to take his company just a few miles north to shoot the first movie ever in a small, tranquil community he was hearing about: Hollywood!

One of the true pioneers of the industry, Griffith has been called "the Man Who Invented Hollywood" and "the Shakespeare of the Screen." He's credited with inventing or perfecting film techniques that are taken for granted in moviemaking today, including the flashback, cross-cutting, the iris shot (the image appearing in just one small circular area on the screen), and masking (covering part of the camera lens while filming to create a special shape so the audience appears to be seeing the action through, say, binoculars or a periscope).

His film career, though, is remembered mostly for two feature-length masterpieces, *The Birth of a Nation* (1915) and *Intolerance: Love's Struggles Through the Ages* (1916), although the former was considered racist by many even in his own day. (Ironically, his investors, which included Hollywood luminaries Louis B. Mayer and Jesse L. Lasky, never seemed to be tainted by its critical condemnation the way Griffith was.)

In 1915 Griffith partnered with Thomas Ince (whose ghost is said to haunt Culver Studios) and Mack Sennett to form Triangle Pictures. Five years later he founded United Artists along with Charlie Chaplin, Douglas Fairbanks, and Mary Pickford.

Though Griffith's career did span the transition into sound, his style soon seemed dated and out of fashion. His last film was 1931's *The Struggle*, and he lived out his final years on the annuity from investments he had made during his glory years.

On July 23, 1948, while standing under the grand crystal chandelier in the Renaissance Revival/Beaux-Arts lobby of the Knickerbocker, Griffith, by then almost completely forgotten in Hollywood, suffered a cerebral hemorrhage and collapsed. He was pronounced dead on the way to the hospital.

Then there's the Knickerbocker's Houdini connection. After Harry Houdini died of peritonitis in Detroit on Halloween 1926, his widow, Bess, moved to Los Angeles, often taking up residence in the guesthouse of the Walker estate on

Laurel Canyon Boulevard. For ten years, from 1927 to 1936, Bess took part in occasional séances in an attempt to contact Houdini's spirit. She announced that the 1936 séance on the anniversary of the escape artist's death would be her last, and it would be conducted on the roof of the Knickerbocker Hotel. He never cam through—at least not using the code they had planned in advance. On that last night in 1936, just as Bess called an end to the final séance, lightning sparked through the sky and an intense thunderstorm poured rain down on all the participants. Was it Harry, reluctant to end the ritual? Or was it his way of saying good-bye?

And now we get to the Knickerbocker's ghosts.

Marilyn Monroe used to sneak through a rear kitchen entrance to avoid the press when she went to the hotel lounge to meet her boyfriend, the retired Yankee slugger Joe DiMaggio. According to most sources, they honeymooned at the Knickerbocker after their marriage in 1954. (They later settled down in Beverly Hills, living next door to the last home of Jean Harlow.) Despite DiMaggio and Marilyn's divorce less than a year later, they remained friends. He's said to have asked her to remarry him just days before her death; and it was he who claimed her body and arranged for the funeral. He had six red roses delivered to her grave three times a week for the next twenty years.

Monroe must have a real fondness for the Knickerbocker, because her spirit supposedly used to return to the bar off the lobby—more specifically, to its ladies' restroom. Several guests to the powder room spotted a beautiful blonde, with skin so clear it seemed translucent, standing by the mirror fixing her makeup. By the time they realized that they were seeing the ghost of Marilyn Monroe, the spectre had vanished.

It's hard today to catch her at the Knickerbocker, because the bar off the lobby is now closed. When the hotel first opened, the Noble Experiment (otherwise known as Prohibition) was in full force, but a little thing like that didn't prevent the speakeasy at the Knickerbocker from serving its elite clientele. As a result, its swanky Art Deco bar, paneled in dark wood and appointed with plush, comfortable divans, made it one of the most popular celebrity nightspots in town.

One of its most frequent guests during the last year of his life was Rudolph Valentino, who loved to stop in to dance the tango. On one occasion, he supposedly rode one of his own horses all the way from his home in the Hollywood Hills to the Knickerbocker cantina.

Known as the "Latin Lover," Valentino was born in Castellaneta, Italy, in 1895. After coming to New York City somewhere around 1912, he became a taxi dancer at Maxim's—meaning he was paid by patrons to dance with them at the club—to make ends meet. The young man soon became involved in a scandal when an heiress he befriended divorced and later shot her husband. To avoid the tabloids, Valentino joined a theatrical company that eventually took him to the Left Coast.

He soon found himself employed as an extra, then in bit roles in the movies. It was in one of these minor parts, in 1919's *The Eyes of Youth*, that screenwriter June Mathis first saw him. She decided on the spot that this swarthy, mysterious—and very sexy—unknown would be perfect for the lead role in her upcoming film at Metro Pictures Corporation, 1921's *The Four Horsemen of the Apocalypse*.

Despite the film's popularity, Metro seemed unwilling or uninterested in trying to build Valentino's career, so the actor moved to Famous Players–Lasky, where Jesse Lasky cast him in the title role of the Paramount movie that would define Valentino forever: *The Sheik*.

By August 15, 1926, when Valentino collapsed in the Hotel Ambassador in New York City, he was one of Hollywood's top movie attractions. Women everywhere fantasized about being his lover; men, though frequently bad-mouthing his silky manner as being unmasculine, copied his appearance. It seemed the whole world wanted to either be with or simply be Valentino.

The superstar was operated on for a perforated ulcer, but peritonitis set in, and the infection quickly spread. He died just eight days after the surgery.

The news seemed unfathomable. He was only thirty-one and at the height of his fame and seeming virility. Women went into mourning; it's said that some even committed suicide. At the funeral home in New York, actress Pola Negri, whom Valentino was dating at the time, dramatically fell to pieces, sobbing uncontrollably in front of his coffin. The actor's body was brought west and, after a second funeral, was interred in what was supposed to be a "loaner" crypt at Hollywood Forever Cemetery owned by Mathis, who had remained his good friend. He's still there.

Valentino's mortal remains may lie in place, but his spirit is one of the most active in Hollywood. His apparition has never appeared in the mausoleum where he's buried, although some have claimed to feel his presence there. More often, his wraith has been seen floating in the costume department at Paramount Pictures (whose lot is next to the cemetery). Usually he's been reported in three of his favorite residences.

Two of them were temporary getaways. While shooting *The Sheik*, Valentino stayed at a private beach house
in Oxnard, a coastal community fifty miles northwest of
Hollywood. Supposedly his phantom, manifesting itself as
a dark, shadowy figure, appears on the cottage's surfside
porch, but the dim form never seems to interact with any
inhabitants.

Santa Maria Inn, eighty miles farther up the coast, was
another hideaway for the legendary actor. His preferred
room, Suite 201, is still the one he likes most. Visitors who
have stayed there overnight have felt his unseen presence
as well as hearing unusual noises in the dark. Sometimes his
weight can be felt sitting on the bed next to the guest who's
lying there. Depending upon your disposition, such a visit
from the notorious screen lover could be quite disquieting—
or not.

The third house haunted by Valentino is his hillside home
in Beverly Hills, Falcon Lair, built in 1923 and named after
his 1924 film *The Hooded Falcon,* which was never completed.
Located on Bella Drive, the sixteen-room Mediterranean-
style mansion was considered opulent for its day, costing
$175,000. By then, Valentino had separated from his third
wife, Natacha Rambova, so he moved into Falcon Lair in 1925
alone. He was dead within a year.

The house was sold to pay off Valentino's debts, but the
subsequent owner never moved in. In fact, it stood empty for
eight years. Since then, the mansion has had several occupants. Actor Harry Carey was perhaps the first to encounter
Valentino's ghost there. The spectre appeared in Valentino's
old bedroom and in the darkened hallways.

A black silhouette, presumed to be Valentino's, stands
at the house's second-story window and has been spied

by passersby. The eight-acre estate also contained stables, which seem to be just as haunted. At least one groom immediately resigned after seeing Valentino's recognizable apparition petting one of the horses.

And, finally, it all comes back to the Knickerbocker. By the end of the 1960s, the once-prestigious lobby bar had been boarded up. It reopened under the auspices of entrepreneur David Fisher in 1993 as the All-Star Cafe and Speakeasy. It operated for eight years as a coffeehouse, quirky club, and nighttime hangout until losing its lease in 2001.

It was during these years that most of the stories about Valentino's hauntings began to surface. Patrons would notice a murky male figure, dressed in fashionable clothes from the early twentieth century, emerge from a dimly lit corner and stride into the room. Just as unexpectedly as it had appeared, it would fade into nothingness. For some reason, over time it was decided that the phantom was that of the Latin Casanova, Rudolph Valentino.

(Interestingly, when the All-Star Cafe had to close, there was talk about relocating it to the lobby of the Vogue Theatre. It seemed like a good idea, moving from one spooky spot to another, but the plan was never realized. Perhaps it's just as well. Spirits usually like to stay in places where they had some connection while alive, so it's questionable whether the ghosts of the Knickerbocker would have followed the hotel's furnishings to the new location anyway.)

Since the 1970s the hotel has been the Knickerbocker Apartments, a residence for seniors. Although there's a restaurant in the lobby open to the public, entrance to the building is otherwise restricted to tenants. As a result, there have been few reports in recent years of visitations from the Beyond.

But who's to say that the spirits don't still call the place home? Maybe they're just biding their time—or hanging out at one of their other favorite haunts—until the moment is right to check back into the Knickerbocker.

Chapter 23
Funny
Business

Where dreams and reality meet, the edges blur. The Comedy Store on the celebrated Sunset Strip is filled with phantoms from the club's former days as the legendary hot spot Ciro's. Spirits may also infest the home of the nightspot's owner, Mitzi Shore.

"It's him. It's him! It's him!"

Sam Kinison wasn't sure whether he had heard it or not. A wild performer, with caustic, jabbing humor, he was building his audience into a frenzy. It was this unpredictable, insane comedy that had gotten him this weekly Sunday-night spot in the Main Room at the Comedy Store, and he was just about to break out in his trademark primal scream.

But then, the voices. Were they just in his head?

Ghosts. They were the only thing, he figured, that could explain what he'd been going through the past few months. Why else would the lights and sound always go haywire when he—and, of all the comics, only he—was onstage at the club? It had to be Denizens of the Dark.

Kinison stopped. Everything. He simply stood still at the microphone, centering his energy. The audience, many of whom were regulars, were stunned to see Kinison's abrupt, unexpected change in mood. *He must be trying something new,* many thought to themselves. That was why they came to the Comedy Store: They never knew what was gonna happen next, or what the comic was gonna say.

"All right. Ya got my attention," Kinison growled. "I don't know what ya want, but you're startin' to piss me off. If ya wanna play, why don't ya come out and let us see ya? Let everyone know you're here."

And with that, black. All of the lights in the club, without warning, instantly and completely cut out. Only for a few seconds, but when the lights suddenly came up full again, it was so startling that the audience gasped. Silence, followed by a few nervous laughs, then an uneasy hubbub broke out as people began to realize that what had just happened was not a "bit" planned by Kinison. They turned to their neighbors, muttering.

"Did you see that?"

"Yeah. What the hell was *that* all about?"

If he had been honest in his heart of hearts, Kinison was a bit shaken, too. It's one thing to be brazen, but he never really expected a response from the ghosts. No one remembers what he ad-libbed next, what he said to break the tension, to pull the audience back within seconds as only a master can, but everyone still talks about the night the spooks came out to party with Sam.

That was in the fall of 1986. But the phantom hecklers dated from decades earlier, back from when the building, and that very room, was one of the swankiest clubs in all of Hollywood, where the Hollywood elite liked to meet and greet.

Ciro's.

William R. "Billy" Wilkerson opened the Sunset Strip nightspot in 1939. It was just down the street from his other famous club, the Cafe Trocadero, which he had opened five years earlier. (Thelma Todd, who haunts the building that used to be her old seaside speakeasy, had her last meal and partied at the Troc the night before her death.)

Both clubs were celebrity hangouts, but there was something about the deceptively bare exterior that really drew the smart set and VIPs from the film world to the ornate Ciro's. Within months of opening its doors, Ciro's became *the* place to see and be seen. Everyone who was anyone came through its doors, knowing that their names would show up in the morning's gossip columns. (It was almost certain with one magazine: Wilkerson owned the trade paper *Hollywood Reporter*.)

Wilkerson had connections, you see, and they weren't always the ones you discuss in public. In fact, like much of the shady side of Tinseltown at that time, the club operated under the all-seeing eye of the mob. (There are still peepholes in the wall that mobsters used to keep track of who was coming and going.)

Bugsy Siegel is often credited with having the dream of building a gambler's oasis in the desert sands of Nevada, but it was Wilkerson who actually began construction on the Flamingo, the first casino hotel in Las Vegas. It was only when he ran short on cash and he turned to the New York bosses that Siegel was sent out west to help oversee the operation.

(Siegel soon muscled his way into control over the project, which wasn't exactly what the boys in New York had in mind. Nor were a lot of his other Hollywood high jinks. Siegel famously died in 1947 in a hail of bullets that burst through the living-room windows of the Beverly Hills home where he was staying—the house owned by his mistress, Virginia Hill. Exactly who ordered and carried out the hit are still a mystery to this day.)

It's said that during Ciro's heyday, gangster Mickey Cohen used the basement for "enforcement." He was not a nice man. After Siegel's murder, and long after Ciro's glory days, Cohen became an L.A. kingpin in the drug trade, studio union racketeering, gambling, and prostitution. Police never found enough evidence to put him away for very long; the feds finally jailed him for income tax evasion. If rumors are true, though, thanks to Cohen, Ciro's cellar saw more than its share of beatings and even murders.

Eventually Ciro's lost its spark. In fact, much of Old Hollywood disappeared with the end of the studio system, in which actors were contract players employed and groomed exclusively by a single studio.

Wilkerson sold Ciro's to a businessman, Herman Hover, but the building remained closed for much of 1942 to 1957. Fade out; fade in. In the 1960s the venue was reopened as a nightclub under a different name.

Then, in April 1972 the place got a new lease on life when comedians Sammy Shore and Rudy De Luca, along with Shore's wife, Mitzi, leased a small room within the sprawling building and opened a ninety-nine-seat comedy club called the Comedy Store.

In August 1974 Mitzi Shore received the club as part of a divorce settlement from her husband. Then, in February 1977 the Comedy Store was temporarily evicted in a dispute with Art Laboe, a popular Los Angeles disc jockey who still held the lease on the section of the building that was Ciro's main room. By the end of March, Shore succeeded in buying the entire property outright.

And with it came a world of difference. Now there were two rooms in the Comedy Store: the Original Room, expanded to seat more than 200, and a new 450-seat theater named, appropriately enough, the Main Room. Eventually, in 1985 the club would also open a Belly Headliner Room where established comedians could drop in to showcase their acts.

It was only a year later that spirits descended on Sam Kinison from The Void.

The ghostly disturbance wasn't the only reminder of death during the comedy club's early years. Before the Main Room opened, performers were happy to work in the small theater for free while they honed their material. But with the debut of the Main Room (in which headliners were paid) and the beginning of the Comedy Store's long contract with HBO to produce a series of annual *Young Comedians* specials, it seemed to many of the struggling comics that they should also be making money for helping to fill the club. Several comedians, including some well-known names, formed an informal "union" and picketed in front of the club. Eventually all the parties were able to come to terms, but that's not to say there were no hard feelings left over. Tragically, one of the comics who was not invited back to perform after the strike committed suicide by jumping from the roof of the Continental Hyatt House located next door. His suicide note read simply, "My name is Steve Lubetkin. I used to work at the Comedy Store."

His ghost has not returned to the club. But many other people's have.

Comedians and security guards have reported seeing chairs slide across the stage on their own, and an unsettling presence is often felt in the dressing room backstage. Talk about stage fright!

Cold spots, long believed to be evidence of spectral activity, appear out of nowhere in the Main Room—sometimes with such an extreme drop in temperature that it's possible for folks to see their breath. Servers have returned to the showroom to find tables they'd just cleared reset with new glasses. The intercom likes to act up as well, with workers getting buzzed by a nonexistent extension. There's never a voice at the other end if they answer, only the sound of heavy breathing.

A spectre dressed in a World War II bomber-style leather jacket was once seen during the day in the offices and later that same night by a different person in the club. On both occasions the employee was able to see right through the apparition before it slowly evaporated. It's also been spied in the kitchen area and moving around the club. The man always seems eager to escape, so legend has it that he was probably one of Cohen's victims.

At another time, during a television taping, the ghosts of three men wearing 1940s-era suits were spotted standing side-by-side in the back of the Main Room; they also visibly vanished without a trace.

And then there are the hauntings in the notorious basement. One night at 3 a.m., a security guard checking out the cellar heard a mysterious growling coming from the back of the room. As he shined his flashlight on a padlocked, fenced-in storage area, the gate slowly started to bend outward as if some invisible force was trying to break free. The fence then suddenly straightened back into place, and a monstrous dark form, emanating evil, appeared by the gate. Needless to say, the watchman was out of there as quick as his legs could carry him.

But whatever the creature was—or is—it's not the only phantom down there. One of the managers has claimed that there are two other angry, lost souls in the cellar. The story goes that one, nicknamed Gus, was once a hit man for the mob, but they turned against their enforcer and killed him. The other is a woman who performed illegal abortions in the basement; she's furious because the mob didn't protect her, and she was arrested.

Various ghost researchers, including Dr. Larry Montz, Daena Smoller, members of the International Society for Paranormal Research, and Dr. Barry Taff, were invited to investigate the club. The team from ISPR also visited Mitzi Shore's house, because some comedians who had stayed there said they encountered shadowy, unidentifiable figures as well as doors that opened and closed by themselves.

In the end, the ISPR claimed to have "cleared" the club of its many ghosts, helping them to Move On. Well, maybe all but one or two. Rumors keep coming back that the place is still paranormally active.

Is it? It's easy enough to find out for yourself. The club is open almost every night of the week. Stop in for the laughs; stay for the screams.

Chapter 24

Just an
Illusion

Opened in 1963 as a private club for magicians, the Magic Castle was originally built as a private-style mansion. Ghosts linger from its time as a residence, and a few more recent spectres have apparently joined in the fun.

Marty Rosenstock took his work at the Magic Castle very seriously. An amateur magician himself, he'd known about the place since he was a kid. It was pretty much the mecca of the magic world.

Opened in 1963, the club for illusionists and their friends was housed in an Edwardian-era mansion (although some say its achitecture is more in the French-chalet style) located at Franklin and Orange Avenues, just a block north of the Hotel Roosevelt and the Chinese Theatre on Hollywood Boulevard. The three-story, towered house had been built between 1908 and 1910 by the banker and real estate tycoon Rollin B. Lane, who modeled it after an estate called Kimberly Crest in Redlands, California. (That home was named for one of its early owners, J. Alfred Kimberly, who was cofounder of the Kimberly-Clark Corporation. It still stands, preserved in its original condition as a Historic Landmark.)

The Lane family lived in the turreted mansion until the 1940s. In 1955, Thomas O. Glover purchased the house and its three acres, and it sat there for years (for the most part without tenants) as an investment property.

Enter the Larsens, two brothers whose father, William W. Larsen Sr., had been a prominent criminal attorney in Pasadena, but whose real love was magic. In the 1920s he contributed original tricks to *The Sphinx*, a magazine for magicians. Then in 1936 he started *Genii, the Conjurer's Magazine.* He gave up his law practice and, with his wife and two sons, began to tour his own illusion show. In 1951 Larsen announced the creation of an Academy of Magic Arts, to foster the appreciation and advancement of all aspects of magic as a performing art, similar to the mission of the Academy of Motion Picture Arts and Sciences. Larsen also advanced the idea of one day establishing a physical home for the society.

Unfortunately, Larsen Sr. never lived to see his vision of a clubhouse for magicians come true. He died in 1955 at the age of forty-eight. His elder son, William "Bill" Larsen Jr., a television producer at CBS, carried on the magazine.

At the same time, Bill's younger brother, Milt, was a comedy writer working on the staff of NBC's *Truth or Consequences*. His ninth-floor window, in an office building across the street from what is now the Hollywood & Highland entertainment and shopping complex, looked out onto the Glover property.

When the brothers resurrected the idea of starting a stylish club where people interested in the conjuring arts could meet socially for food, drinks, and a card trick or two, the possibility of leasing the spooky old mansion came to mind. As it turned out, Glover thought it was a great idea too, and soon a forty-year lease was in place.

In September 1961 Milt and a cadre of friends descended on the old Lane mansion with hammers, paint, and thousands of pieces of salvaged woodwork, stained glass, and other furnishings from razed period structures. Bill concentrated on the business and social end of the academy. On January 2, 1963, with 150 charter members, the Magic Castle officially opened its doors.

To get into the Castle, guests have to say "Open Sesame" to the statue of an owl on the shelf of a bookcase in the lobby. The wall slides open, and visitors pass inside. The ground floor contains a forty-foot bar as well as a twenty-two-seat theater called the Close-Up Gallery, where magicians perform tabletop sleight-of-hand.

In the next room sits a baby grand piano that's said to be "haunted" by the ghost of Invisible Irma, who plays any song called for by visitors. There is, of course, a legend connected with why she's come back from Beyond the Veil. Irma was said to be a frequent guest in the Lane mansion. The family kept a piano in one of their parlors, as was the custom of homes at the time, even though none of the family was musical. Irma loved to sit at the keyboard and play whenever she was there, to such an extent that Mr. Lane, who was no music-lover, had the piano removed from the drawing room and placed in a tower next to the third-floor guest rooms. Irma took this as a personal insult, so before she died in 1932 she swore she would return to haunt the building.

The tall tale continues to say that the piano, covered in dust, was found in the tower when renovations were being done on the mansion to get it ready to become the Magic Castle. The instrument was moved back downstairs to the music room, where it's located today. For good measure, an empty birdcage said to house Irma's phantom pet canary was placed by its side. (Today the spectral bird chirps and its perch rocks whenever a patron slips a tip between the bars of the cage.)

The basement area, christened the Haunted Cellar, has been remodeled to accommodate two small rooms for performances: the Museum as well as a space adjoining the Hat and Hare Pub. On display in the hallway is the prototype built to show Walt Disney how a magical effect known as Pepper's Ghost could be used to create the illusion of spectres flying and dancing in the dining room scene in Disneyland's Haunted Mansion.

The second floor, originally the bedrooms of the Lane mansion, has been converted and subdivided into intimate dining areas. It also contains a small, circular chamber called the Houdini Séance Room that has to be specially reserved by guests. After dinner is cleared, a medium joins the group to try to contact the Spirit World. The room is decorated with original Harry Houdini memorabilia, including handcuffs, a straitjacket, and one of his Metamorphosis escape trunks.

In the 1970s, as membership increased (now hovering around five thousand) and more showroom space was needed, the Castle added two showrooms by building on an annex, which extends from the western side of the mansion on the dining room level. In the Parlour of Prestidigitation, the magician works in a space similar to the one in which he would have performed in a Victorian mansion at the turn of the twentieth century—except that the Castle's Parlour also has spotlights and arena seating for sixty people.

The biggest theater is the 130-seat Palace of Mystery. There, conjurers get to perform larger stage illusions, from producing doves to sawing women in half. Three performers usually share the bill, making up a forty-five-minute show that's repeated throughout the evening.

Just outside the doors to the Palace is a phone booth reputed to be haunted. Anyone entering the old-fashioned wooden booth and closing the door with its frosted panes will suddenly have the reflection of a skeleton appear in the mirror mounted inside.

The underground garage was transformed into a combination performance space and screening room, with an adjoining library and the W.C. Fields Bar, behind which a magician performs on the weekends. The entire floor is decorated with memorabilia from the vaudeville era.

Marty had become one of the hosts at the by-then world-famous clubhouse in the mid-1980s, shortly after he moved out to California from the East Coast. His job was to welcome visitors, facilitate their evenings, and introduce the various performers. Plus, whichever host worked the late shift also had the responsibility of closing up the place when 2 a.m. rolled around.

By the late '80s, Marty knew the routine well. The person who locked up at closing time had to start at the rear of the establishment and work toward the front door, making sure all patrons were out. The host-manager also had to turn down the lights, close doors, and set the security alarms.

Marty pulled on the security bar of the door leading from the annex down to the underground garage. *No one getting in that way,* he thought. Next he walked into the Parlour and slowly turned out all of its lights, which were on separate dimmers. Leaving the room, he passed into the Palace, switched off all the remaining lights in that room, and then cut the electrical breakers for the two rooms.

He was in the process of setting the security system when he noticed that the lights in the area of the Parlour were still on. *Odd,* thought Marty. He had turned out the lights, *plus* the breaker was off. Well, the old place had been rewired so many times, there was no telling where the juice might be coming from. Marty entered the Parlour and was startled to discover that the lights weren't just on: They had been turned up full.

Puzzled, he took one last look around. Satisfied that no one was still inside the Parlour who could be playing tricks on him, he switched the lights off again and left the room, letting the door slam behind him. He hadn't taken more than a few steps when beams of light shot out under the door.

What was going on? Marty had heard that the place was haunted, but this was the first time he had experienced anything unusual for himself. More than a little nervous, he strode back into the room. Exasperated, he called out to whatever invisible spirit might be listening: "All right. Cut that out!"

And instantly, all of the lights went black!

Marty's contact with the Unknown at the Castle was far from unique.

The other showroom in the annex, the Palace, is also haunted. Bryan Lee, the theater's stage manager, was standing at the sound and light console when he heard the animated discussion of a man and woman coming from behind a curtain midstage. Despite the fact he knew he was alone on the stage, he stole a quick glance behind the drape. The talking immediately stopped. A few minutes later the voices started up once more, and again they came to an abrupt halt when he looked behind the curtain.

And that wasn't all. By theatrical tradition, after an evening show has ended, the stage manager places a solitary bulb on a pole stand called a "ghost light" in the center of the stage and keeps it burning all night. Its illumination has practical value as a safety measure, but according to superstition, it also keeps away any ghosts in the house. For a time,

Lee used to set up a ghost light on the Palace stage when closing up. During that period, every time he had a sound or lighting failure backstage during a show, he realized that he had forgotten to leave on the ghost light the night before.

Shortly after Bill Larsen died, Lee was sitting at the Palace Bar outside the showroom with the club's then-entertainment director, Peter Pit. They started to talk about Larsen, and the very second they mentioned his name, the grandfather clock standing by the theater's door started to chime, even though it was not even close to the hour. Was Larsen's spirit listening in?

Former club manager and host Michael Gingras caught the sound of footsteps following him down the grand staircase from the dining area as he was closing the club one night. On a different evening, he was in the downstairs bar area with receptionist Cindy Freeling and one of her friends after shutting down the second floor. Slowly, they became aware of indistinct voices speaking softly in the lobby. They knew no one could be there, because they had already locked the door to the outside. Cindy peeked into the lobby, and the noises stopped as soon as she cracked the door. The room was empty.

They retreated to the bar, but soon the noise started again, this time closer to the wall that separated the two rooms. Cindy's dog, Booker, stiffened and stared toward the entrance. As the three sat there, disembodied, murmuring voices passed in front of them, moved up the staircase, and continued into the dining room overhead. Once there, the sounds faded into nothingness.

Kate Ward, Marty's wife, had started out as a Castle receptionist and later became a host and manager herself. One night while clearing the Close-Up Gallery, she was surprised to hear noises coming from the dressing room area. She knew that the performer had already left the club for the evening. When she peered behind the curtain that separated the showroom from backstage, not only was the dressing room empty, but it was also completely dark.

According to Milt Larsen, several visitors to the Castle have mentioned the bartender they'd just seen pouring libations down in the Haunted Cellar. The scary thing was that, at the time, the Castle didn't have anyone serving behind that particular bar. The man the guests described a burly man with thinning, brownish-gray hair, was Loren Tate, a former bartender who had died some years earlier.

Mark Nelson, another former host and occasional stage manager of the Palace, recalled a time, again after Tate's demise, that he was heading downstairs to collect glassware prior to closing. Judy Williams, the cocktail server at the main bar, called after him, "Say hello to Loren." As Nelson made his rounds through the basement, he was immediately aware of an invisible presence in the cellar, along with a sharp decrease in temperature.

He hurried upstairs and asked Williams why she had made the unexpected remark about the deceased bartender. She had never made the comment before, and, in fact, Tate seldom came up in conversation anymore. She stared blankly and answered, "I have no idea."

When the Magic Castle first opened, it didn't have the number of showrooms and performance areas it does now. Instead, there was one resident magician, Jay Ose, who acted as a combination greeter and performer. To this day, Joan Lawton, a member of the Board of Trustees of the Academy and an early receptionist at the Magic Castle, sometimes is aware of Ose's spirit in the club.

Most often it occurs while she's standing at the fireplace across from the main bar on the entrance level, especially if she's by the end of the mantle closest to the Close-up Gallery where Ose used to perform. Lawton will feel his unseen spectre saunter past her, still carrying his ever-present coffee cup in hand and reciting one of his favorite Yukon poems by Robert Service. There's no particular circumstance under which she senses Ose's presence, but it almost always occurs if one of his best friends, Leo Behnke, is visiting the club.

The Magic Castle isn't the only haunted building with which Milt Larsen has been associated. In 1977 his Society for the Preservation of Variety Arts moved into the Variety Arts Center in downtown Los Angeles. The building was constructed in 1924 as a home for the Friday Morning Club, a women's social and political group. Today it's supposedly haunted by at least two phantoms. An unidentified male actor wearing sixth-century wardrobe appears backstage to cast and crew, and the ghost of Pauline Frederick, the stage and screen star who in 1926 opened the Figueroa Playhouse (also known as the Friday Morning Club Theater) in the building, also roams the facility.

The Magic Castle remains a private club that can only be visited by members and their guests. But if you're fortunate enough to ever wrangle an invitation, never let down your guard once you're inside. That ghost appearing beside you may turn out to not be an illusion at all.

Sitting 250 feet above Franklin Avenue and just up the hill from the Magic Castle, Yamashiro is a Japanese-style restaurant also owned by the Glover estate. It has a commanding view of the city below. (Yamashiro means "Mountain Palace" in Japanese.) The ten-room teak and cedar mansion, built around a courtyard, was constructed by two brothers, Charles and Adolph Bernheimer, between 1911 and 1914 as a private residence and to house their enormous Asian art collection. (Much of the art was auctioned off between 1922 and 1925, after the death of one of the brothers.)

In the late 1920s, the building served as the clubhouse for the film industry elite "400 Club." During the Great Depression it served (allegedly) as a brothel, then a boys' military school. Badly defaced during World War II because of its Japanese design, the main house was broken up into fifteen apartments after the war. Then, in 1948, Thomas O. Glover bought the seven-acre estate. (The Magic Castle property, which Glover acquired from the Lane family in 1955, added another three acres to the parcel.) At first Glover planned to demolish the by-then dilapidated Yamashiro to build a hotel and rental units. When he discovered the original woodwork and silk wallpaper hidden under plywood and wood, Glover decided to renovate instead.

Its ghosts are an open secret. Night security guards frequently hear disembodied voices in the garden and unexplainable footsteps. Because of its panoramic location, the restaurant is a popular venue for special events, especially weddings. Lights turn themselves on in the Groom's Room, and the ethereal cries of a baby often emanate from the closed chamber when it's empty. There's a "Weeping Woman" in the Bride's Room on the second floor, and the chamber has a tendency to inexplicably turn cold. The dining area is also haunted, with many paranormal manifestations occurring around Table 9. Employees have seen plates fly from the shelves, a woman in heels walking in the garden, and shadows disapearing into walls. Those standing on the outside of the building sometimes spot the silhouette of a man as he passes by the window of a second-story room. Some think he is a now-deceased former bartender whose spirit has also been seen near the front entrance. Others claim the dark shade is Thomas O. Glover because the apparition is sometimes wearing a cowboy hat, as was his wont. Glover's ashes, along with his wife's, are buried in the northeast corner of the Garden Court.

Chapter 25

Forever and a Day

Ghosts normally don't hang out in graveyards; they prefer to return to places they frequented when they were alive. Hollywood Forever Cemetery, the burial place for many of filmdom's royalty, is an exception. Walking its grounds are at least two spooks: Clifton Webb and Virginia Rappe.

Emilio ran out of the office waving the map. He jumped into the front passenger seat, and Jonathan put the car into gear.

"They really had one? A map showing where all the stars are buried?"

"Here it is!" Emilio displayed it, almost disbelievingly. "I suppose they decided it was easier than having people wander all over the cemetery trying to find the graves for themselves."

Originally called Hollywood Memorial Park Cemetery, Hollywood Forever Cemetery was founded on approximately one hundred acres in 1899, years before the film industry had taken root. By around 1920, Paramount Studios and RKO had bought up almost half of the property; in fact, Paramount's northern wall still forms the southern boundary of the graveyard.

The cemetery, with its entrance gates located on Santa Monica Boulevard, became "the" place to be buried in early Hollywood. Among its eighty thousand "inhabitants" are some of the founders of the city, including Griffith J. Griffith, who donated the three thousand acres that became Griffith Park.

But it was the stars' tombs that Emilio and Jonathan wanted to see. It was their first time in Hollywood, and if celebrities no longer regularly walked the streets (as they had discovered, much to their dismay), then maybe they could get close to a couple who weren't going anywhere. Like, within six feet.

"So where to first?" asked Jonathan. "It's almost three and the place closes in a few hours. I guess they don't want us here after dark when the ghosts come out."

The guys laughed—never suspecting the graveyard might actually be haunted.

Well, first things first, they decided. They would work their way from the front gates all the way back to the small lake by the far wall. Pulling up first in front of the nearby Abbey of the Psalms Mausoleum, they were impressed by its simple straight lines and tranquility. Inside were the crypts of Jesse Lasky, Victor Fleming, Norma and Constance Talmadge, Darla Hood, Joan Hackett, and finally, about halfway down the first passageway to the left after they entered, the final resting place of Clifton Webb.

Back to the car. Past the graves of Paul Muni, Mel Blanc, Adolph Menjou, Carl "Alfalfa" Switzer, Jayne Mansfield, Hattie McDaniel, Nelson Eddy, and John Huston. Past the Beth Olam Mausoleum, where the notorious gangster Benjamin "Bugsy" Siegel was interred. And past the elaborate sarcophagi of Douglas Fairbanks and Harry Cohn, the bench and sculpture resembling an oversize book that serves as a marker for Tyrone Power, the twin mausoleums of Cecil B. DeMille and his wife, and the elegant tomb of Marion Davies.

The boys decided to peek into the Cathedral Mausoleum, set on the southern shore of the pond. Once within its walls, they quickly located the tombs of H. H. and Daeida Wilcox, Peter Finch, Eleanor Powell, William Desmond Taylor, and Peter Lorre. And there, in a far corner of the mausoleum, was one of its main attractions: Notable for the bright sheen caused by the number of people who had run their fingers across the nameplate was the nondescript tomb of one of Hollywood's earliest superstars—Rudolph Valentino. When he was buried in crypt number 1205 in a silver and bronze coffin in 1926, a crowd estimated to be as large as ten thousand people descended on the cemetery.

Beginning in 1928, a thickly veiled woman in black was often seen visiting the mausoleum—and almost always on the anniversary of Valentino's death—to place roses by the crypt. Her identity has always remained unknown, and in later years the woman was no doubt an imitator of the original mysterious mourner.

By the time Emilio and Jonathan left the mausoleum, the late afternoon sun was starting to disappear behind the tops of the tall palms scattered around the cemetery. They still wanted to walk around the lake—well, it turned out to be more of a reflecting pool with a huge mausoleum on an island in its center—but knew they had to leave the cemetery before long. Soon the front gates would be closing, and they certainly didn't want to be locked inside!

They were halfway around the water, at the northeast bend, when they heard it. A soft sobbing carried on the gentle breeze. It was coming from nearby, but from where—and from whom? There was no one in sight.

The pair looked at each other. Were they both hearing it? Fear crept across their faces as they became aware that, even though they could *see* they were alone, they obviously *weren't*.

Jonathan's eyes tried to focus through the darkening shadows and the light mist that had begun to rise from the damp earth. The sound was coming from over there! Down by that tree at the water's edge. He nudged Emilio and pointed. As they stared incredulously, the low-lying fog seemed to swirl upward, taking form, shape. It was a woman. A ghost!

That did it! Without thinking, the two turned tail and ran to their car. Emilio had barely clambered inside and shut the door behind him before Jonathan stepped on the gas. Was that a speed limit sign they zoomed by? Who cared? They were getting out! No way were they going to be trapped with a spirit from the Other World in Hollywood. Forever.

If the guys had been brave enough to stay longer, they finally might have met a celebrity face-to-face, for the apparition of the weeping woman had been floating over the grave of one of the cemetery's most infamous tenants, Virginia Rappe.

Who?

The death of silent-film actress Virginia Rappe caused the first great Hollywood sex scandal and brought down the career of one of Tinseltown's brightest stars, Roscoe "Fatty" Arbuckle. In 1921 the rotund actor, comedian, screenwriter, and director—his nickname, Fatty, was originally the name of one of his on-screen characters—was at the height of his fame when Paramount offered him a new contract for the amazing sum of $1 million per year. To celebrate, he went to the St. Francis Hotel in San Francisco with two friends and threw a huge party.

On the night of September 5, Rappe turned up at the wild soiree. During the night, she became ill and was briefly allowed to rest on the bed in Arbuckle's room. She was eventually sent to a hospital, where she died four days later from a burst bladder and peritonitis. Maude Delmont, a shady character who had come to the party with the thirty-year-old actress, told the police that Arbuckle had raped Rappe.

The tabloid newspapers, especially those owned by William Randolph Hearst, had a field day. They even suggested that it was Arbuckle's enormous weight that had caused the girl's bladder to rupture as he forced himself upon her.

Despite the fact that there was practically no proof that Arbuckle had anything to do with the girl's sickness or death other than the claims made by Delmont—who was never called to testify in court—Arbuckle was tried three times for manslaughter. The first two trials resulted in hung juries, but the third jury handed down a unanimous verdict for acquittal after just a few minutes' deliberation, along with a written apology to Arbuckle for the great injustice he had suffered.

But it was too little, too late for Arbuckle. His film career had been destroyed.

And poor Virginia Rappe. She was buried in the first row next to the pool in Hollywood Forever Cemetery, and a simple, flat headstone was placed over her earthen grave. Today, a thin, fifteen-to-twenty-foot tall Italian cypress tree rises next to the marker.

So what had the boys seen as the evening chill settled over the cemetery that night?

Paranormalists would insist that it was definitely a manifestation of the unhappy actress. In fact, the guys were lucky—that is, if they had been out to catch a ghost. Rappe's apparition is seldom seen hovering near her grave;

more often people simply hear the disembodied sound of a woman crying.

Is Rappe sobbing because she feels her life was cut short? Or has she returned to impart a message—to tell us what really happened that night at the St. Francis Hotel?

Her ghost is not alone in Hollywood Forever Cemetery, by the way.

Clifton Webb's spectre is perhaps the cemetery's most frequent guest from the Next World. His phantom is said to regularly walk the foyer and the Sanctuary of Peace corridor in the Abbey of the Psalms Mausoleum. Over at Valentino's grave, visitors have felt the actor's presence. They've also sometimes seen a veiled woman—who may or may not be a spectre—kneeling by the crypt.

And a few words have to be said about Bugsy Siegel. Although he doesn't haunt his mausoleum, the mobster's apparition has been spotted in the former Beverly Hills home of Virginia Hill where he was murdered back on June 20, 1947. Some say his ghost also shows up in the Presidential Suite and gardens of the Flamingo Hotel in Las Vegas, even though it's no longer the original Flamingo (which has long since been razed).

For hundreds of years, people around the world have whistled as they passed by graveyards to keep the spirits at bay. If the spectral encounters that take place in Hollywood Forever Cemetery are any indication, maybe that's not such a bad idea.

Appendix A
"BOO"ks and Vide"OHs!"

No ghost researcher does it on his or her own. It's simply impossible to personally check out every purported haunted location for oneself. Fortunately, there's a great deal of paranormal literature available for all levels of followers of the supernatural.

This bibliography includes information about the works that were consulted during the writing of *Haunted Hollywood*. It also lists related books and Web sites that would be of general interest to ghost enthusiasts and fans of Hollywood folklore.

BOOKS

Bartlett, James T. *Gourmet Ghosts—Los Angeles*. City Ghost Guides, 2012. Described as "a guide to the city's haunted bars and restaurants." Ten Hollywood sites and another eight in West Hollywood and Beverly Hills are profiled.

Brooks, Marla. *Ghosts of Hollywood: The Show Still Goes On*. Atglen, PA: Schiffer Publishing Ltd., 2008. Haunted sites described include the Hollywood Roosevelt Hotel, the Magic Castle, and Hollywood Forever Cemetery.

———. *Ghosts of Hollywood II: Talking to Spirits*. Atglen, PA: Schiffer Publishing Ltd., 2008. All the tales in this collection concern spirits that were contacted through séances held at various Hollywood locations or by psychics and paranormal investigators.

Dwyer, Jeff. *Ghost Hunter's Guide to Los Angeles*. Gretna, LA: Pelican Publishing Company, 2007. After giving suggestions on how to look for ghosts, Dwyer describes dozens of sites worth investigating throughout Los Angeles and Southern California.

Guiley, Rosemary Ellen. *The Encyclopedia of Ghosts and Spirits*. New York: Facts on File, 1992. Facts on File became known for publishing one-volume encyclopedias of record, and Guiley's book is no exception. In print (and occasionally updated) for more than twenty years, this book includes entries on ghost phenomena and important figures in the history of paranormal research and Spiritualism, concentrating primarily on the United Kingdom and the United States.

Hauck, Dennis William. *Haunted Places: The National Directory*. New York: Penguin, 1996.

———. *The International Directory of Haunted Places*. New York: Penguin, 2000. *The National Directory* and its companion *International Directory* are perhaps the most popular books in print that list haunted locations throughout the world. Together, more than three thousand sites are contained in the two volumes. Must-own books for amateur and serious ghost hunters alike.

Holzer, Hans W. *Haunted Hollywood*. Indianapolis: Bobbs-Merrill, 1974. This is probably the first work dedicated exclusively to investigations of hauntings in the stars' homes. Holzer, a world-renowned author on the paranormal, relies heavily on the impressions of psychics during his research, but he also conducts firsthand interviews with many who personally experienced the phenomena.

Jacobson, Laurie, and Marc Wanamaker. *Hollywood Haunted: A Ghostly Tour of Filmland*. Santa Monica, CA: Angel City Press, 1994. After more than a decade in print, this fascinating work can now rightly be considered a classic.

May, Antoinette. *Haunted Houses of California*. San Carlos, CA: Wide World Publishing, 2006. As the title suggests, the haunted residences described in these pages are all found in the Golden State, from the far north down to San Diego. Among the stories are tales about Thelma Todd's garage and the Elke Sommer–Joe Hyams home.

Ogden, Tom. *The Complete Idiot's Guide to Ghosts and Hauntings*. Indianapolis: Alpha Books, 2004. In this second edition, the hauntings are separated according to the types of venues the spirits haunt. An entire chapter is dedicated to Hollywood ghost stories.

———. *Haunted Highways*. Guilford, CT: Globe Pequot, 2008. A collection of campfire-style tales based on popular ghost legends about haunted highways, lanes, and trails. Some of the stories involve Hollywood stars, including the cursed car in which James Dean died and the phantom automobile ridden by Telly Savalas.

———. *Haunted Theaters*. Guilford, CT: Globe Pequot, 2009. Many movie stars began their careers in the theater or performed on the stage after they became famous. Some of their stories are told in this collection of tales about haunted playhouses in the United States and the U.K.

Schessler, Ken. *This Is Hollywood*. La Verne, CA: Ken Schessler Productions, 1984. This short paperback lists, describes, and maps historical landmarks in Hollywood and surrounding communities. It includes stars' homes and graves, purported haunted sites, and the locations of celebrity murders and suicides.

Smith, Barbara. *Ghost Stories of Hollywood*. Edmonton, Alberta, Canada: Lone Pine Publishing, 2000. In this volume, Smith, who has written a series of books dedicated to different types of haunted venues, turns her sights on Tinseltown.

VIDEOS

Ghosts Among Us. Crystal Home Video, 2007. DVD.

Haunted sites throughout America are visited on this three-hour DVD. In the Hollywood section, ghost tales associated with the Hollywood sign, Bela Lugosi, Lon Chaney, and the Roosevelt Hotel are explored.

Haunted History: Haunted Hollywood. A&E Television Networks, 2000. VHS.

This show originally aired as a one-hour program on the History Channel on August 25, 2000. The five main hauntings described are those at the Roosevelt Hotel, Hollywood Forever Cemetery, the Knickerbocker Hotel, Raleigh Studios, and the Georgian Hotel in seaside Santa Monica. Commentary is provided by author Laurie Jacobson (*Hollywood Haunted*) as well as paranormal investigators Dr. Barry Taff and Dr. Larry Montz, among others.

Hauntings Across America. The Entertainment Group Video, 1996. VHS.

Hosted by Michael Dorn. Laurie Jacobson introduces the section on Hollywood hauntings. Among the ghost legends examined in this one-hour video are those surrounding Marilyn Monroe, George Reeves, Jean Harlow,

Paul Bern, Jay Sebring, and Sharon Tate. Two private home investigations are documented by paranormalist Dr. Barry Taff: Hollymont Castle in the Beachwood Canyon area of Hollywood and a house in San Pedro, on the Pacific coast about twenty-five miles southwest of Hollywood. *Hauntings Across America* has also been packaged with the 50-minute program *Haunted Places* onto a 110-minute DVD set titled *Hauntings in America*, distributed by Timeless Media Group.

Hollywood Ghost Stories. La Crosse, WI: Platinum Disc, 2005; originally released by Castle Hill Productions and Caidin Film Company, 1986. DVD.

Hosted by John Carradine. This seventy-four-minute DVD explores ghost legends attached to such Hollywood blockbusters as *Poltergeist, The Exorcist, The Omen, The Entity, The Legend of Hell House*, and *The Amityville Horror*; and footage from all of the films is included. There are also on-screen interviews with Elke Sommer, Susan Strasberg, and William Peter Blatty.

Hollywood Ghosts and Gravesites. Delta Entertainment Corporation, 2003. DVD.

This sixty-one-minute DVD, with both color and black-and-white footage, looks at purported hauntings by Harry Houdini, Marilyn Monroe, Bugsy Siegel, and Rudolph Valentino, among others. It also discusses the manifestations that occur on the former luxury liner, the *Queen Mary*, which is now permanently moored in Long Beach, California, about twenty miles southwest of Hollywood.

Hollywood Haunts. Santa Monica, CA: Family Home
  Entertainment, 1999. VHS.
  Originally shot for the Discovery Channel, this fifty-minute video is narrated by Melissa Leebaert. The Hollywood sign, the Roosevelt Hotel, the Knickerbocker Hotel, the Vogue Theatre, and Occidental Studios are among the haunted Hollywood sites that are visited. Three members of the International Society of Paranormal Research are interviewed and take part in a ghost hunt in a private home in the Hollywood Hills.

The Search for Haunted Hollywood. Tulsa, OK: Video
  Communications, 1992; originally released by Gold Key
  Entertainment, 1989. VHS.
  First aired as a television special hosted by John Davidson and starring Patrick Macnee, the video runs ninety-two minutes. Norm Crosby, Susan Ollson, and Jack Carter provide first-person ghost stories, and mentalist Max Maven conducts an on-screen séance. Haunted legends that are investigated include those involving the Hollywood sign and spectral appearances by Marilyn Monroe and Montgomery Clift in the Roosevelt Hotel. In addition, several noted ghost hunters (including Hans Holzer, Richard Senate, Nonie Fagatt, Daniel Hobbit, and Barry Taff) are interviewed.

Secrets of the Unknown, Volume 5. MPI Home Video. Capital
  Cities, ABC Video Enterprises, 1989. VHS.
  This 115-minute video contains five episodes from a History Channel series titled *Secrets & Mysteries*. The "Hollywood Haunting" segment, hosted by Edward Mulhare, looks at several well-known Tinseltown ghost legends, including the haunting of John Wayne's yacht.

WEBSITES

In addition to books and video, innumerable websites—far too many to list individually—were consulted during research for this book. Many are listed in Appendix B, however, in conjunction with the landmarks or locations with which they are associated.

Here are just a few general sites that might be useful:

www.haunted-places.com

This site offers listings (though not terribly detailed descriptions) of haunted locations in both the United States and international destinations. More than a dozen places in Hollywood are mentioned.

www.theshadowlands.net

Online since 1994, The Shadowlands is one of the web's most visited sites for listings of haunted places in specific areas. It shows more than 13,800 locations where ghosts have been encountered. Approximately two dozen of them are right in Hollywood; nearby communities that could be considered "greater Hollywood" are listed separately. Founded by Dave Juliano and now codirected with Tina Carlson.

Two other general sites deserve special mention:

www.findagrave.com

Ever wonder where a particular star is spending Eternity? Now you can find out! You can search for their grave sites by the person's name, his or her claim to fame, birth or death date, or cemetery locations. The site can search twenty-eight million records for non-celebrities as well.

www.imdb.com

The Internet Movie Database (or IMDb) is considered to be the authoritative source for information regarding film production dates and movie casts. I have used this as the definitive source for film release dates, credits, spelling of names, and other movie-related matters during my research.

Appendix B

Map to the Stars' Haunts

Want to visit the places mentioned in Haunted Hollywood for yourself? This is where you'll find all the addresses, telephone numbers, hours of operation, and other pertinent information. Before heading out on a special road trip to see them, however, you may want to check directly with the locations to see if any special arrangements are required.

Many of the sites are on private property, and permission must be granted to visit them. The exterior of some of the stars' current and former homes can be viewed from public streets. Businesses often require paid admissions to visit the interior of their premises.

Before we get into the places found in the individual stories, let's take a look at some general tour information for Hollywood itself.

The Haunted Hollywood Tour
TCL Chinese Theatre
6925 Hollywood Boulevard
Hollywood, CA 90028
(800) 959-3131 or (323) 463-3333
www.starlinetours.com/los-angeles-tour-22.asp

Operated by Starline Tours, the Haunted Hollywood Tour departs at 6:30 p.m., Thursday through Sunday, from the Starline Tours Terminal located at the TCL Chinese Theatre (formerly Grauman's Chinese Theatre). There are also select hotel pick-ups. The two-hour motorized, fully narrated tour passes by many of the most famous haunted sites in Tinseltown and Beverly Hills.

Los Angeles Hauntings
lahauntings@gmail.com
www.lahauntings.com

A newcomer to Hollywood, Los Angeles Hauntings has been operating in the City of Angels since 2013. Tour guides Scott Markus and Connor Bright lead both public and private motorized tours of Tinseltown, downtown L.A., and their surroundings. Before moving to the West Coast, the couple was associated with Windy City ghost expert Ursula Bielski and her popular Chicago Hauntings tour.

Dearly Departed Tours
Ghosts & Legends Walking Tour
(855) 600-DEAD (-3323)
http://dearlydepartedtours.com

Unlike any other sightseeing expedition in the Movie Capital of the World, Dearly Departed Tours explores the dark side of Hollywood. Founded by Scott Michaels in 1998, Dearly Departed offers a variety of themed excursions that visit famous crime scenes and death sites. (The motorized tours deal only peripherally with ghosts and the paranormal, but the company does lead occasional 90-minute, one-mile walking tours down the Boulevard of Broken Dreams (otherwise known as Hollywood Boulevard). Tours depart from the front of the Hollywood Roosevelt Hotel at 7000 Hollywood Boulevard.

Appendix B

Vampira's Haunted Tour
Operated by Skyes Tours
(800) 979-3370 or (212) 209-3370
www.zerve.com/SkyesTours/Vampiras

Operated by Skyes Tours (which was founded by musician and actress Skye Delamey), Vampira's Haunted Tour describes itself as "a dash of year-round Halloween." The motorized excursion drives by such ghost-filled venues as the Magic Castle, Harry Houdini's purported home, the Frolic Room, the Comedy Store, Hollywood Forever Cemetery, the Pig and Whistle, Boardner's, and the Hollywood Roosevelt Hotel. Tours last two hours, and advance ticket purchase is required.

Watson Adventures' Haunted Hollywood Scavenger Hunt
(866) 811-4111 (OvationTix)
www.watsonadventures.com/public/event/the-haunted-hollywood-scavenger-hunt

Watson Adventures operates a Haunted Hollywood Scavenger Hunt. As its name suggests, the "tour" is also a fun, interactive game. Participants are split into small groups and sent out to investigate nearby spook-infested sites by foot. The teams then reconvene about two hours later to compare the results of their exploits. The hunt is offered on select Saturdays, usually about once a month, more often around Halloween. Tours usually depart from the courtyard of Hollywood & Highland Center at the corner of Hollywood Boulevard and Highland Avenue. Advance purchase is required. The Haunted Hollywood Scavenger Hunt can also be arranged as a private event for groups, parties, or other celebrations.

CHAPTER 1: THE PICKFAIR PHANTOMS

The former Pickfair estate
1143 Summit Drive
Beverly Hills, CA 90210

Since 2005 the former Pickfair mansion has been owned by UNICOM International Inc., a private group comprising four corporations in a variety of businesses, including development and marketing of IBM and compatible mainframe system software products, investment, and real estate. The property is not open to the public.

CHAPTER 2: THE HOT TODDY

The former Thelma Todd's Sidewalk Café
(Now the offices of Paulist Productions)
17575 Pacific Coast Highway
Pacific Palisades, CA 90272
(310) 454-0688
www.paulistproductions.org

The private garage in which Todd died is located at 17531 Posetano Road on the hillside above Pacific Coast Highway.

The Cafe Trocadero, where Todd spent her last night, was located at 8610 Sunset Boulevard at the southeast corner of the intersection with Sunset Plaza. Built in 1934 and owned by W. R. Wilkerson, it was one of the most popular nightclubs in Hollywood. The "Troc" closed in 1946 and was eventually demolished.

CHAPTER 3: THE COWBOY SPIRIT

William S. Hart Ranch and Museum
24151 San Fernando Road

Newhall, CA 91321
(661) 254-4584 (museum information)
(661) 259-0855 (park information)
www.hartmuseum.org

Free tours of the main house are available Wednesday through Sunday, though times vary seasonally. Tours of the house and museum are with guides only, but a separate 1910 ranch house on the grounds can be visited on your own.

Newhall is located about twenty-five miles north of Los Angeles, just south of Santa Clarita. Since Hart's death, the County of Los Angeles has expanded the original grounds to its current 260 acres. Although Hart kept horses and dogs, the bison on the property were added as a gift to the park from the Walt Disney Studios in 1962.

CHAPTER 4: THE MAN FROM BEYOND

The Mansion
2451 Laurel Canyon Boulevard
(At the intersection with Willow Glen Road, just north of the junction with Lookout Mountain Avenue)
Los Angeles, CA 90046

At the time that Harry and Bess Houdini would have stayed there, the address for the main mansion owned by Ralf M. Walker was 2398 Laurel Canyon Boulevard. The couple more probably resided in Walker's four-bedroom guesthouse, located across the street at 2435. It, along with the mansion, was destroyed in the four-day Willow Glen wildfires in 1959.

In 2006, the property was purchased by José Luis Nazar, founder of Lexicon Marketing, and the estate has been renamed Houdini Park. Although the grounds remain closed to the public, they are available for special events and film shoots. For now, reports of haunted activity at the site have stopped.

CHAPTER 5: THE HARLOW HAUNTINGS

The former Jean Harlow residence—I
9820 Easton Drive (off North Benedict Canyon Drive)
Beverly Hills, CA 90210

This is the home to which Harlow and Paul Bern moved after their marriage. Two months later, Bern committed suicide there in Harlow's bedroom. It's also the house where Sharon Tate saw the ghostly apparitions the year before her murder.
The former Jean Harlow residence—II
1353 Club View Drive (near Beverly Glen Boulevard)
Los Angeles, CA 90024

This is the house in which Harlow married and where her mother was living at the time of Bern's suicide. Harlow was staying there the night of Bern's death; it is also where she purportedly attempted suicide the next day.

The former (and final) Jean Harlow residence—III
512 North Palm Drive
Beverly Hills, CA 90210

Harlow moved here after Bern's death, and it was to this house she returned after falling ill from uremia. She died of renal failure at Good Samaritan Hospital at 616 Witmer Street in Los Angeles.

Forest Lawn Memorial Park
1712 South Glendale Avenue
Glendale, CA 91205
(800) 204-3131

www.forestlawn.com
Visiting hours are 8 a.m. to 5 p.m. (6 p.m. during daylight-savings time), seven days a week.

Jean Harlow's crypt is among several that may be haunted in Glendale's Forest Lawn Memorial Park. Others include those of Clark Gable and Carole Lombard, Clara Bow, George Burns, Nat King Cole, Alan Ladd, and Jeanette MacDonald.

The former Roman Polanski residence
10050 Cielo Drive
Beverly Hills, CA 90210

This is the address of the home in which members of the Manson Family murdered Sharon Tate, Jay Sebring, and three others. The house has since been torn down and a new one built on the spot. The original Tate–Polanski residence was never haunted, nor is the house now on the site.

Chapter 6: Webb of Mystery

The former Clifton Webb residence
1005 North Rexford Drive
Beverly Hills, CA 90210

The home in which Webb lived was razed by subsequent owners of the property, and a new mansion has been built on the site. There have been no reports of hauntings in the new house.

Clifton Webb is said to haunt the area around his crypt in the Hollywood Forever Cemetery. For more information on the memorial park, see the notes below for Chapter 25.

CHAPTER 7: PRETTY IN PINK

The Pink Palace
1220 Bel Air Road
Los Angeles, CA 90077

Jayne Mansfield's former mansion is no longer standing. It was owned for many years by singer Englebert Humperdinck, who sold the property in 2002. Its buyer, Roland Arnall of Ameriquest Capital Corporation, tore it down along with Esther Williams's former house to expand his other property, the Owlwood estate.

CHAPTER 8: THE WARNING

The former Elke Sommer–Joe Hyams residence
2644 Benedict Canyon Drive
Beverly Hills, CA 90210

Elke Sommer and Joe Hyams moved out of the house due to the disturbances. It is still a private residence.

CHAPTER 9: FASTER THAN A SPEEDING BULLET

The former George Reeves residence
1579 Benedict Canyon Drive
Beverly Hills, CA 90210

This is currently a private residence.

CHAPTER 10: THE DUKE SETS SAIL

Hornblower Cruises & Events
2431 West Pacific Coast Highway
Newport Beach, CA 92663
(888) 467-6256 (main number)

(949) 646-0155
www.hornblower.com

The *Wild Goose*, John Wayne's former yacht, is now owned and operated by Hornblower Cruises, a charter company and special-event organization. The service operates out of (and has offices in) five California ports: San Francisco, Berkeley, Marina del Rey, Newport Beach, and San Diego. The 150-passenger *Wild Goose* is docked in (and sails excursions out of) Newport Beach.

Wayne's Newport Beach mansion, to which the *Wild Goose* is said to have once navigated itself, has since been torn down.

CHAPTER 11: HE WALKS THE FORECOURT

TCL Chinese Theatre
(Formerly Grauman's Chinese Theatre)
6925 Hollywood Boulevard
Hollywood, CA 90028
(323) 464-6266
www.tclchinesetheatres.com

In 2013, a Chinese electronics firm paid for naming rights to the theater; hence it is now officially called the TCL Chinese Theatre. (Most people continue to refer to it as Grauman's, or simply the Chinese Theatre.) That same year, the legendary interior was completely renovated as the movie house was converted into an IMAX theater with stadium-style seating for 932 people. It is the only IMAX theater with a curtain. It's too soon to tell whether the spirit that used to play with the old drapes will continue the habit.

The cinema's forecourt, which features the concrete slabs in which many stars pressed their hand- and footprints, can be visited without charge and is accessible twenty-four hours a day.

Daily tours now visit the interior of the TCL Chinese Theatre, except for special-event dates. For more information, visit www.tclchinesetheatres.com/theatre-tour, call (323) 463-9576, or e-mail tours@chinesetheatres.com.

The Lido Apartments
6500 Yucca Street
Hollywood, CA 90028
(323) 464-4409

Victor Kilian was beaten to death in his apartment here on March 11, 1979, just five days after his eighty-eighth birthday.

The former Ramon Novarro residence
3110 Laurel Canyon Boulevard
North Hollywood, CA 91604

CHAPTER 12: IN VOGUE

supperclub Los Angeles
(Formerly the Vogue Theatre)
6675 Hollywood Boulevard
Hollywood, CA 90028
(323) 466-1900
www.supperclub.la

A nightspot with the name "supperclub Los Angeles" now occupies the completely renovated Vogue Theatre.

El Capitan Theatre
6838 Hollywood Boulevard

Hollywood, CA 90028
(800) DISNEY6 (347-6396)
www.elcapitantheatre.com

CHAPTER 13: WARNER AT WORK

The former Warner Brothers Theater
6433 Hollywood Boulevard
Hollywood, CA 90028

The theater is located within a four-story building that takes up the whole of 6423–6445 Hollywood Boulevard. In a dedication to Sam Warner in its opening night program, the movie palace was referred to as the Warner Brothers Theater. Over the years, however, it has also been known as the Warner Brothers Hollywood Theater, the Warner Pacific Theater, the Hollywood Pacific Theater, and the Pacific 1-2-3.

The spelling of the cinema's name frequently appears differently in print, often with the use of Bros. or Theatre instead of Brothers or Theater, for example. For a time the word Cinerama was part of its official title.

Royal Alexandra Theatre
260 King Street West
Toronto, Ontario
Canada
(416) 872-1212
www.mirvish.com

The theater is thought by some to be haunted by the ghost of Al Jolson.

The former Errol Flynn estate
3100 Torreyson Place
Los Angeles, CA 90046

Set high in the Hollywood Hills just off Mulholland Drive, Flynn's house was once "party central" in Hollywood. It was later owned by country star Stuart Hamblen and singer Rick Nelson. The house has since been torn down and the property subdivided.

Bella Vista
(The former John Barrymore estate)
6 Beverly Grove
Beverly Hills, CA 90212

Located at the very uppermost end of Tower Road. The 1930 census report gives the address of the sprawling estate as 9897 Tower Road.

The former Ozzie Nelson residence
1822 Camino Palmero Street
Los Angeles, CA 90046

The house is a private residence but can be seen from the road behind a high fence.

Hollywood High School
1521 North Highland Avenue
Hollywood, CA 90028
(323) 993-1700

School property may not be visited without permission.

CHAPTER 14: PLAYING THE PALACE

The former Hollywood Palace
(Now known as Avalon)
1735 Vine
Hollywood, CA 90028
(323) 462-8900
www.avalonhollywood.com

CHAPTER 15: THE HUGHES HAUNTING

Pantages Theatre
6233 Hollywood Boulevard
Hollywood, CA 90028
(323) 468-1770

The Frolic Room
6245 Hollywood Boulevard
Hollywood, CA 90028
(323) 462-5890

Palace Grand Theatre
255 King Street
Dawson City, YT (Yukon Territory)
Canada Y0B 1G0

The current Palace Grand Theatre, built by Parks Canada in 1962, is an exact replica of the original. It's open for tours as well as occasional shows and concerts in the summer season.

For more information, contact one of the following:
Heritage Presentation & Visitor Services
Dawson Historical Complex NHS, Dredge No. 4 NHS, and
S.S. Keno NHS
(867) 993-7237

Klondike Visitors Association
P.O. Box 389C
Dawson City, YT
Canada Y0B 1G0
(867) 993-5575
www.dawsoncity.ca

Parks Canada
(867) 993-7200
www.pc.gc.ca

CHAPTER 16: WITHOUT A WORD

The Silent Movie Theatre
611 North Fairfax Avenue
Los Angeles, CA 90036
(323) 655-2520 (box office)
(323) 655-2510 (offices)
www.silentmovietheatre.com
www.cinefamily.org

Now owned and operated by the Cinefamily group, the movie house continues to show silent movies as part of a mixed program of contemporary arthouse films and popular fare from the sound era.

CHAPTER 17: THE MAN IN THE BOWLER HAT

Culver Studios
(Formerly the Thomas H. Ince Studios)
9336 Washington Boulevard
Culver City, CA 90232
(310) 202-1234
www.theculverstudios.com

Sweet Lady Jane Bakery
8360 Melrose Avenue
West Hollywood, CA 90069
(323) 653-7145

The ghost of actor-writer-director Orson Welles, replete in black cape, is said to haunt this bakery. Even when Welles isn't seen, servers and patrons have sometimes detected the odor of his brandy and cigar by the window table the auteur used to frequent—even though neither alcohol nor tobacco is now allowed in the eatery.

Universal Studios Theme Park and Studio Tour
3900 Lankershim Boulevard
Universal City, CA 91608
(800) UNIVERSAL (800-864-8377)
www.universalstudioshollywood.com

The theme park offers a tram-operated tour of the working back lot as part of its admission price. Please note that this is a motorized (not walking) tour, and no interiors of actual working stages are visited.

For many, the name Universal is synonymous with the horror genre in the motion picture industry. Lon Chaney haunts Stage 28, where he filmed the 1925 silent classic *The Phantom of the Opera*. The route of the tram changes depending upon shooting schedules, so the tour guide may or may not be able to point out Stage 28 as it passes by. (Lon Chaney's ghost was also said to haunt a bus stop on the north side of Hollywood Boulevard just east of Vine Street. His visitations stopped when the bench was replaced.)

Route of Bela Lugosi's stroll
Hollywood Boulevard west of Vine Street
Hollywood, CA 90028

The apparition of Bela Lugosi, another Universal star, has been seen walking the sidewalk along Hollywood Boulevard.

The former Bela Lugosi residence
5620 Harold Way
Los Angeles, CA 90028

This is the site of the apartment building where Lugosi was living at the time of his death. At least one person has claimed to have seen his spirit there.

Paramount Studios
5555 Melrose Avenue
Hollywood, CA 90028
(323) 956-5000 (general information)
(323) 956-1717 (guest relations and studio tour)
www.paramountstudios.com

Paramount offers guided two-hour tours, Monday through Friday; advanced reservations are required. All guests must be at least twelve years of age. To get to Paramount Studios from the 101 (Hollywood) Freeway, take the Melrose Avenue exit and travel west. Cross Western Avenue, then turn right into the Windsor Street gate.

In addition to its studio tour, Paramount offers complimentary tickets to television shows taped in front of live audiences. For a schedule of shows, check with guest relations.

The former Lucille Ball residence
1000 North Roxbury Drive
Beverly Hills, CA 90210
This is a private residence.

Raleigh Studios
5300 Melrose Avenue
Los Angeles, CA 90038
(323) 466-3111
www.raleighstudios.com

GMT Studios
5751 Buckingham Parkway
Culver City, CA 90230
(310) 649-3733
www.gmtstudios.com

Occidental Studios
201 North Occidental Boulevard
Los Angeles, CA 90026
(213) 384-3331
www.occidentalstudios.com

CHAPTER 18: HOLLYWOODLAND

The Hollywood sign is located on Mount Lee overlooking the city. Due to vandalism and for security reasons, hiking to the sign itself is no longer permitted. There are trails, however, that allow access to a viewpoint behind and above the sign.

The sign can be seen throughout Hollywood. If you don't want to venture into the hills, it's possible to have a clear view from a pedestrian bridge located in the shopping complex Hollywood & Highland Center.

Hollywood & Highland Center
Corner of Hollywood Boulevard and Highland Avenue
Hollywood, CA 90028
www.hollywoodandhighland.com

No parking areas in the Hollywood Hills have been specifically set aside for tourists wishing to view the Hollywood sign, and the unfamiliar narrow, winding roads in the hills can be difficult to negotiate. In addition, some of the short streets have no outlets, and many of the curbs, including the space on Deronda described in this appendix are posted as tow-away zones. Perhaps the closest place to safely and legally park to see and photograph the sign from a totally unobstructed viewpoint is Lake Hollywood Park at 3160 Canyon Lake Drive above the Hollywood Reservoir.

The former Peg Entwistle residence
2428 North Beachwood Drive
Hollywood, CA 90068

The house at which Peg Entwistle was living at the time of her death is now a private residence. Her ghost is said to haunt the stretch of Beachwood Drive between the house and the Hollywood sign but not the residence itself.

CHAPTER 19: THE CURSE OF DONA PETRANILLA

Griffith Park
4730 Crystal Springs Drive
Los Angeles, CA 90028

(323) 644-2050 (visitor center)
(323) 913-4688 (ranger station)

Griffith Park, administered by the City of Los Angeles Department of Recreation and Parks, is free of charge to the public. It's open from 6 a.m. to 10 p.m. daily, although many of the roads are posted as closed from sunset to sunrise. All hiking trails close at sundown.

The park is bounded on the north by California SR 134, on the east by the I-5 (the Golden State Freeway), and, for a large portion of the southern border, by Los Feliz Boulevard. The grounds have a number of entrances, depending upon which attraction you plan to visit.

Crystal Springs Drive off Los Feliz Boulevard is considered the main entrance to the park. The street address given is the headquarters, ranger station, and visitor center—part of which (the Park Film Office) is housed in the adobe built by the Feliz family. Though original, the old building dates to the 1830s and was extensively remodeled in the 1920s. The visitor center is generally staffed during regular business hours.

Bee Rock is a sandstone cone (more or less in the shape of an upside-down beehive) that juts out of the surrounding hillside. It's located in the eastern end of the park and can be accessed by foot along the 2.2-mile Bee Rock Trail that begins in the general vicinity of the old zoo picnic area. Information and park maps are available at the visitor center.

Please note that trails within Griffith Park are seldom marked, including the trailheads. Over the years, hikers have honeycombed the hills with intersecting minor trails, making it all the more difficult to stick to a particular path. Be sure to check with the visitor center or a park ranger before setting out on your own. Wear comfortable shoes, a hat and sunscreen if necessary, and take plenty of water. The more than fifty miles of trails, though not dangerous, are not individually patrolled every day, so it would also be wise to carry a cell phone, especially if traveling solo.

Griffith Park is an urban wilderness, so it's very possible that you will come in contact with wildlife such as snakes, skunks, bobcats, or coyotes. Just so you know.

CHAPTER 20: THE PHANTOM OF THE PINES

Runyon Canyon Park
2000 Fuller Avenue
Los Angeles, CA 90046
(323) 913-4632 (park services information, Monday–Friday, 9 a.m.–4 p.m.)
(323) 666-5046 (park maintenance)
www.laparks.org
Open daily, dusk to dawn. Admission is free. Operated by the Los Angeles Department of Recreation and Parks.

Runyon Canyon encompasses 160 acres, 90 of which have been designated off-leash for dogs. The terrain is not suitable for biking. There are three entrances to the park and its numerous hiking trails. All have limited parking nearby. The main Fuller Avenue entrance is located at the southern end of the canyon; two blocks to the west is another entrance near the north end of Vista Street. The trails along the ridges of the two slopes of the canyon meet at the top, from which there is another trail leading to the northernmost entrance near the 7300 block of Mulholland Drive (just west of Outpost Drive). Round trip, the hiking loop is approximately 3.5 miles.

The haunted ruins are a few hundred yards past the gates of the Fuller Avenue entrance to the left.

Wattles Mansion
1824 North Curson Avenue
West Hollywood, CA 90046
(213) 485-8744
www.lapark.org

Adjacent to Runyon Canyon Park. The mansion, park, and gardens are maintained by the Los Angeles Department of Recreation and Parks.

CHAPTER 21: FROM HERE TO ETERNITY

Hollywood Roosevelt Hotel
7000 Hollywood Boulevard
Hollywood, CA 90028
(323) 466-7000
(800) 833-3333
www.thehollywoodroosevelt.com

Now owned by Thompson Hotels, the Hollywood Roosevelt Hotel is one of the best-known and most fabled hotels in the Film Capital of the World. Haunted locations in the hotel include Room 928 and its adjacent corridor, the twelfth floor Gable-Lombard penthouse suite, the Blossom Room, and around the pool. Many of the areas are open only to residents and for special events.

Marilyn Monroe is said to haunt at least three places besides the Hotel Roosevelt: the sidewalk outside her Brentwood home, her crypt in the Corridor of Memories section of Westwood Village Memorial Park, and the Knickerbocker Hotel (detailed below in the "Knickerbocker Holiday" notes).

The former Marilyn Monroe residence
12305 Fifth Helena Drive
Los Angeles, CA 90049

Pierce Brothers Westwood Village Memorial Park
1218 Glendon Avenue
Los Angeles, CA 90024
(310) 474-1579

CHAPTER 22: KNICKERBOCKER HOLIDAY

Knickerbocker Hotel
(Now the Hollywood Knickerbocker Apartments)
1714 Ivar Avenue
Hollywood, CA 90028
(323) 463-0096 or (323) 462-8202 (rental office)

Falcon Lair
1436 Bella Drive
Beverly Hills, CA 90210

The Falcon Lair stables
10051 Cielo Drive
Beverly Hills, CA 90210

Valentino's beach house
224 Cahuenga Street
Oxnard, CA 93030

Falcon Lair and the beach house Valentino visited are now private residences.

Santa Maria Inn
801 South Broadway
Santa Maria, CA 93454
(805) 928-7777

Valentino's presence is felt and heard in Room 210, where he most often stayed.

The spirit of the mysterious woman in black who visited Valentino's crypt for decades is sometimes seen in the Hollywood Forever Cemetery mausoleum where the star was buried. (See details below in the "Forever and a Day" notes.)

CHAPTER 23: FUNNY BUSINESS

The Comedy Store
(Formerly Ciro's nightclub)
8433 West Sunset Boulevard
West Hollywood, CA 90069
(323) 656-6225 (show information)
(323) 656-6268 (office)
www.thecomedystore.com

Bugsy Siegel murder site/former Virginia Hill residence
810 Linden Drive
Beverly Hills, CA 90210

The Flamingo Hotel and Casino
3555 Las Vegas Boulevard South
Las Vegas, NV 89109
(702) 733-3111

Bugsy Siegel's ghost has been said to materialize in the former Virginia Hill home where he was murdered. A spectre seen in the Presidential Suite and the rose garden of the Flamingo Hotel in Las Vegas may or may not be Siegel: The current casino bears the same name but is not the original Flamingo hotel whose construction Siegel oversaw. The modern resort that bears its name is owned and operated by Harrah's.

CHAPTER 24: JUST AN ILLUSION

The Magic Castle
7001 Franklin Avenue
Hollywood, CA 90028
(323) 851-3313
www.magiccastle.com

The Magic Castle is a private club for magicians and interested associates. To enter, you must be a member, be accompanied by a member, or have a guest card from a member. The Castle does not provide private tours.

Variety Arts Center
938 South Figueroa Street
Los Angeles, CA 90015

The Variety Arts Center was once the home of the Society for the Preservation of Variety Arts, which was founded by Milt Larsen (who also cofounded the Magic Castle). The building is not currently operating as a theatrical venue.

Yamashiro Hollywood
(also known simply as Yamashiro)
1999 North Sycamore Avenue
Hollywood, CA 90068
(323) 466-5125
www.yamashirohollywood.com

Chapter 25: Forever and a Day

Hollywood Forever Cemetery
6000 Santa Monica Boulevard
Hollywood, CA 90028
(323) 469-1181
www.hollywoodforever.com

Founded in 1899, Hollywood Forever Cemetery is one of the oldest graveyards in greater Los Angeles and is the burial site of many pioneers of both Hollywood itself and the film industry. A map to the graves of the stars is available at the cemetery offices by the front gate.

Today the grounds are immaculate, but by the 1980s the graveyard had fallen into disrepair. Lawns went untended, and necessary repairs, even to some of the crypts and tombstones, were ignored. Eventually the cemetery was threatened with bankruptcy. Forever Enterprises, which maintains several cemetery properties across the United States, purchased the sixty-two-acre memorial park in 1998 and renamed it Hollywood Forever Cemetery. Today it has been restored to its former beauty and is once again able to accept new applicants for "residency."

Clifton Webb is interred in crypt 2350 in Corridor G-6 in the Sanctuary of Peace within the Abbey of the Psalms Mausoleum, which is to your right after you enter the main gates of the cemetery.

Rudolph Valentino's crypt is found in the last aisle in the extreme southeast corner of the Cathedral Mausoleum, near the pond.

Virginia Rappe rests nearby between the first row of graves along the eastern side of the small lake. Her grave is marked with a simple headstone and lies beneath a single, tall cypress tree.

Hollywood Forever Historic Walking Tour
(818) 517-5988
www.cemeterytour.com

Since 2002, Karie Bible has offered occasional two-hour walking tours of Hollywood Forever Cemetery, designed under the guidance of Marc Wanamaker, co-author of *Hollywood Haunted*. This is a daytime historical walk, not a ghost tour, although the graves of Valentino, Webb, and Rappe might be visited. Available as either a group or private tour.

Although it's possible to visit the final resting places of many of the other celebrities mentioned in this book, there are no organized ghost tours in Los Angeles that visit graves on cemetery property. The location of the burial sites can be found at www.findagrave.com.

Appendix C

On Location

Still dying for a few more haunted sites to visit? Here are capsule descriptions of fifteen additional Hollywood venues inhabited by ghosts and spirits.

Barney's Beanery
8447 Santa Monica Boulevard
West Hollywood, CA 90069
(323) 654-2287
www.barneysbeanery.com
Although it now has sister restaurants in several locations, the "original" Barney's Beanery is in what is now West Hollywood. John "Barney" Anthony established his first eatery in Berkeley, California, in 1920, but he moved it to the Beanery's current spot on Santa Monica Boulevard (U.S. Route 66) in 1927. A solitary, ghostly male figure in a white shirt has been spied throughout the building, everywhere from the cellar to outside the rooftop office. The spectre seems to frequent the area in and around the basement cooler. Interestingly, the apparition never sets off the motion detector floodlights. The spectre doesn't always materialize: Sometimes servers simply feel an invisible presence brush against them as it walks by. Now and then the motion is accompanied by a whooshing sound. In the kitchen, knives will spin on their own. Late at night while closing up, one of the cooks encountered the shades of two small boys with long teeth and fingernails. Another cook transferred to one of the other Beanery sites after hearing kegs of beer being dragged across the floor in the cellar's walk-in refrigerator

and then seeing them rock back and forth without being touched. At least three murders—a shooting death and two stabbings—have occurred in the bar and restaurant in West Hollywood, but it's unknown if they have anything to do with the hauntings.

Boardner's

1652 North Cherokee Avenue

Hollywood, CA 90028

(323) 462-9621

www.boardners.com

This storied bar less than a block off Hollywood Boulevard was built in 1927 by singer Gene Austin, who named it My Blue Heaven after one of his hit tunes. Within a few years it was The Cherokee Men's House, one of Hollywood's first gay bars. In the 1930s it became Morressy's Hair Salon, but the shop was really a front for a secret speakeasy and card club. In 1942, Steve Boardner bought the premises, added the neon sign out front, and transformed it into an Art Deco, dark, cozy watering hole, which quickly became a hangout for film stars during filmdom's Golden Era. It was also a hangout of Elizabeth Short, the movie wannabe who became known as the Black Dahlia after her gruesome murder in 1947. These days the bar is connected to a dance club, and they share a Spanish-style courtyard complete with fountain. Paranormal activity includes doors opening and closing, disembodied footsteps in the office, and music and the TV playing when the power is off. The hideaway's main ghost is a murky phantom who haunts the small women's restroom, often with its face appearing in the mirror. The spectres of an old man in a top hat and a woman wearing a shawl have also been spotted walking in the alley out back.

The Cat & Fiddle
6530 W. Sunset Boulevard
Hollywood, CA 90028

Although the pub closed in December 2014, The Cat & Fiddle was a fixture in Hollywood for many years. The authentic English bar and restaurant was housed inside the Thompson Building, which was constructed around 1927 with a Spanish/Mediterranean exterior. Over the years, the space was occupied by a costume and make-up warehouse and at least two restaurants, Mary Helen's Tea Room and the later Gourmet Hollywood, which welcomed movie stars in the 1940s and 1950s. Owners Paula and Kim Gardner opened The Cat & Fiddle in Laurel Canyon in 1982 but moved it to its Sunset Boulevard location two years later. (Kim Gardner named it after a favorite pub just west of London. The phrase "Cat & Fiddle" may have been derived from a nickname for King Henry VIII's first wife, Catherine of Aragon, who had the sobriquet "Catherine La Fidèle.") The Hollywood pub's most frequently seen ghost was a man smoking a cigarette. He was usually spotted near the front gate, leaning against a wall, or walking up the stairs toward the office. Paranormal activity in the pub's Victoria Room included a jukebox turning itself on, a lamp tipping over, and glassware shattering. Then there was the Casablanca Room, in which a mob hit occurred in the 1930s, when one of Meyer Lansky's men shot a member of a Chinese Tong gang. (Another story says that the gunfight broke out among mobsters having a party there in the 1940s. One person was killed, but rather than spoil the fun, his body was simply dragged to another room.) A pint mug has been known to fly into the bar area from the empty room after the place was closed, glasses have fallen from a shelf, light switches worked themselves, and saloon-style doors would swing open and shut. There were cold spots and breezes, occasional strange noises coming from the room, and even a dark shadow walking toward the rear door. In early 2015, the former Cat & Fiddle space was leased by Biergarten, a popular garden-restaurant in San Francisco. No one knows yet whether the phantoms will stay to haunt the next venture to open in the building.

Chateau Marmont
8221 Sunset Boulevard
West Hollywood, CA 90046
(323) 656-1010
www.chateaumarmont.com
Fred Horowitz, a Los Angeles attorney, opened Chateau Marmont as an apartment building in 1927. The architecture of the seven-story, L-shaped building was loosely based on a Gothic chateau he had seen on the Loire River. Unfortunately, it opened in February 1929, just months before the Great Depression hit. The place had to be sold, and the new owner, Albert E. Smith, converted it into a hotel with sixty-three rooms and suites. In the 1940s, nine Spanish-style cottages adjacent to the property were acquired by the hotel. In 1976, Chateau Marmont was named a Los Angeles Historical-Cultural Landmark. The hotel is famous as a hideout for the rich and famous and for the hijinks that sometimes take place there. Most notoriously, on March 5, 1975, actor-comedian John Belushi died there of a drug overdose in Bungalow 3. Strange things have taken place in that cabin ever since, including the time a little boy's parents asked him why he kept giggling. He told them he was laughing at "the funny man," even though no one else was in the room. The youngster later saw a photograph of

Belushi and identified him as the prankster. Paranormal activity takes place all over the Chateau Marmont, however. Phenomena include windows opening, furniture shifting, faucets that turn themselves on and off, cold spots, unusual noises and voices, the sound of people walking down the hallway, disembodied floating heads, the sensation of being watched, a spectral woman who floats above one of the beds, and even spirits who get in bed with occupants.

El Cid

4212 West Sunset Boulevard

Los Angeles, CA 90029

(323) 668-0318

www.elcidla.com

In 1915 pioneer filmmaker D. W. Griffith filmed scenes for *The Birth of a Nation* in cornfields at the eastern edge of Hollywood behind the spot now occupied by El Cid. Ten years later, a prison-themed restaurant named Jail Café (complete with waiters dressed as guards) opened there. Even the tall stone wall that lined Sunset Boulevard resembled a jailhouse. In 1932, the eatery was converted into the Gateway Theatre. Between 1950 and 1961 it was the Cabaret Concert Theatre. Then, in 1963, Flamenco aficionado Margarita Cordova and her husband, singer/guitarist Clark Allen, along with dancers Marta Amaya and Armando Media, transformed the theater into El Cid, a sixteenth-century-style, Spanish-themed tavern featuring Flamenco music and dancing. Flamenco is still performed there on weekends, but during the day, when the theater is empty, employees will often hear the distinctive strumming sounds of a ghostly Flamenco guitar. Some believe that the spirit of Allen, who died in 2008, has returned to play a few encores for his fans.

El Compadre Restaurant

7408 Sunset Boulevard
Los Angeles, CA 90029
(323) 874-7924
www.elcompadrerestaurant.com

El Compadre Restaurant has offered drinks and fine Mexican cuisine since 1975, but its South of the Border–style building just west of Hollywood on Sunset Boulevard has housed a bar and restaurant since the 1920s. In the 1950s, the place was known as Don Pepe's, and it was often frequented by folks who lived, say, south of the law. During a robbery, three or four men shot into the crowd of customers and staff, and two men were killed instantly. Their ghosts now float around the room, appearing as shadows. They most often hover close to the piano. They've been known to move objects and flick the light switches in the restaurant area, and patrons have heard footsteps and disembodied voices. A third phantom, who may or may not be associated with the hold-up, hangs out around a mirror near the bar, sometimes as a full-form materialization, sometimes as a shadow in the glass, and other times as a mist covering its surface. Even when the spirit isn't seen, patrons frequently sense that they're being watched or that an invisible presence is standing nearby.

The Haunted Intersection

North Sierra Bonita Avenue and Hollywood Boulevard
Los Angeles, CA 90046

Modern-day motorists driving through this intersection on the western edge of Hollywood have had to swerve to avoid hitting ghosts from the nineteenth century. The spectres include covered wagons, arrows and tomahawks zipping through the air, Native Americans on foot and on horse-back, and Mexican bandits. Pedestrians have seen the spirits as well.

The Holly Mont House

6221 Holly Mont Drive

Hollywood, CA 90068

Located in the Hollywood Hills East, the "Holly Mont House" (as it's known in ghost literature) is one of the most thoroughly investigated haunted houses in America. The two-level, Mediterranean-style, five-bedroom, four-bath Holly Mont House was built in 1925. It was owned by Don Jolly when Dr. Barry Taff, a paranormal researcher associated with the then-active UCLA Parapsychology Lab, first began his observations in 1976. Taff reportedly experienced an extraordinary amount of paranormal activity, much of it telekinetic or poltergeist-like in nature, such as the sudden appearance of objects, things flying through the air, and items repositioning themselves. There were electrical disturbances, inexplicable fires, doors unlocking and locking themselves, and odd noises. A houseboy saw apparitions and strange shadows out of the corner of his eye; he eventually quit when the incidents became too frightening. Taff was able to revisit the house throughout the mid-1980s, and over the course of a decade, he amassed a truly astounding record of unexplainable events. In 2008, the house's new owner, Abdi Manavi, allowed Taff to return, and the researcher discovered that paranormal activity was still occurring, though to a lesser degree. The property has been on and off the market since, and real estate listings refer to the structure as a fixer-upper. Perhaps the spirits have taken their toll.

The Hollywood Tower

6138 Franklin Avenue

Hollywood, CA 90028

(866) 352-5623

www.thehollywoodtower.com

The French Normandy–style apartment building known as the Hollywood Tower was built in 1929. It has two wings configured in a V-shape with a tall tower where they meet, giving the edifice seven stories and fifty-six apartments (three of them penthouses). The exterior of the structure is said to have been the inspiration for the Twilight Zone Tower of Terror at Disney World. (The theme park attraction's storyline about an elevator accident that killed five people has no basis in fact.) When the Hollywood Tower opened, its sophisticated and elegant design drew members of the Hollywood A-list to its door. It was added to the National Register of Historical Places in 1988. The most-frequently reported ghost is a man in 1930s clothing who appears on the seventh floor, staring out toward the Hollywood Hills. When he senses he's being watched, the apparition disappears.

Hotel Hollywood

(Formerly the Oban Hotel)

6364 Yucca St.

Hollywood, CA 90028

(323) 466-0524

www.thehotelhollywood.com

Known as the Oban Hotel when it opened in 1922, the three-story lodging was refurbished and renamed the Hotel Hollywood in 2002. Among the stars who stayed there when they were first starting out were James Dean, Clark Gable, Fred

MacMurray, Glenn Miller, Paul Newman, Orson Welles, and Marilyn Monroe. The building has at least two ghosts. One is a failed actor named Charles Love who became a props manager. On February 15, 1933, at the age of thirty-three, he wrote a farewell letter to silent film comedian Harry Langdon (for whom he was a screen double), then shot himself with a single bullet to the brain. Instead of haunting the room where he died, his spirit moved to the basement, the steps leading down to the basement, and the first floor at the top of the staircase. He usually appears as a cold spot or a strong odor similar to that of rotten eggs. When his spectre does materialize, it's only in the form of a dark shadow—black, brown, or rust-colored. Another spectre that appears at the top of the staircase may be a former owner of the hotel. Some say there is also a female apparition on the second floor in one of the front rooms.

The Hudson Apartments
6533 Hollywood Boulevard
Hollywood, CA 90028
(323) 860-7404
www.hudsonapartments.com
Jesse L. Lasky (co-founder of Paramount Pictures) and Samuel Goldwyn (the "G" in MGM, Metro-Goldwyn-Mayer) opened the Hudson Apartments in 1917 as the Hillview Hollywood. The rooming house was specifically built to cater to actors, which was considered risky at the time. Rudolph Valentino, Stan Laurel, and Charlie Chaplin were among its early residents. Seriously damaged in the 1994 Northridge earthquake, the apartments have been completely renovated. The Hudson's ghost is a man dressed in 1920s attire, and he usually appears downstairs. He even shows

himself to prospective renters, much to the chagrin of the management.

Miceli's
1646 North Las Palmas Avenue
Hollywood, CA 90028
(323) 466-3438
www.micelisrestaurant.com
Miceli's was founded as Miceli's Pizzaria [*sic*]—Hollywood's first pizza parlor—in 1949 by Carmen and Sylvia Miceli, with the assistance of their siblings Angie, Millie, Tony, and Sammie. Expanding its menu to include Sicilian family recipes, Miceli's soon prospered and has become a Hollywood landmark. There is now a branch restaurant in Universal City, but it's the Tinseltown eatery that's haunted. One employee reported being lightly poked in the ribs by an invisible hand and saw a door slam on its own. Occasionally, glasses will fall and break without being touched. The spectre is thought to be a longtime server, Antoinette "Toni" Colavecchi Hines, who died in 2003 just shy of her 89th birthday. The phenomena occur most often in November around the dates of Toni's birth (the 24th) and death (the 18th).

Musso & Frank Grill
6667 Hollywood Boulevard
Hollywood, CA 90028
(323) 467-7788
www.mussoandfrank.com
Open Tuesday through Saturday, 11 a.m. to 11 p.m.
Founded as Frank's Café in 1919, Musso & Frank Grill is named for early co-owners Joseph Musso and Frank Toulet. The menu was created by French chef Jean Rue, and

it remains basically the same cuisine to this day. During the heyday of the studios, the legendary restaurant drew the most famous names in Tinseltown. Luminescent orbs have appeared in modern-day photographs taken of Charlie Chaplin's favorite booth: Number 1, located in the Old Room in the back. Upon closer examination, some of the photos reveal what appear to be a man's left eye and a long, straight nose. The waitstaff has also seen the spectre of a woman without a head at various spots in the restaurant.

Pig 'N Whistle

6714 Hollywood Boulevard
Los Angeles, CA 90028
(323) 463-0000
www.pignwhistlehollywood.com
John H. Gage founded the original Pig 'N Whistle bar and restaurant in downtown Los Angeles in 1908. When the Egyptian Theater opened on Hollywood Boulevard in 1922, Gage sensed a unique opportunity. He established a new Pig 'N Whistle, complete with ornate wooden beams and a ceiling full of ceramic tiles decorated with—what else?— pigs and whistles, right next door to the cinema on July 22, 1927. It soon became a popular stop for those going to the movies, including celebrities attending movie premieres. By the 1950s, the restaurant had fallen out of favor and closed its doors. (In the meantime, another Pig 'N Whistle had opened next to the El Capitan Theatre just down the street in 1929, but that location closed within a decade.) New owners bought the space in 1999 and re-opened Pig 'N Whistle, completely restored to its former glory, in 2001. Its ghost has never been seen, but employees will feel an invisible spectre tugging at their pants leg or simply get

the feeling of a nearby presence. For some reason, everyone seems to agree that the spirit is a little girl. There's a separate legend that the ladies' restroom is home to a woman whose young daughter died in a fire in the building in the 1950s. (Although there was a fire at the location, there are no newspaper accounts of any fatalities.)

Ripley's Believe It or Not! Odditorium
6780 Hollywood Boulevard
Hollywood, CA 90028
(323) 466-6335
www.ripleys.com/hollywood
Housed in what was once a bank building, Ripley's Believe It or Not is visited by the ghost of a little girl. Legend has it that several people were gunned down in the building many years ago during a bank robbery, but the youngster survived because she was in the bathroom at the time. She came out of the restroom to find the bodies of the victims, including those of her parents, and the trauma has resulted in her spirit returning to the scene of the crime after her death—back in the form of a little girl. She has been seen throughout the building, both day and night, but she most frequently appears to staff members who remain on "rain duty" after the museum has closed for the evening. Supposedly there are many leaks in the roof, and during a severe downpour an employee is asked to stay in the building overnight to place buckets and empty them. One of the phantom's favorite haunts is the ladies' room in which she hid during the hold-up. On occasion someone sitting in one of its stalls will see a girl's feet pass by, but if, as she leaves, the woman happens to look toward the stall where the girl would have been, it is empty.

Appendix D

Peek-A-Boo: Celebrity Encounters

In *Haunted Hollywood* you've read about many celebrities who either saw or in other ways experienced phantoms. But those stars were far from alone.

Dozens of well-known personalities have gone on record saying that they either witnessed an apparition or were convinced by some other paranormal phenomenon that invisible entities do exist. And some other stars are themselves the apparitions in popular ghost legends. Here's a representative sampling of each.

DAN AYKROYD

One of the writers and stars of *Ghost Busters* and *Ghostbusters II*, Aykroyd has said that he thinks his home, once owned by Cass Elliot of The Mamas and Papas fame, was haunted—perhaps by Mama Cass herself. His StairMaster would turn on by itself, and jewelry would move across bureau tops on its own. He's even felt the weight of an invisible spirit getting into bed beside him. Aykroyd's mother claims that when she was nursing him the ghosts of Sam and Mary-Ellen, his great-grandparents, appeared at the foot of her bed to welcome him into the family.

SANDRA BULLOCK

While filming *Gravity* in London, Bullock stayed at a converted church. After several sleepless nights, she was reportedly convinced that ghostly presences were to blame. She asked her producers to have the lodgings investigated.

NICOLAS CAGE
This actor of more than fifty movies is a true believer in the paranormal. He's even played supernatural beings: an angel in *City of Angels* and the title character in *Ghost Rider*. When he was young, he supposedly encountered a ghost in the attic of the home of his uncle, director Francis Ford Coppola.

JAMES CAGNEY
This film legend, who's best known for a string of gangster movies as well as portraying George M. Cohan in *Yankee Doodle Dandy*, believed that he was saved from a fatal car crash when the disembodied voice of his father, who had died years earlier, gave him a warning.

NEVE CAMPBELL
It's said that a woman was murdered in one of the houses where Campbell later lived and that visitors to the home have run into the victim's ghost. No wonder the actress was such a good choice for *The Craft* and the *Scream* movie trilogy.

BELINDA CARLISLE
As one of the members of The Go-Gos, Carlisle made her name as a singer of pop and new wave–inflected rock. She appeared as an actress in *Swing Shift* and made a cameo in *She's Having a Baby*. Back in 1975, when she was seventeen, she had an out-of-body experience while falling asleep in a chair at her parents' house. More recently, she witnessed a hazy, ghostlike form floating over her bed.

DAVID CARRADINE

The late actor revealed that after he married his fifth (and final) wife Anne, strange noises would emanate from their bedroom closet. The small room would also turn "icy cold." He was convinced that his wife's deceased husband, Dana, was producing the phenomena.

JACK CARTER

Comedian Jack Carter and his wife were frequent guests of Sydney and Georgia Shelton, whose home had once been owned by Conrad "Nicky" Hilton Jr. Though he was one of the sons of Conrad Hilton, founder of the hotel chain, Nicky is best remembered as being the first of Elizabeth Taylor's many husbands. During one of his visits to the Sheltons', Carter saw Hilton's ghost in his old study/library. On another occasion, the Carters saw the liquor cabinet in the kitchen shaking on its own, rattling bottles and spilling liquids. Another time they spotted bloodstains that had inexplicably appeared on the carpeting. Supposedly the stains returned even after the carpeting was replaced. It's said that subsequent owners have seen ghosts in the house.

JOAN CRAWFORD

Christina Crawford, Joan's daughter who wrote the tell-all book *Mommy Dearest,* says that when she was a little girl she heard children's voices inside the walls and their ghosts walking the hallways of their house at 426 North Bristol Avenue in Brentwood. Apparently Joan also heard the voices and at one point had a priest come to the home to perform an exorcism. After the Oscar-winning actress died in 1977, spontaneous fires would sometimes burst out in her bedroom, but firefighters were never able to find a cause.

No apparition has ever appeared, but subsequent owners, including Donald O'Connor and Anthony Newley, felt an evil (or at least uneasy) presence in the residence.

NORM CROSBY
Comedian Norm Crosby has gone on the record as saying a year or two after his grandfather died, the man's spirit visited Norm's wife in a dream. The elderly man told the woman that he was feeling "disturbed." The Crosbys visited the grandfather's grave and found out that the root from a tree in the next lot had grown under the man's coffin and begun to force it upward. They immediately had the root removed and the grave site restored. Soon after, Norm's grandfather returned in a dream to say that he was feeling much better.

RICHARD DREYFUSS
According to reports, for several consecutive nights during a period back in the late 1970s, the Oscar-winning actor was visited by the apparition of a little girl.

CARRIE FISHER
In 2005, Carrie Fisher's friend, Republican lobbyist Greg Stevens, died from a drug overdose in her bed—while she was sleeping next to him. She was sure that his spirit remained in the house. Eventually her friends brought in an exorcist to "clear" the house.

MITZI GAYNOR
The blonde actress/singer and star of the movie *South Pacific* and her husband Jack Bean (who passed away in 2006) saw the ghost of a maid, whom they named "Mrs. Walker,"

cleaning around their house. Apparently the phantom loved to dust the crystal chandeliers, because the glass would often begin to tinkle, seemingly on its own. The house is located at 610 North Arden Drive in Beverly Hills.

ROBIN GIVENS
After her divorce from Mike Tyson in 1989, the actress moved into a West Hollywood house once occupied by John Lennon. Givens claimed in a *Boston Herald* interview to have sensed the spirit of the ex-Beatle still inhabiting the space. She first became aware of the ghost when she was awakened by the disembodied sound of a man singing—only to realize it was Lennon's voice.

HUGH GRANT
In the mid-1990s, the British actor bought a $1.7 million home in Los Angeles that was once owned by Bette Davis. Both he and guests heard the moaning and screams of a disembodied spectre in the house. Although the film diva was a major Warner Bros. star in the 1940s and 1950s, by the end of her career Davis became known for a slew of over-the-top eccentric performances in such films as *The Watcher in the Woods*, *Return from Witch Mountain*, *Hush . . . Hush, Sweet Charlotte*, and *Whatever Happened to Baby Jane?* Was she trying to make a comeback?

ALYSON HANNIGAN
The *Buffy the Vampire Slayer* and *How I Met Your Mother* star told interviewers in 2003 that a polite male ghost haunted the Los Angeles home she shared with her husband. The anonymous apparition was seen first by one of Hannigan's friends as they left the house one evening.

ETHAN HAWKE AND UMA THURMAN
Although the stars deny it, neighbors suggested that the couple sold their new apartment in Sneden's Landing, New York, when spirits began to make themselves uncomfortably known.

KATE HUDSON
In 2014, the Academy Award–nominated actress told the host of the British television show *Alan Carr: Chatty Man* that both she and her mother, Goldie Hawn, can sense when ghosts are present. Hudson explained that "it is not really seeing; it is feeling a spirit. A fifth energy." She suggested that the best thing to do in such a situation is to let the entity know what year it is and remind them "that they don't belong there." For a time she lived in a haunted house in London that had been rented by her mother. Hudson has seen the apparition of a woman with no face, which she said was "really creepy." In addition, she's been visited by her grandmother at least once in a dream.

MICHAEL JACKSON
During Dr. Conrad Murray's trial for the involuntary manslaughter of Michael Jackson, Lionel Richie's ex-wife Brenda testified that the pop star's spirit told her that he accidentally took his own life. Many people believed that a shadow resembling Jackson—his ghost?—was seen walking down a corridor in Larry King's "Inside Neverland" special on CNN, which aired in 2009.

JANIS JOPLIN
On October 4, 1970, the famed singer died of a heroin overdose in Room 105 of what was then the Landmark Hotel

in Hollywood, California. Today, the hotel is known as The Highland Gardens. Joplin's ghost has been seen in the room where she passed on as well as in the hotel. It's claimed that if you say her name in the lobby, photographs sometimes move and doors slam shut.

KE$HA
In 2012, singer-songwriter Ke$ha told interviewer Ryan Seacrest that she had had sex with a ghost multiple times and that she was "very open to it." The following year on *Jimmy Kimmel Live!*, she told the host that as a result of her supernatural indiscretions, her vagina was haunted. She said that if she ran a "ghost meter" over her body, its alarm would go off whenever it neared her genitals.

STEPHEN KING
Although he never saw an apparition while staying in Room 217 at the allegedly haunted Stanley Hotel in Estes Park, Colorado, Stephen King says that he was overcome with an unexplainable anxiety. The incident inspired him to write *The Shining*, in which the fictional Overlook Hotel stands in for the Stanley.

LADY GAGA
Lady Gaga spent close to $5,000 purchasing electronic field sweepers and other apparatus to sweep the premises of "bad energy" before her Monster's Ball concert in London in 2010. Months later she held a séance to get rid of a spirit named Ryan whom she believed was pestering her.

JESSICA LANGE
During a Reuters interview about her role as a mysterious

neighbor during the premiere season of FX's *American Horror Story*, Jessica Lange said, "I've lived in my share of haunted houses, so I believe they exist. Most of them have been fairly benevolent, but some have been troublesome."

ARTHUR LAURENTS

Arthur Laurents, best known for his librettos of *West Side Story* and *Gypsy*, began to see the ghost of Tom Hatcher after his fifty-two-year life partner's death in 2006. The first time was on the ski slopes at a resort the two frequented, then in a twelve-acre park Hatcher had created in Quogue, Long Island. When Laurents was considering a revival of *West Side Story* in which some of the Puerto Rican characters' dialogue would be in Spanish, the playwright ran across a Spanish translation of the show that had Hatcher's handwritten notes in it. Coincidence?

DEMI LOVATO

Lovato remembers several strange paranormal occurrences in her home when she was growing up, including (at the age of eight) seeing the apparition of a little girl, dressed in 1800s clothing, standing in her closet. When she told her mother a week later, her mom confessed that she had caught her daughter talking to an imaginary friend three years earlier. Demi had completely forgotten the incident. At the time, Lovato had told her mom that her invisible playmate was her friend, Victoria. And, interestingly, there was a framed photo of a girl in nineteenth-century clothing in the room.

PAUL MCCARTNEY

In 1995, McCartney got together with George Harrison and

Ringo Starr to record John Lennon's 1977 song "Free as a Bird" as part of their *Anthology* project. According to McCartney, during the session there were unusual, unaccounted-for noises in the studio and mechanical interference with the recording equipment. They finally chalked up the phenomena to the playful meddling of Lennon's spirit.

MATTHEW MCCONAUGHEY

Investigating an odd noise in his Hollywood home, the well-chisled McConaughey was startled to run into the ghost of an older woman whom he nicknamed Madame Blue. The two co-existed peacefully the whole time he lived there—perhaps because the handsome young actor had a penchant for walking around his house in the nude.

TAYLOR MOMSEN

Gossip Girl's Taylor Momsen became an amateur ghost-hunter when visiting Devil's Lake, North Dakota. Her mother had grown up there, and after a wealthy next-door neighbor died, Momsen snuck over to her house to look around. The woman's ghost turned up in two photos she took. One showed her hand on a typewriter, and the spirit's entire form was seen standing at a window in the other.

DOROTHY PARKER AND HARPO MARX

Parker was a member of the famed group of writers known as the Round Table that met for lunch at New York City's Algonquin Hotel beginning in 1919. (In Hollywood, she was best known as the co-writer of the 1937 film *A Star in Born*.) Years later after the renovation of the hotel attic, odd noises were heard coming from inside the empty room, and at one point Parker's photograph fell from a wall. Some believed

Parker had made a return. Harpo Marx's spectre has also been spotted around the hotel.

KATY PERRY
Katy Perry was living in a rented Beverly Hills mansion while shooting a commercial for her new perfume in 2013. She ran from the master bedroom suite in terror when she looked into a mirror and saw the face of a mustached man staring back at her. She reportedly agreed to remain in the house, but all of the mirrors on the property were covered and a security guard was hired to stay on the premises.

ELVIS PRESLEY
The King of Rock 'n' Roll played a series of concerts at the Las Vegas Hilton from 1969 through 1976. Many have claimed to see his apparition standing around backstage, as if waiting to go back on for another bow.

KEANU REEVES
Reeves still vividly recalls the night an apparition walked into his room when the film star was a boy growing up in New Jersey. The spectre was a white, double-breasted suit—just a suit—which moved as if it were being worn, but there was no human form wearing the cloth. The figure soon disappeared but not before it was seen by Reeves's nanny as well.

JOAN RIVERS
After her husband's suicide in 1987, Rivers moved into an apartment in New York that, for some reason, had been slow to sell. During renovations, the comedy legend visited the apartment to find pornographic writing and other marks

written on the walls, and her dog refused to go inside. The elevator operator suggested that it was the ghost of a Mrs. Spencer, a previous tenant who had died there. Rivers enlisted the help of a New Orleans voodoo priestess to exorcise the entity. The spirit left for a time but eventually returned, staying for at least twenty more years.

TIM ROBBINS
Back in 1984, feeling the mere presence of an unseen spirit was enough for this levelheaded actor to move out of an apartment after just one day.

CYNTHIA ROWLEY
Designer Cynthia Rowley encountered an apparition several times in a country home she bought in Greenwich, Connecticut. The wraith's face was always covered by a gray scarf, but her identity soon became apparent. One Christmas season, as Rowley began to light a set of candles she had placed on a mantle, her husband, without knowing why, blurted that she shouldn't. She nevertheless felt compelled, and when she struck the match its flame jumped to a wreath hung above the fireplace. Soon the room was burning. The blaze was quickly extinguished, and no one was hurt, but one of the firefighters who arrived on the scene told Rowley that the mansion had been built by an heiress to the Diamond Match Company who had been burned and disfigured in her father's factory as a teenager.

TELLY SAVALAS
One night in the early 1960s, long before his tenure as television's *Kojak*, Savalas was hitchhiking in the rain on a deserted Long Island road around three in the morning.

His car had just run out of gas. As he later told the story, a man wearing a tuxedo and driving a black Cadillac picked him up. The stranger dropped him off at the nearest open gas station a few miles down the road and loaned the young actor (who had also forgotten his wallet) money for the gas. When Savalas stopped at the address the man had given him to return the money, he discovered that the person had died some years before.

FRANK SINATRA AND MARILYN MONROE
The crooner's apparition has been spotted in Lakeview Cabin #5 at the Cal Neva Resort & Casino, which was owned by the singer from 1960 to 1963. The bungalow on the shore of Lake Tahoe was the home-away-from-home for the recording star when he visited the hotel. Another frequent guest during that period, Marilyn Monroe, has returned to her favorite getaway, Lakeview Cabin #3, as well as the swimming pool.

ANNA NICOLE SMITH
The spectre of the former Playmate and model has been seen roaming the corridors of the Seminole Hard Rock Hotel and Casino, where she died in her room from a prescription drug overdose on February 8, 2007, at the age of thirty-nine.

BARBARA STANWYCK
Barbara Stanwyck's career spanned fifty years, from the Golden Age of Movies through her time in television. She was nominated for four Academy Awards, was given an honorary Oscar in 1982, and notably portrayed the matriarch in TV's *The Big Valley*. For many years, she and film star Robert Taylor were lovers. After his death in 1969, the actress began to see his spirit in her Beverly Hills home, and visitations

continued right up until her own death in 1990. Her house was at 1055 Loma Vista Drive, off Sunset Boulevard.

STING
The rock singer, former front man for The Police and star of the movie *Dune,* has seen phantoms in one of his five homes. His wife, Trudie, encountered them as well.

EMMA STONE
Stone, who portrayed a fake medium in the Woody Allen movie *Magic in the Moonlight,* believes that the spirit of her deceased grandfather is leaving quarters that seem to appear out of thin air around the house. If the story is true, the coins are examples of an "apport," the paranormal appearance of a solid object. The phenomenon was most often seen in séance rooms during the heyday of Spiritualism.

SUSAN STRASBERG
In the 1960s, actress Strasberg, the daughter of acting guru Lee Strasberg, lived in a Beverly Hills home once owned by the British actor Sir Cedric Hardwicke. She, her father, and her husband ran into the ghost of a woman in one of the house's upstairs bedrooms.

JEAN CLAUDE VAN DAMME
While brushing his teeth, Van Damme once caught a ghost staring back at him from his bathroom mirror. Remind anyone of the haunted mirror on John Wayne's yacht and the Marilyn Monroe mirror at the Hollywood Roosevelt Hotel? "Mirror, mirror on the wall" indeed!

AMY WINEHOUSE

After Amy Winehouse's death, her father told reporters that he believes the singer's presence is still around. He pointed to one incident that may or may not have been a paranormal manifestation: While he was delivering the eulogy at her funeral, a black butterfly flew into the room, briefly alit on Kelly Osbourne's shoulder, then flew up around Winehouse's father on the podium.

NEAR-DEATH EXPERIENCES

Many paranormalists believe that a person's soul or spirit can sometimes separate from and return to the body while the individual is still alive, allowing for an out-of-body experience (OBE) or a near-death experience (NDE). Because the person isn't dead, the entity isn't a ghost, at least not in the common sense of the term. Instead, many refer to the traveling aura as an "astral body." Regardless of what the spectre is, the phenomenon is of great interest to ghost enthusiasts.

Perhaps the most famous film star to admit to having had an NDE was Elizabeth Taylor. During the filming of *Cleopatra* in 1961, she contracted pneumonia. The actress fell into a coma, and at one point her heart stopped. For a time, she was clinically dead. Afterward, she spoke of having had an out-of-body experience in which she saw herself floating above her body. Her astral body then traveled down a long tunnel toward a white light until voices told her to return.

Another celebrity who has reported having an NDE is **Gary Busey,** who had an NDE while on the operating table following a motorcycle accident in 1988. He found himself encircled by angels in the form of balls of light. **Eric Estrada,** best known for his work on television's *Chips*, also had an NDE following a motorcycle crash. Halfway down a corridor filled with lights and music, a voice told him that he had to return because he hadn't "achieved personal happiness and peace of mind." **Ozzy Osbourne** "died" twice while in an eight-day coma following a bike accident. Although he saw the clichéd white light, he said there were "no [expletive] angels, no one blowing trumpets, and no man in a white beard."

Eric Roberts's out-of-body moments came following a near-fatal car accident in Westport, Connecticut, in June 1981. At the age of nineteen, actor **Robert Pastorelli** was in an automobile accident that rolled his car four times. He recalls his pain suddenly ceasing as he realized he was floating in the air looking down at his unconscious body. It was only the look of sadness on his father's face that made his spirit return.

In the late 1970s, **Tony Bennett**'s career was in a slump, and at one point he nearly overdosed. He had a brief NDE encounter, in which he saw himself wrapped in a golden light. When he came to, he found the strength to make the necessary changes to turn his life around.

Chevy Chase was almost electrocuted in 1981 while working on the movie *Modern Problems*. He underwent acute depression after returning from an NDE: The Next World seemed much more blissful than the reality of life.

James Cromwell's NDE during a near-drowning at the age of five resulted in a lifetime of recurring dreams, which he believes are connected to previous incarnations.

When **Rebecca DeMornay** was seven years old, her spirit left her body while she was lying ill from a peptic ulcer in a Mexico City hospital. The doppelganger went to the window, looked out, and saw barefoot children dancing around a lamppost, singing and playing in the snow. In 1983 on a return to Mexico she discovered that the lamppost never existed.

Lou Gossett Jr. has had five OBEs, including one at the age of twelve. He also claims to be able to remember tidbits from previous lives.

During a suicide attempt (by taking an overdose of Nembutal and Seconal), **Sally Kirkland**'s lungs and heart stopped. She feels she was "given a second chance" by a life-affirming NDE, which led to her swearing off drugs.

About a near-death experience he had preceding his liver transplant in 1995, **Larry Hagman** said, "I didn't see a light some people see, but I had a wonderful feeling of bliss and warmth. ... That sounds corny, but it was just lovely, uplifting."

While performing in a play in Chicago, *CSI*'s **William Petersen** cut his finger so badly that it required surgery. He briefly lost his vital signs and later recalled entering that archetypal white tunnel filled with white light. A disembodied male voice told him "it's not your time" and that he had to go back.

Burt Reynolds's eight- or nine-hour coma from an overdose of sleeping pills may have been accidental, but he also had an OBE.

During the first of eight heart attacks in 1964, **Peter Sellers** left his body. He saw the proverbial "white light" and started moving toward it. He was clinically dead, and the actor saw a hand reach toward him through the light. He wasn't able to identify the entity, but when a doctor was able to start Sellers's heart, its voice told Sellers it wasn't his time. The hand withdrew, and Sellers sensed himself float back into his body.

Jane Seymour's NDE occurred during a severe allergic reaction to an injection of penicillin. Her spirit double floated out of her body and looked down at the people gathered around the table frantically trying to resuscitate her. She claims it was the love for her children that drew her back.

Sharon Stone also saw that white light when she was knocked out from a brain hemorrhage—a tear in an artery at the base of the skull. Stone even started to see friends on the Other Side. But the experience was brief. Soon she was conscious and back in the room.

Donald Sutherland died for a short time during a bout with meningitis in 1979. He saw himself floating above his body bathed in blue light. He began to float down a long tunnel before being revived.

Finally, a paranormal reality show entitled *Celebrity Ghost Stories* premiered on BIO (formerly The Biography Channel) on October 3, 2009. In each episode, an assortment of famous and lesser-known guest stars told of their encounters with the Unknown. After four years the show moved to the Lifetime Movie Network for a fifth season before going on hiatus. Many of the episodes can be seen on YouTube or are available for purchase online.

About the Author

Tom Ogden is one of America's most celebrated magicians. He has performed professionally for forty years, from the tinsel and sawdust of the circus ring to the glitter and sequins of Las Vegas, Atlantic City, and Lake Tahoe. He has opened for such acts as Robin Williams, Billy Crystal, and the Osmonds.

Ogden's television work has included appearances on NBC's *The World's Greatest Magic II* and FOX's *The Great Magic of Las Vegas,* and numerous commercials. He has twice been voted Parlour Magician of the Year at the famed Magic Castle in Hollywood and has received an additional dozen nominations in other categories.

Ogden's books include *200 Years of the American Circus* (which was named a Best Reference Work by both the American Library Association and the New York Public Library), *Wizards and Sorcerers, The Complete Idiot's Guide to Magic Tricks, The Complete Idiot's Guide to Ghosts and Hauntings,* and *The Complete Idiot's Guide to Street Magic,* as well as eight books in Globe Pequot's Haunted series. He has also been profiled in *Writer's Market.*

A recognized expert on the spirit world, Ogden lectures at colleges and universities about ghosts and the paranormal.

He resides in Los Angeles.